KEY TERMS

IN SECOND
LANGUAGE ACQUISITION
(SECOND EDITION)

二语习得核心术语

(第二版)

（美）Bill VanPatten　（意大利）Alessandro G. Benati　著

陈亚平　注

外语教学与研究出版社
FOREIGN LANGUAGE TEACHING AND RESEARCH PRESS
北京 BEIJING

京权图字：01-2017-7146

© Bill VanPatten and Alessandro G. Benati, 2015
This Licensed Edition is published by arrangement with Bloomsbury Publishing Plc

图书在版编目（CIP）数据

　　二语习得核心术语：第二版：英、汉／（美）比尔·范巴腾（Bill VanPatten），（意）亚历山德罗·G.贝纳蒂（Alessandro G. Benati）著；陈亚平注. —— 北京：外语教学与研究出版社，2017.12（2023.1重印）
（外语学术核心术语丛书）
　　书名原文：Key Terms in Second Language Acquisition (Second Edition)
　　ISBN 978-7-5135-9737-1

　　I. ①二… II. ①比… ②亚… ③陈… III. ①第二语言－外语教学－名词术语－英、汉 IV. ①H09-61

　　中国版本图书馆 CIP 数据核字 (2018) 第 001445 号

出 版 人　王　芳
项目负责　冯丹丹
责任编辑　毕　争
责任校对　陈　阳
封面设计　孙莉明　高　蕾
版式设计　吴德胜
出版发行　外语教学与研究出版社
社　　址　北京市西三环北路 19 号（100089）
网　　址　http://www.fltrp.com
印　　刷　北京九州迅驰传媒文化有限公司
开　　本　889×1194　1/32
印　　张　8.5
版　　次　2018 年 1 月第 1 版 2023 年 1 月第 7 次印刷
书　　号　ISBN 978-7-5135-9737-1
定　　价　33.90 元

购书咨询：(010) 88819926　电子邮箱：club@fltrp.com
外研书店：https://waiyants.tmall.com
凡印刷、装订质量问题，请联系我社印制部
联系电话：(010) 61207896　电子邮箱：zhijian@fltrp.com
凡侵权、盗版书籍线索，请联系我社法律事务部
举报电话：(010) 88817519　电子邮箱：banquan@fltrp.com
物料号：297370001

记载人类文明
沟通世界文化
www.fltrp.com

To Janizona My Name Is Murphy, Too

—BVP

To Orazio Benati and Anna Maria Ferrari

—AB

Contents

总 序

　　我国外语教学与研究出版社与国际著名 Bloomsbury 出版集团在 2016 年联合推出了"外语学术核心术语丛书"。本丛书是为初涉各个专业领域的学习者——包括高等院校本科生、硕博士研究生、年轻教师等，特别是外语语言文学专业学习者——准备的专业入门丛书，意义深远。

　　本丛书最初由总部设在伦敦的 Continuum 国际出版集团发行，自 2011 年该出版集团隶属于 Bloomsbury 出版集团后，改称 "Bloomsbury Key Terms Series"。经与 Bloomsbury 出版集团商谈后，外语教学与研究出版社结合我国高校情况和需要邀请国内专家撰写导读，并将英语的核心术语译成中文在国内出版。

　　"外语学术核心术语丛书"中的"核心术语"意义上不同于英国学者雷蒙·威廉斯（Raymond Williams）在 *Keywords: A Vocabulary of Culture and Society*（1976）一书中的 "keywords"（关键词）。威廉斯所著之书着重考察有关文化和社会的 100 多个关键词在时间长河中的意义和用法变迁，特别是从马克思主义的政治斗争视角进行论述。本丛书的"核心术语"也不同于当今学术期刊文章中出现的"关键词"（key words）。学术期刊文章要求作者在摘要之后列有"关键词"，一般为 3—5 个，每个关键词为 2—6 个字，关注这些核心词的出现频率并便于搜索。与此二者不同，本丛书的编写注重构成某个学科（如哲学或语言学）或理论（如系统功能语言学）的核心术语，为读者提供有关核心词的简易解释和互参方法。这类专业书籍的理论基础为连续体（Continuum）理论，即一个学科或理论与核心词汇构成连续体的关系：一端是某学科或理论，经过精密度的逐步分析后，到达由核心术语组成的另一端。这是因为一个学科或理论的存在必然要通过一定数量的专业性术语来论述，而对一个核心术语的理解，必然要通过它和其他术语的区分与比较，最后在该学科或理论的体系中去理解其意义、功能和价值。也只有在这个基础上，我们才得以初步理解和掌握某学科或理论的整体。这是本丛书与传统专业书籍不同的编写原则。

本丛书的另一特色表现在选题时既注重学科性，也考虑到多学科性和跨学科性。这是学术界对当代知识传授与学科发展的崭新认识。从本丛书已经选定的 14 个选题中，有关哲学的有 2 部，即心智哲学和艺术哲学；有关语言和语言学的有 8 部，即语言学、语义学、句法与句法理论、语用学、系统功能语言学、文体学、话语分析和符号学。此外，也有文学理论、翻译学、伦理学和逻辑学的选题。"外语学术核心术语丛书"的出版目的之一就是为了帮助学生摆脱传统专业的概念，扩大视野，了解学科的多层次的复杂联系。正如束定芳和田臻在《语义学核心术语》导读中指出，语义学是研究自然语言的意义，实际上它涉及语言学、哲学、符号学、逻辑学、心理学等诸多领域的学科。可见非外语专业学生也可阅读本套丛书。

有鉴于此，"外语学术核心术语丛书"的编写框架体现了因材施教和由浅入深的基本原则。为了帮助各个专业的学习者理解和掌握相关学科或理论，本丛书编写体例基本一致，大致包括以下 5 个方面：

（1）引言：参与编写某学科或理论的作者应对该专题的基本内容作浅显介绍和解释，如《心智哲学核心术语》的作者在引言中以清晰、简洁和易懂的方式说明心智哲学与哲学的关系，在此过程中提供有关该学科发展的情境和背景。《语言学核心术语》的作者则在引言中对语音学、音系学、词汇学、句法学和语用学均作了简单介绍，进一步向学生推荐社会语言学、心理语言学、应用语言学、语料库语言学和话语分析等课程内容，最后介绍语言学的主要流派。

（2）核心术语：对某学科或理论认真选择最重要最有密切关系的术语，以引导学生初步了解该学科或理论，如《话语分析核心术语》一书收录了309个术语；《系统功能语言学核心术语》收录了342个术语。这些术语有理论的，也有描述的。对每个术语均提供了精确的定义、出处及其与其他术语的关系。就收词量来说，会出现有些重要词语没有收录的情况，如现代逻辑各分支中的许多重要术语没有出现，对此我同意《逻辑学核心术语》导读作者郝兆宽的解释，"对读者而言这应该是好事，不至于一开始就迷失在海量而且极为技术的细节中"。

（3）重要学者：这一部分的内容主要说明，每个选题除了某专业的核心术语外，还向新入门者提供了与某学科或理论有关的权威学者和理论家。如《话语分析核心术语》一书收录了42位重要学者，其中除话语分析各种理论和方法的代表人物外，还有与话语分析有关的哲学家、社会学家、心理学家、人类学家、认知语言学、语用学家、计算机中介交流研究者、语料库语言学家、法律语言学家等等。他们都在不同方面、不同程度上对话语分析理论的发展有所建树。在具体内容上，选题的编写者介绍了这些权威学者的简历，包括他们的生平、研究方向、代表作品以及对话语分析的主要贡献。

（4）代表性论著：这部分内容是有关某学科或理论的重要论著，如《话语分析核心术语》一书在本部分介绍了24部代表作品，基本上概括了话语分析不同时期、不同领域的研究成果，其目的是引导学生有目的地去直接阅读原著，以便深入学习或研究。

（5）索引：在本套丛书的索引中，对出现在核心术语和权威学者这两部分的重要术语和人物均提供了页码，这也是本丛书关注术语与人物互参这一重大原则的体现。

除上述内容外，外研社"外语学术核心术语丛书"与英语原版有所不同，它增加了由中国学者撰写的中文导读，并提供了核心术语的中译文。这些内容不仅仅是用中文复述有关选题的基本内容，而且为中国学生提供了更多的有关该学科或理论的信息。这表现在：

（1）尽管中文版的中文导读与原版的英文引言有相通之处，中国学生经由他们熟悉易懂的中文内容可更方便地进一步阅读、理解和掌握原著。

（2）中文导读提供了英语原著作者的信息，如黄国文和刘明介绍了《话语分析核心术语》一书作者英国兰卡斯特大学语言学教授保罗·贝克（Paul Baker）的生平、研究方向、主要著作等。

（3）中文导读补充了几年前出版的英文原著未谈到的重要情况，又增加了原著出版后的近况，特别是中国学者的科研成果。前者可以束定芳和田臻有关《语义学核心术语》的导读为例，他们在谈到H. P. 格赖斯（H. P. Grice）于1948年演讲中提出的意义理论时，在附注中补充了有关意义的讨论，可参阅格赖斯在1957年发表于 *The Philosophical Review* 的文章；后者如《符号学核心术语》的导读作者张凌介绍了我国符号学的发展情况。

（4）难能可贵的是我国学者能对有关学科和理论发表自己的观点，供学生参考。如《语言学核心术语》导读作者蓝纯总结了原作者选词的3个依据，即多年的从教经验、现有的工具书和编者本人对各领域的熟悉程度。《文学理论核心术语》导读作者张剑对该书与此前出版的威廉斯所著的《关键词：文化与社会的词汇》和 M. H. 亚伯拉姆斯（M. H. Abrams）编辑的《文学术语汇编》两书进行比较。黄国文和陈瑜敏在《系统功能语言学核心术语》一书的导读中指出，在该学派内部对"语法隐喻"（grammatical metaphor）是否包括"语篇隐喻"（textual metaphor）存在着不同观点。

如本序言在开篇时所述，外研社"外语学术核心术语丛书"的出版具有深远意义。除了具有很高的实用价值外，它还是一部让学生按自己兴趣、以自学为主的读物，是为学生攀登知识高峰搭建的平台。我们也会发现，"外语学术核心术语丛书"与已有的专业书籍有所不同。它是教材，又非教材；它是辞书，又非辞书；它是专著，又非专著。在这个意义上，它是外研社在出版界引进和推出的一个崭新的语类。考虑到当前我国学术界和教育界正在讨论酝酿高等教育和人才培养的改革，本丛书的出版给高等教育改革指引了一个重要的方向。

胡壮麟

北京大学

2016 年 3 月

导　读

　　二语习得是一个涵盖性术语，指学习者在掌握母语之后的任何一门或多门语言的习得，它既包括目标语环境下的语言习得，也包括外语环境下的外语学习。1972 年 Larry Selinker 在《应用语言学国际评论》上发表了"中介语"一文，指出二语学习者的语言是介于一语和二语之间的过渡性语言，有其独特的内部语言系统，应该单独拿出来研究。该文的发表标志着二语习得研究作为一个独立学科的正式开始。

　　二语习得研究要回答三大问题：（1）什么是二语能力？（2）二语能力是如何获得的？（3）为什么二语学习者的最终学习状态存在差异？这些问题都非常难回答，因为里面牵扯到语言本质、学习者和学习过程等诸多方面，涉及语言学、认知心理学、社会学、生物学等学科。这种多学科多视角的研究已经让我们对二语习得这一复杂的过程有了较为深刻的认识，对一些关键因素有了较为深入的理解，例如输入、输出和互动的作用，习得发展阶段、习得顺序等。随着研究的不断深入以及高科技的不断使用，越来越多的谜团正在逐渐被揭开。但同时研究者们也意识到，二语习得就像盲人面前的大象，从不同的部位下手去摸，得到的对大象的认识会不同，摸到尾巴的人说它像绳子，摸到身躯的人说它像一堵墙，摸到大腿的人说它像柱子。然而，要想对二语习得有一个全面透彻的了解，必须首先对这头大象的尾巴、鼻子、大腿等进行深入细致的研究，了解各自的特点及属性。

　　二语习得研究目前还处在对大象不同部位进行深入研究的阶段，不同视角得出的结论不尽相同，有的甚至还互相矛盾，当然也有不少研究正在整合来自不同视角的结果，并获得了不少新的发现。初入二语习得领域的读者可能会有不少疑虑，也很容易因为只看到部分学者的研究就持一孔之见，认为二语习得研究很简单。本书专为入门读者而著，是一本很好的答疑解惑的教科书，既能让读者粗略了解二语习得如大象般庞大复杂的概貌，又让读者欲罢不能，循着书中提供的线索去继续深入阅读。

本书包括五章：引言、二语习得关键议题、主要理论和研究框架、核心术语、代表性论著。内容的编排遵循这样一个原则，第一、二、三章出现的核心术语都用黑体标明，读者碰到这些术语时可以去第四章查阅。这种编排方式使作者可以在一开始就使用专门术语对所介绍的议题进行较为专业的讨论。

下面我们逐章进行介绍。

第一章：引言

首先界定二语习得这个概念及其与外语学习的区别，前者指目的语环境下的语言习得，后者指外语环境下尤其是课堂上的语言学习。作者指出这种区分从语言学或心理学角度来看并没有多大意义，因为二语习得最基本的问题是学习者如何内化除母语外的一种语言体系并将之运用到语言的理解和产出中去。随后，作者简要回顾了二语习得研究的发展历史，介绍从 20 世纪 70 年代开始的每个阶段的研究重点及其对二语习得的贡献。最后，作者指出二语习得研究关注的是学习者及其语言的发展，其研究成果并不一定能直接指导二语教学，但一个合格的语言教师必须要对二语习得有所了解。

第二章：二语习得关键议题

作者列举了二语习得的九大议题，这些议题都围绕一个核心问题，即一语习得和二语习得在多大程度上相似，是否涉及相同的学习者内部加工机制和习得机制。议题的编写体例基本一致，首先是基本概念介绍，然后是围绕议题的主要立场和观点，最后是简要评价。通过阅读本章，读者可以对二语习得的研究范畴和当前研究重点有所了解。

第一个议题是二语习得的初始状态，即学习者用于二语习得的初始语言知识。一语初始状态假说认为学习者从一开始就将一语的所有语言知识迁移到二语的学习中；普遍语法初始状态假说则认为学习者一开始使用的是普遍语法，并不受一语迁移的影响，或受的影响极为有限。作者认为第一种观点得到了普遍的接受和不少实证研究的支持，但同时指出初始状态的研究多依赖自发的口语语料，针对潜在语言能力进行测试。我们平常观察到的学习者语料中的一语使用现象，不是迁移而是交际策略。

第二个议题是二语学习者能否获得类似本族语者的语言能力。除了能与不能这两种截然不同的观点外，第三种观点认为在某些方面可以获得类似本族语者的语言心理表征，但在深层能力与产出的外界面处可能存在问题。作者认为问题的关键应该是为什么多数学习者不能获得类似本族语者的能力，但一个潜在的问题是类似本族语者的选择标准不一问题，这也会导致该问题的不同答案。

第三个议题是关键期问题。这个问题最早是针对一语习得提出来的，后来被应用到二语习得，主要有三种观点：有关键期，因为二语学习者一般不能像一语者习得母语那样成功习得二语；无关键期，语言学习能力的衰退是一个逐渐的过程，不与某一特定时期相连；部分存在关键期的观点则认为普遍语法原则没有关键期，但二语参数的重新设定会在某一关键期后受损。作者认为完全支持或否定关键期的存在都很难获得数据支持，一语的影响或许是造成二语习得普遍不成功的罪魁祸首。

第四个议题为二语发展的路径。二语发展的路径呈现三大主要特征，第一是阶段性发展，在句子结构的习得上尤其如此，例如英语不规则动词过去时的 U 型发展；第二是屈折语素习得有一定的顺序，例如英语进行体 -ing 的习得要先于规则动词的过去时，而后者又先于不规则动词的过去时。这两个特征似乎不受学习环境和课堂教学的影响。第三是语言特征的习得过程中会出现自由变异和系统变异现象。作者指出，尽管学习者的一语背景无法改变二语的发展路径，但对二语发展的速度以及最终的习得状态还是有影响的。至于二语发展为什么具有这些特征，目前尚无定论。

第五个议题是显性学习和隐性学习，分别指对输入信息的有意识加工和无意识加工。关于二者在二语习得中的作用，目前有三种主要观点：二语习得在很大程度上是隐性的；二语习得在很大程度上是显性的；二语习得既包含隐性学习也包含显性学习。第一种观点源自 Krashen 对习得和学得的区分：习得是隐性的，其所获得的知识构成语言能力；学得是显性的，学得的知识只能用来监控学习者的语言运用。普遍语法框架下的二语研究者都认为语言习得是隐性的，语言能力是普遍语法原则与输入信息相互作用的结果；联结主义习得观也认为语言习得是隐性的，但认为语言能力是学习者在频率的影响下对输入信息进行无意识抽象加工的结果。第二种观点认为二语习得始于显性学习，但持该观点的人数较少。第三种观点认为显性学习和隐性学习在习得中都起作用，以 Dekeyser 为代表的技能学习理论认为二语发展是陈述性知识程序化的过程，学习者通过显性学习获得陈述性知识，但程序化过程涉及隐性学习；还有的学者则强调注意在习得中的作用，认为学习者首先必须注意到输入信息中的语言特征，才能习得该特征。作者与普遍语法框架下的研究者持相同的观点，但也承认显性的课堂教学还是有作用的，只是不清楚这种显性学习在普遍语法遭遇输入信息时是否有互动以及如何互动。

第六个议题为输入和输出的作用。关于输入，不同流派的学者意见基本一致，输入是必不可少的。对于形式主义流派来说，输入触发参数的定值，而对于联结主义流派来说，学习者必须接触大量的输入才能抽象出语言规律来。自从 20 世纪 80 年代中期 Merrill Swain 提出输出假说以来，学界对输出作用的辩论一直没有停息，一部分人，包括 Merrill Swain，认为输出是必要的，能导致习得，也有人，如 Krashen，以及形式主义流派的学者，认为输出与习得没有关系。以 Michael Long 为代表的学者则认为与学习者的互动对习得有促进作用，互动能产生反馈，而反馈能让学习者注意到语言形式，因此输出和习得之间存在间接的因果关系。Merrill Swain 近年来的观点也有所改变，她不再强调输出是必要的，但仍认为输出可以促进习得。作者认为互动确实能促进习得，但目前的研究似乎只能证明互动对词汇和语音的习得有帮助，没有特别强的证据显示互动能导致句法的习得，因此将互动与语言能力或语言心理表征的发展联系起来似乎还为时过早。

第七个议题是学习者个体差异及其对习得的影响。二语发展尽管呈现出某些普遍特征，但学习者最终学习状态的差异性很大，学习者的个体差异研究因此成为二语习得研究的一个重要部分，主要集中在四个方面：语言学能、动机、学习风格和学习策略。语言学能指的是学习者用于语言习得的认知能力，包括感知能力、语音编码能力、语法敏感度和工作记忆等，传统上它被看作一个整体的概念，将之与学习成绩等变量进行相关分析研究。近 20 年来语言学能研究发生了明显变化，一些学者开始突破研究传统，重新审视学能的结构问题，如 Robinson 提出了语言学能综合体假说，认为学能是一个动态的结构，不同条件下的语言学习需要运用不同的认知能力或学能组合。动机指的是学习的意愿，过去多从社会心理角度来研究，现在从学习者内部挖掘的研究日益增多，出现了许多与认知学和心理学相关的概念，如学习者的心理自我、自尊和自我调节等。学习风格又叫认知风格，指个体在学习过程中表现出来的习惯化的行为模式。这方面的研究集中在课堂教学环境下，探讨教师的教学风格是否与学生的学习风格一致的问题。学习策略研究主要关注四个问题，（1）学习策略在多大程度上与成功的学习相关；（2）什么样的学习者使用什么样的策略；（3）学习策略是否可教；（4）学习策略都有哪些。作者认为个体差异的研究目的是找出他们与最终习得状态的关系，例如，个体差异对习得发展路径有什么影响？学习风格和策略与学习者的内部加工机制有什么关系？但研究成果缺乏理论支撑，此外个体差异与习得的关系到底是什么也不清楚，作者比较看好学能研究，认为它能在一定程度上揭示二语习得的核心问题，即二语习得与一语习得的异同以及二语学习者的最终学习状态为何存在如此大的差异。

第八个议题是二语教学。关于教学是否有用有四种观点：无用、作用有限、有益、有必要。Krashen 是持无用观点的代表，他认为无意识的学习才是最重要的，课堂的有意识学习对习得没有促进作用，教学不能改变习得顺序和二语发展路径。也有学者认为习得是普遍语法原则与输入相互作用的结果，教学不能让学习者设定参数。此外，关于教学效果的研究多是短期的，鲜有长期的研究来证明教学的效果。以 Pienemann 为代表的学者持第二种观点，认为教学有作用但作用有限。一方面语言特征的可加工性制约着习得，教学不能改变习得顺序；另一方面契合学习者加工能力的教学可以加快习得的步伐。Michael Long 是持第三种观点的代表，他在总结大量研究的基础上指出，教学以及教学和自然习得相结合的方式比纯自然习得更有效，教学能影响习得速度和最终习得状态。Schmidt 从教学能提升学习者注意力的角度支持此观点。Norris 和 Ortega 在 2000 年对 40 多篇课堂教学论文的元分析发现，课堂教学总体上有效果。认为教学是必要的观点在上 20 世纪 80 年代比较盛行，主要证据是自然状态下学习者的语言系统会出现僵化现象，而教学是解决该问题的唯一出路。但迄今没有任何证据证明没有教学学习者就无法习得语言。教学是二语习得尤其是外语学习的重要手段，进入 90 年代后，学者们不再纠结于教学是否有用，而是把重点转移到了什么样的教学才能促进习得，输入强化、输入加工和重形式教学等教学改革应运而生。

第九个议题是二语习得的制约因素。从形式主义语言学的角度来看，语言的发展受到普遍语法的制约，学习者与生俱来的普遍语法限制了他们的假设空间，使得他们不去犯某些语言错误。类型共性也对语言发展有制约作用，它指的是在多语种语料的基础上对语言某些方面进行归纳研究后高度概括出来的蕴含共性，即，如果某种语言中存在某一种语言现象，则一定会存在另一种语言现象，反之则不然。例如，如果关系代词可以在关系从句中作宾语，那么它一定能在关系从句中作主语。与此相关的一个概念是标记性：假如，A、B 是属于同一范畴的两个项目，如果 A 的存在蕴含 B 的存在，反之不然，那么，A 具有标记性，B 是无标记的。标记性会制约习得，无标记的语言特征比有标记的语言特征要先习得。从认知角度来说，大脑的加工机制也制约习得。研究显示疑问词作主语的 wh- 疑问句要先于疑问词作宾语的疑问句的习得，William O'Crady 从加工机制的角度解读说这是由于疑问词作宾语从结构上来说需要更多的移位，因此计算起来更复杂。Pienemann 的可加工性理论也是从加工程序的角度来研究输出加工对习得的制约，他认为输出加工包含六级加工程序，严重制约了学习者输出中语言特征出现的顺序。此外，输入的可及性、互动的可及性和一语迁移都是制约二语习得的因素。

第三章：主要理论和研究框架

本章之所以取名主要理论和研究框架，是因为作者特意强调理论和框架不是同一个概念。理论是对自然发生的现象的一整套解释，其首要目的是解释现有现象，其次是作出预测。框架和模型是建立在不同理论的融合基础上的，比理论涉及面更广，其目的不是解释和作出预测，而更多的是描述。一个好的理论能让我们作出能证伪的假设，但假设也可以在没有理论的情况下作出，因此理论和假设也不是同一概念。按照作者的定义，本章包括五大理论：普遍语法理论、涌现论和基于使用的理论、可加工性理论、社会文化理论、技能学习理论；一个假说：互动假说；两个模型：陈述／程序模型、输入加工模型；以及一个框架：复杂理论。

本章的编写模式基本一致，首先介绍基本概念，然后列举主要主张，最后是结论，包括简要的评论和代表学者名单。我们以涌现论和基于使用的理论为例。涌现论是认知心理学的一个理论，强调生物体与环境的相互作用，否认任何先天的领域专用的机制或能力。涌现论认为语言与自然界中存在的绝大多数复杂系统一样具有层级结构，当相对简单的发展程序暴露在大型复杂的环境当中时，语言的复杂性就自然出现了。就语言习得来说，我们一般的广域学习机制足以让我们获得复杂的语言表征。在这一认识上，涌现论与基于使用的其他二语习得理论不谋而合，都认为语言学习主要基于语言使用，学习者通过广域认知机制从输入中抽象出二语的规律。作者在基于使用的二语习得理论后面加了一个复数，因为它不是一个理论，而是指遵循相同理念的多个语言学理论，如认知语言学、构式语法等。作者以涌现论为例列举了基于使用的二语习得理论最重要的两个理念：语言学习是隐性的统计学习；语言以及语言特性都是简单的认知学习机制与环境作用而涌现的结果。在结论部分，作者指出，尽管涌现论受到了很多学者的关注，但还是缺乏实证研究的支持，有些研究采用电脑来模拟二语习得，但是否适用于二语学习者还不清楚。另外，作者指出，涌现论无法解释刺激贫乏问题，即学习者是如何获得超出他们所接触的语言知识之外的知识的，也无法解释为什么有的语言特征出现频率很高，学习者却习得很晚。在这点上作者可能陷入了对该理论常见的误解，即认为它只在意数字，过于注重语言构式的频率，但实际上它主张构式的习得受目标构式和学习者语言发展状态影响，并不认为频率越高，构式就越显著，就越易习得。

另一个值得一提的是输入加工模型，该模型的构建者是本书的作者之一 Bill VanPatten。该模型认为学习者在理解语言材料时，会使用一套加工策略将语言形式与意义相联结，这些加工策略遵循四大普遍原则：实义词优先原则，词汇优先原则，第一名词原则和句子定位原则。例如第一名词原则对那些严格执行主、谓、宾或主、宾、谓句子结构的语言很适用，但不是所有语言都遵循这个语序，因此学习者在学习宾、谓、主这样的句子时，就容易把第一个名词当成主语。显然这种加工策略制约了学习者二语的习得，输入加工模型就是针对这个问题提出来的。该模型融合了不同理论的观点，如普遍语法理论和涌现论关于输入与心理表征关系的观点。因为其强调教学干预对学习者输入加工初期联结形式与意义的影响，在二语教学领域获得了不少关注。但作者也承认该模型对一语在二语习得中的影响关注不够，也没有充分考虑其他影响习得的因素，如输出或互动。

二语习得理论需要围绕语言的本质、学习者和学习过程三个核心方面来建构，但目前还没有任何一个理论能将这三个方面完美地整合在一起。本书介绍的九个理论和框架中，有八个针对的是学习者和学习过程，只有一个对语言的本质进行了非常详细的阐述，这就是乔姆斯基的普遍语法理论。普遍语法理论其实不是习得理论，而是语言理论，即关于语言本质的理论。它认为语言知识是天生的，是语言使用者大脑里抽象的隐性的构成语言系统的大脑表征。一个重要的概念就是普遍语法，人类独有的与生俱来的普遍语法使儿童先天就具备在短时间内掌握母语的能力，语言是靠语言输入触发习得的，而不是学得的。将该理论运用到二语习得，有三个重要主张：（1）所有人类语言，包括二语中介语，都受普遍语法的制约；（2）二语习得环境与一语习得环境一样都存在刺激贫乏问题；（3）尽管普遍语法制约二语习得，但它不能保证学习者都能获得本族语者那样的语言能力。因为普遍语法理论对语言本质进行了非常清楚的界定，因此研究者们可以依托该理论构建可证伪的假设或作出预测，但其弱点是它不是一个习得理论，无法对学习者中介语的发展过程进行解释。

其他八个理论和框架针对学习者和学习过程。例如，可加工性理论认为，二语句法的发展受到加工机制的约束，学习者只能理解和产出当前阶段语言处理器能处理的语言形式。该理论能较好地解释二语发展的阶段性特征，也是目前唯一清晰地阐述语法特征如何在学习者的产出中逐渐出现的理论，能预测二语的发展轨迹。陈述/程序模型认为陈述记忆和程序记忆在一语和二语习得中起着关键作用，词汇知识依赖陈述性记忆，语法知识最初储存在陈述性记忆中，在足够的语言接触后，基于程序性记忆的语法加工会超越陈述性加工，语法知识逐渐自动化。青春期后，程序性记忆慢慢减退，陈述性记忆占主导，加上语言输入的减少和语言学习经历的改变，成人二语习得和加工更多地依赖陈述性记忆。该模型较好地解释了一语和二语习得的异同，对二语学习者为什么难以获得本族语者同样的语言能力有较强的解释力。社会文化理论从社会心理角度来解释学习的发生，认为高级心理活动是一个在社会文化环境影响下，借助中介通过调节的作用而发展的过程。中介、内化和最近发展区是该理论的三个基本概念，它强调知识构建过程中个体对社会环境和社会活动的依赖性，强调个体借助针对其最近发展区的中介将高级心理活动由人际间向心理内转变的过程。语言学习作为人的一种高级心理活动，也必然遵循这样一个从外部心理间的社会活动层面向内部心理内活动层面转化的发展过程，从这个角度来看，二语学习者的语言发展就是从由互动中的他人调节转移到自我调节的过程。

复杂理论是本章介绍的唯一研究框架，它将语言习得的认知观和社会观结合起来，把二语习得系统看成一个复杂、开放、自组织、自适应的动态变化系统。语言学习不再是往恒久不变的系统里增加新知识，而是在教师、学生、环境等多种要素的交互作用下重构系统。学习者不是被动的输入吸收者，他们的语言发展是不断重构语言系统以适应新的语境的结果。学习者的语言不是目标语的残次版本，而是一个不断自我修正的自然发生的系统。二语学习没有终点，二语发展变化的过程永无休止。作者认为该理论不是针对某个特定现象而构建的，而是可以整合来自不同理论的预测和发现，让我们更好地体会语言习得这样一个受多因素影响、涉及面广的复杂活动。

第四章：核心术语

第四章是本书的主要内容，按照字母顺序一共介绍了 139 个核心术语。术语的收录比较全面，基本上囊括了二语习得领域的基本概念以及各流派重要研究所涉及的关键术语，使读者能够比较全面地了解该领域的大致轮廓。编写的结构和细节层次大致相同，术语多以简洁的定义开始，然后是较为细致的相关议题或研究的描述，有的还有研究案例，多数术语还提及了相关研究的代表学者。另外，几乎所有的术语都与前面的引言、关键议题和主要理论三章交叉参考，使读者能够尽快地找到想要找的内容，也使整部作品的结构更有条理，更加紧凑。

第五章：代表性论著

本章按照论著作者姓名的字母顺序列举了二语习得的重要文献，依托这些文献，读者能对该领域的研究范畴、关键议题和主要理论有更深入的了解。但从目标读者角度来看，这部分或许易读性不如其他部分。部分文献在前面核心术语部分提到过，读者可以借助这些线索结合文献作进一步阅读，但也有不少文献在书的其他地方并未涉及，加上没作任何注释，也未按主题分类，对于一个在该领域涉猎不深的读者来说，其用途可能有限。尽管如此，该部分选录的文献都是论及二语习得领域重大议题的代表作，对于想在此领域进行系统深入学习的读者来说，不失为经典的参考文献。

参考文献

Gass, S. M. & Selinker, L. (2008). *Second Language Acquisition: An Introductory Course* (3rd ed.). New York and London: Routledge.

Muriel Saville-Troike, (2012). *Introducing Second Language Acquisition* (2nd ed.). New York: Cambridge University Press.

VanPatten, B. & Williams, J. (eds.). (2015). *Theories in Second Language Acquisition: An Introduction* (2nd ed.). New York: Routledge.

陈亚平

北京外国语大学

Acknowledgments

We would like to thank the many folks at Bloomsbury for their help in the preparation of this book. Our special thanks go to Gurdeep Mattu, Andrew Wardell, and Balaji Kasirajan. In addition, we would like to thank our colleague Wynne Wong, who read portions of the first-edition manuscript and offered feedback and suggestions. To be sure, we do not hold her or anyone else responsible for any omissions or errors contained in this book. We also thank the anonymous reviewers who provided ideas during the planning stage of the second edition. Finally, we would like to thank our families and friends who put up with our hectic work and writing schedules. In a world that doesn't always appreciate academic efforts, it is comforting to have those around us who understand why we academics do what we do.

Introduction

What is second language acquisition?

Second language acquisition (SLA) is a research field that focuses on learners and learning rather than teachers and teaching. In the bestselling text *Second Language Acquisition: An Introductory Course*, Gass, Behney, and Plonsky (2013, p. 1) define SLA as "the study of how learners create a new language system." As a research field, they add that SLA is the study of what is learned of a second language and what is not learned.

An examination of any other introductory or overview texts would reveal similar definitions and discussions of the scope of SLA research (e.g., Doughty & Long, 2003; VanPatten, 2003; White, 2003; Lightbown & Spada, 2006; Gass & Mackey, 2012; Ortega, 2015; VanPatten & Williams, 2015). Moreover, such definitions would include a concern for both processes and products involved in how languages are learned, as the field is informed by a variety of disciplines such as linguistics, psychology, and education. These different influences are most easily seen in the edited volume by VanPatten and Williams (2015) on theories in SLA. The mainstream theories represented in that volume reflect the multifaceted nature of SLA, as well as the various parent disciplines that have come to inform research on language learning.

Some make the distinction between *foreign* language learning and *second* language acquisition. The former is used to refer to language learning in contexts in which the language is not normally spoken outside the classroom, such as learning French in Newcastle, United Kingdom, or Greek in Omaha, Nebraska, in the United States. SLA is used by some to refer to those contexts in which the language is used outside the classroom, as in the case of learning English in the United States or learning Spanish in Spain. While such distinctions are useful from a sociological perspective, they have little linguistic or psychological validity. As has been argued repeatedly in the literature, people and the mechanisms they possess for language learning do not change from context to context. The mind/brain still has to do what it has to do whether instruction in language is present or not, and whether there is presence or absence of opportunities to interact with speakers of the language. To be sure, context impacts rate and ultimate proficiency, but context does not impact the underlying processes involved in learning another language. Thus, it is common in the field of L2 research to place all contexts of learning under the umbrella term *second language acquisition.*

Looking at the various definitions of SLA, what emerges is a concern about learners and learning. The field of SLA addresses the fundamental questions of how learners come to internalize the linguistic system of another language and how they make use of that linguistic system during comprehension and speech production. Although, we can draw some pedagogical implications from theories and research in SLA, the main objective of SLA research is learning and not teaching, although we will touch upon the relationship between SLA and language teaching later in this introduction.

A brief history of SLA

Contemporary research in SLA has its roots in two seminal publications. The first is S. Pit Corder's (1967) essay "The Significance of Learners'

Errors." Concerned largely with teaching, Corder noted that advances in language instruction would not occur until we understood what language learners bring to the task of acquisition. Influenced by L1 research—which had repudiated any kind of strict behaviorist account of child language acquisition—Corder suggested that like children, perhaps L2 learners came equipped with something internal, something that guided and constrained their acquisition of the formal properties of language. He called this something "the internal syllabus," noting that it did not necessarily match the syllabus that instruction attempted to impose upon learners. Corder also made a distinction between **input** and **intake**, defining input as the language available from the environment, but intake as that language that actually makes its way into the learner's developing competence. This distinction is still held today in the field.

The second seminal work is Larry Selinker's "Interlanguage," published in 1972. In this article, Selinker argued that L2 learners possessed an internal linguistic system worthy of study in its own right, a language system that had to be taken on its own terms and not as some corrupted version of the L2. He called this system an **interlanguage** because the system was neither the L1 nor the L2, but something in-between that the learners were building from environmental data. Selinker also posited a number of constructs still central today in L2 research, notably L1 **transfer** and **fossilization**—each of which is described elsewhere in this book.

Thus, these two critical thinkers laid the foundation upon which the next decades of work on SLA was forged.

The 1970s

The 1970s was marked largely by descriptive studies that sought to refute behaviorism and to apply the basic ideas of Corder and Selinker. During this time frame, we saw the emergence of research on **acquisition orders** (the famous **morpheme studies**) that replicated both the methodology and the findings of L1 acquisition research in the L2 context. We also saw the emergence of research on **transitional stages** of competence, which again replicated important findings from L1 research. The picture that began to take shape was that indeed L2 learners possessed built-in syllabi that directed their course of development just as Corder had previously suggested. This time period also gave birth to **error analysis**, the careful examination of learner output with particular attention to "errors" (categorized as deviations from L2 normative language). From error analysis scholars began to minimize L1 influence on SLA; that is, researchers revealed that L1 transfer was not as widespread as once thought. To be sure, this period was heavily marked by research on English as a second language, especially by non-classroom learners, leaving some professionals in other languages to dismiss the findings as inapplicable to classroom learners and to learners of other languages.

However, research in the 1980s and 1990s would subsequently demonstrate that the general tenets of SLA were applicable to all languages in all contexts.

The 1980s

By the early 1980s, Krashen's ideas on acquisition (see **Monitor Theory** and **acquisition versus learning**, and **Input Hypothesis**, for example) were mainstream. He had posited that learners acquire language through interaction with language, most notably through comprehension of the input they are exposed to. While fundamentally true, Krashen's ideas left a good amount of acquisition unexplained and the 1980s overall is marked by a critical review of his ideas and the quest for more explanatory models about the specifics of acquisition. For example, if L1 influence is limited, why was it limited? If learners had a built-in syllabus, what was this built-in syllabus and where did it come from? And if all learners needed was exposure to input, why were so many

L2 learners non-native-like after so many years of interaction with the language?

It is in this time frame, then, that we see the application of theories from other domains. For example, Lydia White led the charge to use linguistic theory to describe learner competence and to speculate why that competence looked the way it did. Manfred Pienemann began to explore the use of Lexical Functional Grammar and speech processing models to explain the developmental nature of learner output. We also see the beginnings of the application of cognitive theory and other psychological approaches (e.g., connectionism) to SLA, applications that would not reach any real impact until the 1990s. The point here is that SLA researchers began looking seriously at the nature of theories and what theories needed to do in order to explain SLA.

The 1990s

The 1990s witnessed a burgeoning of competing theoretical ideas and approaches regarding SLA, with an additional plethora of isolated hypotheses that took hold in the general literature (e.g., **noticing**, the **Output Hypothesis**, the **Interaction Hypothesis**—all of which had roots in the 1980s). Nonetheless, two major approaches dominated the field: the application of linguistic theory and the application of certain psychological approaches—namely, skill theory and the modern version of associationism (see **connectionism**). The linguistic theoretical approach continued to be concerned with an adequate description of interlanguage as well as its explanation. That is, scholars in this camp focused on the nature of the learner's internal mental representation and what constrained it. A central tenet of this approach is that language is special. By "special," these scholars meant that language is uniquely human, is encapsulated in its own module in the mind/brain, and comes equipped from birth with a set of language-specific constraints called **Universal Grammar**. Thus, acquisition was a particular kind of experience for humans that involved the interaction of Universal Grammar with data from the outside world.

Scholars in the psychological camp tended to eschew any linguistic description of an interlanguage and indeed some went so far as to say that there was no mental representation at all. Interested largely in behavior, this camp did not concern itself with underlying knowledge per se but more with what learners did with language. Because they saw language as just another instance of human behavior, the belief was that theories of behavior should be sufficient to account for SLA and thus there was no need to posit unique faculties of the mind that dealt exclusively with language. As such, there was nothing special about language—and if indeed the learner had any mental representation that could be called language, it was an artifact of learning, a latent structure that emerged based on data the learner had encountered in the environment. Language acquisition was the interaction of general human learning mechanisms with data from the outside world.

Again, other approaches emerged such as Processability Theory (see **processability**), **input processing**, and others, but in many ways these theories could be seen as compatible with either linguistic theory or cognitive theory, depending on the particulars of each theory. One theory that emerged in the 1990s largely due to concerns with educational practice was **Sociocultural Theory**. As an account of SLA, it dismissed both linguistic theory and cognitive theory as being too "mind/brain" oriented and instead situated the learner as an active agent in learning within particular social contexts.

The 2000s and beyond

It is fair to say that as of the writing of this book, SLA looks pretty much like it did in the second half of the 1990s in terms of foci. As a discipline, it is splintered, with certain camps not in dialogue with others. Both linguistic and cognitive approaches continue to dominate the field—although social and sociocultural perspectives have made significant inroads into the discourse on SLA—and we do not envision this changing in the near future, largely because of the sheer number of people working within these fields and also because of the healthy research agenda both camps enjoy outside the field of SLA; that is, linguistic theory is alive and well and is applied to a range of endeavors from child first language acquisition to natural language processing, and psychology as a discipline is very well situated within academia and has been for over a century. Thus, we see the field of SLA staying largely focused on the mind/brain. After all, that's where language resides, either as a special mental representation as the linguists would have it or as some manifestation of behavioral imprints as the psychologists would have it. In the end, even those who take a strong social context approach to acquisition would have to admit that language is a property of the mind and although learning may happen through interaction and through "dialogic discourse," language ends up in the mind/brain of the learner.

Second language acquisition and second language teaching

Because the contemporary field of SLA research has its roots in concerns for language instruction, it is natural for many language-teaching professionals to look to SLA research for insights into teaching. In the early days of SLA research, for example, people wondered how information on acquisition orders could be applied to language teaching. Should we teach language structures in the order in which they are acquired? Because these structural elements are acquired in a fixed order anyway, should we forget about teaching them altogether and just let them emerge on their own? These and similar questions have "stalked" the field since the mid-1970s and by the 1980s there seemed to be some pressure on SLA specialists to "produce applicable results" for language teachers. To this end, Patsy Lightbown published a widely-cited piece titled "Great Expectations: Second Language Acquisition Research and Classroom Teaching" in 1985. In that paper, she described the tension between teacher expectations about research and what researchers were interested in and what they researched. It was clear from her discussion that there was a gap, and that SLA had emerged as a vibrant field of research that may or may not have immediate implications for instruction.

Nonetheless, a subfield within SLA research emerged to address the role of formal instruction on second language development: instructed SLA. Unlike general SLA research, which focuses on the learner and the development of language over time, instructed SLA focuses on the degree to which external manipulation (e.g., instruction, learner self-directed learning, input manipulation) can affect development in some way. Since the mid-1980s, a good deal has been learned about the effects of formal instruction, some of which are described elsewhere in this book. The point here is that the picture that now exists is this: Any focus on instruction must consider what we already know about SLA more generally. That is, both instruction and instructed SLA cannot ignore the findings of SLA research and must be informed by it. Here is one example: If we know that particular linguistic structures are acquired in a particular order over time, what is the purpose of instruction on those same structures? If an instructor believes he or she can get learners to learn something early that is normally acquired later in acquisition, is that instructor making the best use of his or her time? When researchers in instructed SLA choose to examine the effects of formal instruction, how do they select the linguistic features and why do they select the ones they do? These are important questions, and it is SLA research that can help to inform instructors and researchers about the choices they make.

Our perspective, then, is that even though a significant gap exists between research on SLA and teacher expectations, there is enough of

SLA research in existence that is useful for general teacher edification. The more one understands the nature of the object of one's profession, the better one is situated to make choices, answer questions, and to best utilize one's time and efforts. Unfortunately, from our perspective, language teachers are often woefully undereducated in the general findings of SLA. While a general course on SLA often forms the background for those prepared at the graduate level in TESOL, this is not the case for those who teach other languages and is certainly not the case for those who enter the language-teaching profession with a baccalaureate degree or equivalent. Even though the present book is not about instructed SLA or language teaching, hopefully it will inspire language teachers to learn more about acquisition and to reflect on language teaching more generally.

About this book

Key Terms in Second Language Acquisition is divided into four major sections: Key Questions, Key Theories and Frameworks, Key Terms, and Key Readings. In Key Questions, we present nine of the major questions that confront SLA research today. Our presentations are necessarily brief as our goal is not to be exhaustive but rather to sketch the basics for the novice readers. Citations provided within this section will lead the readers to original and more thorough treatments. In Key Theories, we briefly introduce the readers to the dominant current theories in the field of SLA, outlining basic ideas in each as well as their basic claims. In Key Terms, we provide encyclopedia-like descriptions of a good number of terms used in the SLA literature. To be sure, this list is not exhaustive and we apologize in advance for any terms we may have left out. In preparing a book like this, one has to make the cut somewhere in order not to have a large collection of all terms used in SLA research.

Finally, in Key Readings, we provide information on not only the references cited elsewhere in this book, but also additional references that may be of use to the novice readers. Again, we apologize if we are not all-inclusive. Our hope is, though, that we have provided enough for the beginner to bootstrap himself or herself into a complicated field of inquiry.

The readers will note that throughout the book, certain words and phrases appear in bold as in the following passage taken from an earlier paragraph in this introduction:

"The 1990s witnessed a burgeoning of competing theoretical ideas and approaches regarding SLA, with an additional plethora of isolated hypotheses that took hold in the general literature (e.g., **noticing**, the **Output Hypothesis**, the **Interaction Hypothesis**—all of which had roots in the 1980s)."

The boldface signals a key term that can be found in this book. Thus, when reading the above, the reader can turn to the Key Terms section and find descriptions of noticing, the Output Hypothesis, and the Interaction Hypothesis. At other times, the reader may see a key issue referenced within the text as in the following example: "How far learners get in terms of acquisition is open to debate (see **Can L2 learners become native-like?**)." Again, in such cases the reader can turn to the Key Questions section and find the relevant information.

Key Questions in Second Language Acquisition

Like any field of inquiry, SLA research is driven by a number of major issues or questions. These include the following:

1. What is the initial state? That is, what do learners bring to the task of acquisition in terms of underlying knowledge related to language?
2. Can L2 learners become native-like?
3. Is there a critical period?
4. What does development look like?
5. What are the roles of explicit and implicit learning in SLA?
6. What are the roles of input and output in SLA?
7. What are individual differences and how do they affect acquisition?
8. Does instruction make a difference?
9. What constraints are there on acquisition?

To be sure, there are other questions that scholars address, but many of these are related to the above questions. For example, some scholars are deeply interested in the role of interaction (e.g., conversation) in language acquisition. We see this topic related to the role of output more generally and will treat it in that section.

We would also like to state here that all of the questions listed above are themselves related to an overarching question that lurks in the background of SLA: To what extent are first and second language acquisition the same thing (i.e., involve the same learner-internal processing and acquisition mechanisms)? Everyone knows that first and second language acquisition must differ due to contextual differences: quality and quantity of input and interaction; topic and focus of interactions; exposure to formal rules; differences between children and adults; and so on. But ultimately, acquisition is something that happens in the brain/mind as it processes and stores language. Is SLA like first language acquisition in this regard, or is SLA guided by fundamentally different internal mechanisms? And if there are processes and mechanisms common to L1 acquisition and SLA, then why do SLA learners vary so much in terms of outcome, while L1 learners all seem to converge on the same linguistic system and same general abilities (metalinguistic and educational knowledge regarding language notwithstanding)?

So, in a sense, all of the questions listed above (as well as related questions) are various manifestations of the issue of L1 versus L2 acquisition in one way or another. Because of their interrelatedness, the readers may see some overlap in discussion of each question and for sure will see the interconnectedness of the issues presented. We hope that this brief overview of key questions in SLA inspires the novice readers to pursue SLA research to a greater degree. There are some excellent overview texts as well as handbooks that provide much more detailed information and evaluative comments that we cannot provide here (e.g., Doughty & Long, 2003; Kroll & de Groot, 2005; Gass, Behney & Plonsky, 2013; VanPatten & Williams, 2015). The reader ought to consider our short descriptions here as "advanced organizers" for reading more detailed and sometimes more technical materials on SLA.

Question 1: What is the initial state?

The concept of initial state refers to the starting point for L2 learners, namely, what they bring to the task of acquiring another language. There are two basic positions on the initial state of SLA: (1) The learner transfers all properties of the first language at the outset (the L1 = initial state hypothesis); (2) The learner begins with "universals of language" and does not transfer L1 properties at the outset. All other positions are some variations of these two (e.g., there might be partial transfer). Under no scenario does any theory or framework believe that the learner comes to the task of acquisition as a "blank slate." Everyone believes something is there at the beginning of SLA; the question is *what*.

L1 = Initial state

A number of scholars believe that from the very beginning, all the properties of the L1 are transferred into SLA (e.g., Schwartz & Sprouse, 1996). Under this scenario, the learner assumes (unconsciously) that the L2 is just like the L1. This is commonly referred to as *full transfer*. The job of the learner subsequently is to replace L1 properties with appropriate L2 properties. Within one theory (**Universal Grammar**) this is often called "parameter resetting" (see, for example, White, 2003). We will illustrate with a simple example from English and Spanish.

Spanish is what linguists call a null subject language. Null subject languages allow free omission of subject pronouns in finite sentences or clauses (i.e., sentences that have tense). Thus, *Habla mucho* 'He talks a lot' is a perfectly fine sentence as is *Él habla mucho* (*él* = the overt subject pronoun 'he'). English is a non-null-subject language, and thus 'Talks a lot' is not normally permitted; the subject pronoun 'he' is required as in 'He talks a lot.' Compare (an asterisk indicates a sentence is not well formed):

SPANISH

María: ¿Conoces a Juan? 'Do you know John?'

Julieta: Sí. Habla mucho. 'Yes. He talks a lot.'

ENGLISH

Mary: Do you know John?

Juliet: Yes. *Talks a lot.

At the same time, there are sentences in Spanish in which a null subject is actually required and an overt pronoun is prohibited. These include weather and time expressions: *Está lloviendo* 'It's raining,' *Es la una* 'It's one o'clock'; impersonal expressions with "it's": *Es imposible* 'It's impossible,' *Es difícil* 'It's difficult'; and existential statements such as *¿Hay café?* 'Is there coffee?' That is, in these kinds of sentences, an overt subject pronoun is not allowed (e.g., *Ello es la una). In English, these kinds of expressions require the dummy subject 'it' or 'there' (in existential sentences): *It's one o'clock/*Is one o'clock* and *There's lots of food/*Is lots of food*. We would say that Spanish has the parameter set to +null subject, while English has it set to –null subject.

Proponents of the L1 = initial state position would claim that speakers of Spanish begin acquisition by unconsciously assuming that English is +null subject, and thus it has all the same null subject properties as Spanish. At the beginning, these learners would believe that *Is raining* is a perfectly fine sentence in English. Researchers would also claim that speakers of English would begin acquisition assuming that Spanish is –null subject, again with all the properties associated with this **parameter**. These learners would initially believe that *Ello está lloviendo* is fine. In each case, it would be the job of the learners to reset to the appropriate parameter during acquisition.

Various theories would talk about the properties of the L1 in different ways: that is, not all would talk about parameters. Some would talk about **form-function** relationships and meaning (e.g., as in **functional approaches** or **connectionism**); others might refer to **processing** and **parsing** routines (how learners compute syntactic relationships in real time while listening or reading), claiming that L1 processing routines are transferred into SLA. Still, other theories might claim that something different is transferred. The point here is that regardless of the theory, they would all agree that the L1 is the starting point and that learners must "overwrite" the properties (or processing routines or whatever) to create a new system. Errors that learners make should reveal influence from the L1. In addition, researchers could administer certain kinds of tests (e.g., **grammaticality judgment** tests, truth-value tests) to probe the underlying competence of learners for L1 influence.

Universals = Initial state

Proponents of the universals = initial state hypothesis believe that L2 learners begin acquisition much like children learning their first language. That is, they come to the task of SLA with whatever internal mechanisms guiding language acquisition that L1 learners have and little else in terms of "linguistic baggage." This can be called the *no transfer* position. Depending on the theory the researcher uses, these internal mechanisms can be linguistic or cognitive in nature. Returning to the earlier example of null subjects, proponents of the universals = initial state hypothesis would say that learners begin acquisition without making any assumptions; that is, learners are "open" to the language being either +null subject or –null subject. Rather than "reset" the parameter, learners would simply "set" it based on the evidence they receive. Errors made by the learners would not necessarily reflect influence from the L1, and tests that scholars would give them to probe their underlying competence should likewise not reveal L1 influence.

For those researchers who do not ascribe to a linguistic theory like Universal Grammar, the universals may be of some other sort. For example, they could be processing universals related to *computational complexity*. Computational complexity refers to structural complexity. The more "stuff moves around" in a sentence and is syntactically far from its starting point, the more difficult it is to process and thus acquire. An example would be *wh*-movement in questions with subjects and objects. *Wh*-elements (question words such as *who, what,* and *where*) are said to move from a point of origin in a sentence to occupy a spot higher in a syntactic tree. In practical terms, this means the *wh*-element moves to the front of the sentence. The subject *who*, for example, moves from the subject position before the verb to the front of the sentence and is represented like this (note that this is not how syntacticians would annotate the sentence; we are taking liberty here for illustration): *Who* $[_S [_{VP}$ *met Mary]]?* The subscript $_S$ stands for 'sentence,' the $_{VP}$ stands for 'verb phrase,' and the stands for the place where *who* originated. This contrasts with object *who* which originates behind a verb and within a verb phrase: *Who* $[_S$ – *did Mary* $[_{VP}$ *see* – *]]?* The object *who* has to travel a longer syntactic distance: It crosses a verb phrase and a subject node to get to where it is. The subject *who*, however, crosses only the sentence node. Thus, it is syntactically easier to compute in acquisition. Research on both first and second language acquisition has shown this to be the case (see, for example, O'Grady, 2003) and subject *who* appears in speech before object *who*.

Thus, processing accounts are more concerned about how learners compute syntactic relations during comprehension and how this affects acquisition (remembering that acquisition is input-dependent, learners have to process the input before they can actually acquire anything). Computational complexity falls under universals because the complexity is seen as the same for all learners regardless of first language; that is, all learners will have more difficulty computing grammatical information that crosses multiple syntactic boundaries compared to computing those that cross only one, for example.

Limited or partial L1 transfer

Some scholars working from a linguistic perspective believe that there is L1 transfer but that it is limited. For example, Vainikka and Young-Scholten (1996) have advanced the idea of *partial transfer*. They claim that learners transfer the **lexicon** and its syntactic properties (e.g., arguments that a verb requires for the sentence to be grammatical, such as *put* requires three arguments—a putter, something put, and the place it is put—while *die* requires only one—the entity experiencing the death) but not the functional features of language related to things such as tense, person-number, and agreement. They predict that learners would make limited L1-influenced errors such as basic word order. For example, an L2 learner of Japanese with English as L1 would begin acquisition transferring subject-verb-object word order, while Japanese is subject-object-verb. However, that learner would not transfer the features related to how English makes agreement on verbs or how English encodes pastness on verbs.

Pienemann (1998), coming from an output processing perspective, believes that L1 output procedures (how people put together syntax and lexicon in real time while speaking) are not fully transferred into SLA. In his framework (see **processability**), learners must acquire L2 output processing procedures that interface with the learner's developing grammar, and that these are responsible for learners' spontaneous production. L1 output procedures can only be transferred when the learner is at a point in acquisition where he or she has acquired the L2 processing routine *and* there is similarity between the L1 and L2 structure in question. (The issue is more complex than this and the reader is invited to review the work on processability and L1 transfer.)

Assessment

Based on the published literature to date, it seems that the L1 = initial state position is more widely accepted and appears to have the most empirical support. This is especially true of researchers who use linguistic theory (such as Universal Grammar) as their framework, but is also true of researchers coming from cognitive or processing perspectives. The exception would be Pienemann's framework, which continues to limit transferability of L1 because of his focus on processing procedures for speech and not on the underlying competence of L2 learners.

The reader should be aware that research on the initial state relies on spontaneous spoken data as well as tests that attempt to tap underlying competence. Language instructors may see much more evidence of L1 influence in learners because they tend to deal less with spontaneous data and less with concern for underlying competence. Because classroom learners may be pushed to produce beyond their current capacity, they will often create utterances by relying on their L1 and "dressing it up" in L2 words. However, this is not transfer as understood here. This type of language production may be classified more as a communication strategy used by someone who is not linguistically ready to produce needed language.

Question 2: Can L2 learners become native-like?

Most L2 learners have some kind of perceptible accent, and it is not uncommon for someone to ask "Where are you from?" when detecting something in the non-native's speech. One major question that has been researched extensively in the L2 literature is the degree to which an L2 learner can develop native-like ability with the language. Currently there are three positions: (1) L2 learners cannot develop native-like L2 ability; (2) L2 learners can develop native-like ability; and (3) L2 learners can develop native-like underlying competence in some if not all domains, but there may be problems in terms of the interface between underlying competence and production. These positions are tied to the concept of **ultimate attainment**: How far can learners get in acquisition? This issue of ultimate attainment may also be linked to the concept of a **critical period**, which we will discuss in a different key question.

L2 learners cannot become native-like

This position holds that L2 learners are unable to achieve native-like ability, and the bulk of evidence comes from research on grammatical development as well as **phonology** (sound system and pronunciation). Typically in this research, very advanced native-like L2 learners are compared with native speakers on a variety of grammatical features (e.g., **tense, aspect,** syntactic structures). The researcher first determines if someone is native-like by recording them and having a panel of judges (all natives) listen to the recordings and rate the speakers on a scale of, say, 1–5. To be considered a native-like speaker, the participant has to receive a score that is statistically not different from that given to native speakers who have also been recorded and mixed into the fray. Subsequently, the researcher administers a battery of tests designed to tap the underlying competence of the participant. These are usually paper and pencil tests designed to get at intuitions about the language that native speakers typically possess, but more recent research has begun to examine processing and parsing (how learners create syntactic structure in real time while listening to or reading sentences).

Research from this side of the question has shown, for example, that few if any native-like speakers demonstrate native-like underlying competence. Their scores on the tests of intuitions may yield scores that are significantly different from those of a group of native speakers. One of the most widely cited studies in this camp, which was foundational in nature, is by Coppieters (1987). He tested very advanced learners of French L2 on morphological, syntactic, and semantic properties and compared them with native French speakers. On his measures, he found considerable deviation between natives and non-natives. A number of other studies have echoed Coppieters' work, all in the realm of syntactic properties of language. Another widely cited study is by Johnson and Newport (1991). In that study, Chinese learners of English L2 were found to differ substantially from native speakers on their intuitions about **subjacency** violations.

In terms of phonology, a number of studies suggest that non-natives cannot achieve native-like pronunciation. James Flege and his colleagues, for example, have demonstrated that early L2 learners (i.e., children) can attain a native-like accent but that late L2 learners (i.e., adolescents and adults) cannot. To be sure, Flege does not wholeheartedly endorse that learners "can't" become native-like; his conclusion is that native-likeness decreases with the age of learning an L2.

L2 learners can become native-like

On the other side of the question are those researchers who have found some support that L2 learners can become native-like. On the question of phonological properties of language, Theo Bongaerts and his colleagues have produced a number of studies that demonstrate that L2 learners can become native-like in pronunciation; that is, their pronunciation is consistently mistaken by native judges to be native-like, and these judges mark them as 'native' on the measures Bongaerts has used.

One name associated with the idea that L2 learners can become native-like in the **syntax** and **morphology** of language is David Birdsong. His well-known 1992 study was a direct response to Coppieters' work (discussed earlier). He found problems with Coppieters' research design and addressed these in his own work, also on L2 learners of French. The result was that he found a significant number of his participants who were indistinguishable from natives on his tests. His conclusion was that L2 learners can become native-like.

Another well-known study that is a direct response to Johnson and

Newport's study (see earlier discussion) is that of White and Genesee (1996). They tested learners from a variety of L1 backgrounds on subjacency violations in English and compared their performance to that of native speakers. They found that non-natives can attain native-like intuitions about language. One main difference between their study and Johnson and Newport's is that White and Genesee used independent measures to establish that the L2 learners seemed native-like to begin with (i.e., native speaker ratings of their pronunciation). Johnson and Newport relied on years of residence in the United States and quality of exposure to English as their measure of who to include in their "near-native" L2 group.

L2 learners can achieve native-likeness in some domains

Other research has suggested that learners can achieve native-likeness in some domains but not others, or that their underlying **competence (mental representation of language)** may be native-like but for some reason there is a disconnect between competence and **performance**. Donna Lardiere is one such person associated with this position. She studied a Chinese speaker, Patty, with English L2 whom she had known for over twenty years (Lardiere, 2007). Lardiere documents that Patty's speech is marked by a number of non-native structures, some of which we list here:

(1) that my cousin ask me to come
(2) that's how he interact people
(3) because he give us sad, you mean?
(4) so I wrote and speak fluently
(5) I met him and he go out ...
(6) I went to school and learn English

(Lardiere, 2007, pp. 74, 95)

As Lardiere scrutinized the data, she found dissociation between morphosyntactic competence (including inflections) and phonological representation or possibly phonetic representation. For example, the native speaker of English is not likely to omit past tense endings on verbs when they are required. Patty, however, did make omissions, but not consistently. Lardiere compared Patty's production of past tense in her oral speech with that in her written email messages. What Lardiere found was that in spoken speech, Patty produced past tense endings anywhere between 34 percent and 41 percent, but in the written emails, she used almost 78 percent of past tense correctly. Assuming Patty was writing spontaneously and didn't self-correct (which is evident from other aspects of her emails), Lardiere suggested that Patty's production of past tense may be tied to phonological problems rather than morphosyntactic ones. That is, Patty's mental representation and/ or phonetic representation for syllable endings seemed to be working against her. Lardiere reasoned that Patty's phonological representation was constrained by transfer from her L1, Chinese, which does not allow syllable final clusters. English past tense endings, however, are often part of a consonant cluster as a /t/ or /d/ sound is added to a word final consonant: *watched* /wačt/, *looked* /lœkt/, *called* /kald/. Phonological matters, then, would explain in large part her production patterns with verb endings. In short, Patty may be native-like in terms of morphological and syntactic representation of tense, but because she is non-native-like in terms of phonological competence and/or ability, her past tense use was uneven and non-native-like in terms of production.

Lardiere also found that Patty was lacking in certain discourse and pragmatic representations that included foregrounding (i.e., making an event prominent in the discourse) versus backgrounding (e.g., making an event non-prominent) in English. Because these concepts are germane to how people structure narratives in the past, Patty seemed to be omitting past tense markings not because of a morphological or syntactic deficit in her competence, but because of deficits in her discourse–pragmatic representation of English.

In a somewhat different approach to the matter, Sorace (2003) has discussed the issue of optionality. Optionality refers to the idea that in a grammar, a speaker may have a choice between two options to express the same meaning, but actually may have strong preference for one over the other. Thus, in L1 English, speakers have the choice to drop the complementizer *that* as in *I think that Paul is very clever* and *I think Paul is clever*. Sorace points out that such options are well established in L1 grammatical systems (or what she calls "mature grammars"), and she applies the concept to L2 development. Sorace has noticed how near-native speakers of Italian do not use pronouns the same way as natives. She provides the example of being asked questions, such as:

(7) Perchè Lucia non ha preso le chiavi?'Why didn't Lucia take her keys?'

(8) Che cosa è sucesso?'What happened?'

The L1 Italian speaker would answer as in (9a) and (9b), whereas her research documents the near-natives answering as in (10a) and (10b):

(9a) Perchè pensava di trovarti a casa. 'Because she thought she'd find you at home.'

(9b) Ha telefonato Paola. 'Paola telephoned.'

(10a) Perchè lei pensava di trovarti a casa. 'Because she thought she'd find you at home.'

(10b) Paola ha telefonato. 'Paola telephoned.'

In (9a), the Italian speakers omit the subject pronoun whereas the near-natives do not in (10a). In (9b), the Italian speakers postpose the subject noun whereas the near-natives in (10b) leave the subject in preverbal position. She claims, however, that the near-natives have the option of producing (9a) and (9b), but that their grammars show strong preference for one over the other, and that preference is not native-like. Optionality, then, means that the grammars themselves contain native-like syntactic options but that they also contain non-native-like preferences.

Assessment

For obvious reasons, we cannot review the entire body of literature on the matter of ultimate attainment. However, a substantial body of research does provide clear evidence that non-natives *can* become native-like. At the same time, the research also suggests that most *do* not. Thus, we think native-likeness is possible but its probability is not high. We think the question is not whether learners can become native-like but why more do not.

At the same time, we see something else emerging in the literature: that native-likeness is possible, but that it may be masked by matters unrelated to the focus of inquiry. In the case of Lardiere's Patty, native-like mental representation is possible, but issues related to language production mask this. Also, native-likeness in syntactic representation is possible, but discourse features or preference for one structure over another may not be native-like (Sorace's optionality). We think this is the direction that research on ultimate attainment may take us.

We also note here one potential problem in this line of research: determining who should be included in a pool of near-natives. As we noted, some research uses native judges who are "fooled" by non-native speakers. These non-natives are then designated as near-natives and used in the kind of research discussed here. In other cases, length of residence or time spent in the L2 environment is used as a determinant. Sometimes, both measures are used. But testing someone who appears to be near-native and then scores differently from natives is only a score for that non-native at that point in time. What would happen if that learner were tested five years later? Ten years later? What is the cutoff period to know that learning has ceased? This is not a trivial question and one that will continue to plague research on ultimate attainment, **fossilization**, and the **Critical Period Hypothesis**.

Question 3: Is there a critical period?

The notion of a critical period and the **Critical Period Hypothesis** (CPH) have been with SLA research for almost four decades. As originally formulated, the CPH was concerned with first language acquisition, the idea being that a language was impossible to acquire past a certain age. In other words, the biologically endowed mechanisms for language acquisition are operational only during a certain period of time. If children did not receive sufficient linguistic input prior to a certain age (puberty), then those mechanisms would cease being available and language acquisition would be severely hampered if not be impossible. This hypothesis was subsequently extended to the L2 context in that, even though a person may have successfully acquired an L1, the mechanisms used to acquire that L1 "turned off" by a certain age and thus SLA did not have access to the same mechanisms. SLA would be either impossible (i.e., native-like ability and knowledge would be impossible to obtain), or people could reach reasonable levels of proficiency, but not by using the mechanisms required for L1 acquisition.

As the reader might guess, there are several positions taken by scholars on the CPH applied to SLA. The first is that there is a CP for SLA. Again, the consequences are that native-like ability is impossible and the learner must use nonlinguistic learning mechanisms to acquire something that looks like a linguistic system. The second position is that there is no CP for SLA and thus L1 acquisition and SLA are fundamentally similar at their core (i.e., both use the same linguistic mechanisms for acquisition). Difference in outcomes—namely, that L1 acquisition is universally successful while SLA varies in terms of how far learners get and what their underlying competence is—would be due to factors residing outside the domain of the learning mechanism. The third position is that there is no one critical period but various critical periods, or perhaps critical periods for certain dimensions of language but not others.

There is a critical period

Scholars who believe that there is a critical period generally rely on one kind of evidence: namely, that L2 learners are not uniformly successful at acquisition the way L1 learners are. That is, each and every unimpaired child winds up with a native linguistic system. To be sure, people vary on matters such as vocabulary size, rhetorical ability, and discourse styles, but these are not (strictly speaking) matters related to the formal properties of language, which is the concern of the CPH. L2 learners, however, vary greatly in how much of the formal properties of language they acquire and can use. What is more, they seem to differ in significant ways from native speakers on a variety of measures and in a variety of language domains. In the discussion on ultimate attainment, we made reference to work by Coppieters as well as Johnson and Newport, in which very advanced and near-native-like L2 learners did not perform like native speakers. Some scholars take this as evidence that there is a critical period. There is much additional evidence that gets marshaled for the CPH.

DeKeyser and Larson-Hall (2005), for example, review the research on near-natives with an eye toward what that research might say about the CPH. Their conclusion is that the robustness of the data (i.e., too many non-natives are not native-like) argues against any outright rejection of the CPH. Based on DeKeyser's previous work (DeKeyser, 2000), as well as the work they review, these authors suggest that the issue comes down to this: Children rely largely on implicit processes to get language, and adults (or rather, post-CP learners) rely on explicit processes. Because the linguistic mechanisms posited for children only work implicitly, the conclusion is that post-CP learners are not engaging those mechanisms if they are learning explicitly. (See the Key Question **What are the roles of explicit and implicit learning in SLA?**) In DeKeyser's 2000 study, for example, he found a strong correlation between language aptitude measures (which relate to explicit learning) and learning outcomes in post-CP learners but did not find such a correlation with pre-CP learners. He takes this as evidence that children and adults engage different learning mechanisms.

The major difference between pre- and post- CP learners can be summarized in Robert Bley-Vroman's **Fundamental Difference Hypothesis.** Bley-Vroman claims that L1 acquisition and adult SLA are not the same and vary along a number of dimensions. Focusing on the characteristics of SLA he lists the following:

- lack of success and general failure;
- variation in success, course, and strategy;
- variations in goals;
- fossilization;
- indeterminate intuitions;
- importance of instruction;
- importance of negative evidence;
- role of affective factors.

These all point, he claims, to the fact that SLA in adults is different from L1 acquisition in children. Thus, adults do not have access to **Universal Grammar**, and thus use general cognitive-learning mechanisms for getting language (or language-like behavior).

Other scholars fall on the same side of the CPH argument, and evidence can be marshaled from a number of studies.

There is no critical period (or at least, it's questionable)

A number of scholars reject the notion of a critical period. These scholars either offer evidence that non-natives indeed can obtain native-like ability (see the Key Question **Can L2 learners become native-like?**) or they reanalyze the data from the pro-CPH side to show how the data can be interpreted in a different way.

As we discussed in the key question on whether learners can become native-like, researchers such as Birdsong and White and Genesee, among others, show that they can. Such results can be taken as evidence against a CP. This would mean that adults do have access to **Universal Grammar** and that they also have access to the linguistic mechanisms guiding acquisition that are present in L1 acquisition.

In a 2005 essay, David Birdsong reviews a number of studies related to the CPH, and in conducting a more fined-grained analysis of (1) the linguistic structures studied, (2) how the effects of age play out in the data, and (3) in noting that there are indeed native-like performers among the non-native group, he comes to the conclusion that the CPH is unsustainable as formulated. Notably, he finds that the loss of language ability is not linked to a particular period; instead, the ability to learn language declines steadily over time. It is progressive and thus does not fit within a "critical period." He also finds that a number of variables come into play that affect how the data appear in the aggregate. When looking at individuals, he finds that "not everybody is losing it to the same degree." Such findings would lead to the conclusion that a critical period doesn't really exist. His ideas are echoed in the review of the CPH data by Bialystok and Hakuta (1994). They, too, demonstrate how the decline in native-likeness for L2 learners is not a function of a cutoff period, but instead is more gradual. That is, the later the age of acquisition, the further one is likely to fall from native-likeness. Put another way, the earlier the age of acquisition, the more one is likely to be closer to native-likeness.

Herschensohn (2008) arrives at a similar conclusion, but also focuses on the possibility that the existence of an L1 plays a role. What she suggests is that the "deficits" observed in later L2 learners are not necessarily attributable to the loss of the language-learning mechanisms used in L1 acquisition. Instead, she argues, the "excellence" of the L1 linguistic system and the mental architecture that surrounds it may inhibit complete acquisition of an L2. Because older learners have such well-worn machinery in their brain for the L1, this machinery gets in the way of the processes and mechanisms utilized for language acquisition in children. It's not that later L2 learners don't have access to them; they just have extra baggage.

There are critical periods for some things

In a different vein, some argue that the construct of a monolithic critical period is wrong, largely because the concept of language used by scholars is not clear enough. Eubank and Gregg (1999), for example, have argued that language is componential in nature. Not only does it consist of **syntax**, **morphology**, **phonology**, and so on, some of which may have critical periods and others not, but some components have subcomponents. We can illustrate with syntax and Universal Grammar. Within Universal Grammar, there are **principles** and **parameters**. They argue that it is possible that universal principles are still available to L2 learners but that new parameters are not. Because universal principles must govern an L1, they cannot disappear once the L1 is set. These principles remain with speakers for their entire lives. But once parameters are set for the L1 values, other values are lost and cannot be retrieved in adult SLA. Thus, there is no critical period for universals (principles inherent to all languages) but there is a critical period beyond which resetting parameters is impaired.

Assessment

If one were to examine the vast array of studies conducted within the CPH (and in ultimate attainment more generally), it would appear that a strong notion of a critical period is untenable. Does this mean there is a "weak" version of the CPH? Not really. A weak version would be vacuous, at best, and would be hard to sustain by data. The notion of differential critical periods as put forth by Eubank and Gregg is appealing, but we would have to reconcile their "no new parameters" concept of a critical period with studies in which parameters do seem to be reset.

We think that Herschensohn's idea that the L1 is the culprit in lack of success (rather than access to Universal Grammar and its principles and parameters) has promise. As an explanation of the overall data, it is more compelling than a critical period in which access to linguistic learning mechanisms has been switched off. However, it remains to be seen what predictions can come of her hypothesis.

Question 4: What does development look like?

There are three principal characteristics of development in SLA over time. One is that there is stage-like development, particularly in the realm of sentence structure, but not exclusively so. A second characteristic is ordered development—that is, A precedes B which precedes C and so on. A third characteristic is that even within a stage of development of the acquisition of a particular linguistic feature, there can be variation. We will take each of these in turn.

SLA includes stage-like development

Staged development in SLA has been documented since the early days (1970s) of contemporary research. Stages (also called **developmental sequences**) have been found for negation, question formation, and other sentence structures in English, negation as well as sentence word order in German, direct object pronouns in French, copular verbs in Spanish, relative clauses in a variety of languages, among other features. One of the most well-known developmental sequences is negation in English. The stages are as follows:

Stage	Description	Example
1	negation external to the sentence (e.g., no + X)	No drink beer. No you eat that.
2	negation moves inside the sentence (e.g., S + no + X); 'don't' appears as an alternate of 'no'	I no can do these. I don't can do these.
3	appearance of modals and attachment of negation	I can't do that one.
4	appearance of analyzed 'do' with negation attached	She didn't like that one. He doesn't eat it.

Staged development is widely attested in both classroom and non-classroom contexts and is taken as a given in SLA. What is more, instruction has no effect on stages. That is, learners do not skip stages because of instruction; instruction does not alter developmental sequences (see the Key Question **Does instruction make a difference?**).

To be sure, stages are not neat and tidy such that learners abruptly drop something like *No drink beer* and go directly to *I no drink beer*. Although we will treat variation later, we note here that as learners traverse stages, they may produce structures from stage 1 as they enter stage 2, and while in the middle of stage 2, occasionally produce a stage 1 structure or a stage 3 structure. What determines the stage is the preponderance of the structure produced. A person is in stage 2 because the majority of what he or she produces for a given structure is stage 2-like for that structure.

Some staged development obeys U-shaped behavior (see **U-shaped acquisition**). U-shaped behavior occurs when a learner produces something correctly, then begins to produce that same thing incorrectly (usually due to learning something else), and then regains the ability to produce that thing correctly. The classic example comes from irregular past tenses. In the beginning, learners produce highly frequent irregular past tense forms such as *went* and *ate*. In the next stage, they begin to produce incorrect irregulars because of (unconscious) influence from regular past tense forms: *wented/goed*, *eated/ated*. Subsequently, they reacquire the correct irregulars.

We also note here that there is a good deal of overlap in the acquisition of some structures when we compare L1 and L2 learners. For example, L2 acquisition of negation in English looks amazingly similar in terms of staged development to L1 acquisition of the same.

Ordered development

In addition to stages of particular structures, there also exists what are called **acquisition orders**. While staged development refers to the acquisition of *one* particular structure, acquisition orders are concerned with the relative order in which *different* structures are acquired over time. Thus, while we have staged development for the acquisition of irregular past tense forms, where does irregular past tense fit within other verbal inflections in English such as third-person -*s* and progressive -*ing*? Also, different from staged development that includes non-native performance, acquisition orders are concerned with when learners begin to do things correctly most of the time. The standard measure is 90 percent accurate. For English verbal inflections, the following acquisition order is firmly attested:

- progressive -*ing*;
- regular past tense;
- irregular past tense;
- third-person -*s*.

This acquisition order means that learners first gain accuracy with -*ing*, then gain accuracy with regular past tense, then gain accuracy with irregular past tense, and gain accuracy last with third-person -*s*. As in the case of staged development, acquisition orders are unaffected by context and instruction.

To be clear on the distinction between acquisition orders and staged development, we can look at it this way. For each item in an acquisition order, we can ask, "How is that particular thing acquired over time?" As we saw earlier, there is staged development for irregular past tense forms before learners gain accuracy with them. Thus, at any given time, learners behavior exhibit both acquisition orders and staged development.

Acquisition orders are by and large concerned with **morphemes** and not sentence structure. There is, for example, an acquisition order for nominal (noun) morphemes in English as well: plural -s is acquired before articles which in turn are acquired before possessive -s. Together with staged development, acquisition orders are taken as evidence that learners possess internal mechanisms that process and organize language over time. However, the precise reasons for the orders themselves remain open for discussion. In Goldschneider and DeKeyser (2001), for example, a number of factors working together seemed to be good predictors of these orders of acquisition (e.g., frequency, **salience**, reliability of the **form-function** mapping).

Variation and variability

As learners enter a stage of development or begin to acquire a new morpheme or formal feature of language, they may demonstrate variable performance. Researchers have posited two kinds of **variation**: free and systematic. Free variation refers to the seemingly random use of two or more formal features to perform the same linguistic function. For example, a learner might use *No look my card* and *Don't look my card* to perform the function of telling someone to keep his eyes to himself (the example comes from Rod Ellis's work). Although it has been documented in learner speech, free variation does not seem to play a major role in production and generally seems to disappear as learners' L2 systems develop and organize. That is, free variation might be fleetingly transitional as the learner enters a new stage of development.

More studied and of more interest to linguists is systematic variation, which refers to the use of two or more formal features that on the surface look to perform the same function but actually do not. Schachter (1986), for example, examined the data on negation from one learner and discovered that he used *I don't know* for the function of expressing a lack of information but used *no + verb* in the context of denials. Thus, in one recording session it might look like the learner was randomly using two structures for negation when in fact it seems they were distributed across different functions or intended meanings.

Variation does exist with native speakers, to be sure, and what is unclear is to what extent native speaker models can explain L2 learner variability. The source of systematic variation has been debated, with scholars examining everything from task-induced variation to context-related variation. Some approaches have taken a multifactor analysis, with promising results. Unfortunately, variability is not nearly as studied as it was in the late 1970s and throughout the 1980s. The thrust of SLA research has been directed toward other aspects of learner language.

A comment about first language influence

We have described stages, orders, and variation without reference to influence from the L1. The reader may infer that we mean there is no L1 influence in development. This is not the case. Although acquisition orders don't seem to be influenced by the L1—that is, whether you speak Chinese or Spanish does not determine the overall order of acquisition of morphemes in English—the rate at which learners acquire morphemes and possibly even how well they do with particular morphemes might be influenced by the L1, especially L1 phonological properties. For example, let's take the case of third-person *-s*. There are two issues here which involve the L1: (1) Whether or not the L1 has verbal inflections for tense and person-number; (2) Whether or not the L1 allows consonant clusters at the ends of words/syllables. Chinese, for example, does not have tense and person-number inflections, and it does not allow consonant clusters at the ends of syllables/words. German, however, has both. Thus, the German learner of English L2 might have an advantage in acquiring third-person -s. At the same time, this advantage does not seem to disrupt the overall order of -ing first, past tense next, third-person -s last. The German L1 speaker just might get to third-person -s a little sooner than the Chinese speaker, but it is still the last verbal morpheme that he or she will acquire. We are, of course, simplifying for this book, and so our goal here is only to inform the reader that the L1 may play a role, but it is not the only role nor the most important one when it comes to developmental sequences and acquisition orders. To what extent, however, such a "minimized role" poses a challenge to concepts such as L1 = initial state is unclear, largely because it is not clear to what extent acquisition orders and developmental sequences are tied into concepts related to linguistic theory and thus **Universal Grammar**.

Assessment

L2 learners clearly create linguistic systems in an organized way that seem little affected by external forces such as instruction and correction. One of the main endeavors of SLA research has been to explain development. To this end, SLA research has not been as successful as one might hope. Although acquisition orders, for example, are now an accepted phenomenon, there is no widely accepted explanation for why they exist and why they exist in the orders they do. Application of current linguistic theory to explaining development (something that was absent in the 1970s and 1980s when the bulk of this research was conducted) has been minimal. Hawkins (2001), for example, has discussed the possibility that verbal morphemes, such as -ing, tense inflection, and third-person -s, develop as a result of how abstract features of syntax develop in learners' competence. He posits that syntactic competence involves gradual building up of different phrases over time, and as these phrases emerge, the verbal morphemes associated with them are acquired. Pienemann's Processability Theory has been used to explain the emergence of morphemes over time, but emergence (when a formal feature appears with any regularity) and acquisition (when that form comes under 90 percent control) are two different beasts. Thus, it is not clear in the end to what extent **processability** will explain such orders. It has been much more successful in explaining developmental sequences and stages, however.

Multifactor approaches such as the one taken by Jennifer Goldschneider and Robert DeKeyser suggest that a combination of factors as salience, frequency, and others better account for acquisition orders. However, since their 2001 call to re-examine acquisition orders, little interest has been shown. The field of SLA has moved beyond the accepted findings of the 1970s and early 1980s, and it is unlikely that we will see the same interest in acquisition orders or developmental sequences that we saw in the early days of SLA research.

Question 5: What are the roles of explicit and implicit learning in SLA?

Explicit and implicit learning have been discussed both in cognitive psychology and in SLA. Definitions of the two kinds of learning are problematic, as Hulstijn (2005) points out. However, he offers one definition that we adopt here for the purpose of discussion. "Explicit learning is input processing with the conscious intention to find out whether the input information contains regularities and, if so, to work out the concepts and rules with which these regularities can be captured. Implicit learning is input processing without such an intention, taking place unconsciously" (p. 131).

One can adopt one of three potential positions regarding explicit and implicit processes or learning: (1) SLA is largely or exclusively implicit; (2) SLA is largely or exclusively explicit; (3) SLA consists of both implicit and explicit learning.

SLA is largely implicit

That SLA is largely implicit is a position of a number of scholars. Krashen (1982, and elsewhere) has argued repeatedly that SLA is largely implicit. He distinguishes between **acquisition** and **learning** in adults; the former involves implicit learning and results in **competence** as we normally define the term, while the latter involves explicit learning and results in a learned system, available for **monitoring**. Although few scholars still follow Krashen's **Monitor Theory**, many argue that acquisition is largely implicit using a variety of theoretical approaches. Most persons working within a **Universal Grammar** framework would contend that acquisition is implicit, as underlying competence is a result of the interaction of processed input data with the principles and parameters of Universal Grammar. This interaction happens outside of learner awareness. (See, for example, White, 2003.)

Within nonlinguistic theories—those that are based on psychological accounts of learning such as **connectionism**—acquisition is largely implicit as well. Within these approaches, learning is the result of unconscious processing of linguistic tokens in the input, with unconscious frequency tabulation by the learner's internal mechanisms playing a major role in acquisition. As N. Ellis (2005) has stated, "the bulk of language acquisition is implicit learning from usage. Most knowledge is tacit knowledge; most learning is implicit" (p. 306).

Such positions, to be sure, do not rule out explicit learning completely, or that it plays absolutely no role in SLA. What we mean to underscore here is that such positions suggest a primary and fundamental role for implicit learning in SLA; explicit learning plays a secondary or helpful role, if at all.

SLA is largely explicit

Few scholars believe that SLA is largely explicit, although some may claim that SLA *begins* with explicit learning (see below). The main reason that so few believe that SLA cannot be largely or exclusively explicit is that explicit processes are relatively cumbersome and do not result in an implicit linguistic system that can be used with rapidity and ease during communication. Again, this does not mean for some scholars that explicit learning is completely out. We treat this issue below.

SLA involves both implicit and explicit learning

Those who ascribe to roles for both explicit and implicit learning in SLA fall into two major groups. The first involves the use of skill theory, a general theory of learning that claims that adults begin learning something through largely explicit processes, and, with subsequently adequate practice and exposure, move into implicit processes (see **Adaptive Control of Thought model** and **skills**). Within this theory, development involves the use of declarative knowledge followed by procedural knowledge, with the latter's automatization. The use of declarative knowledge involves explicit learning or processes; learners get rules explicitly and have some kind of conscious awareness of those rules. The automatization of procedural knowledge involves implicit learning or processes; learners begin to proceduralize the explicit knowledge they possess (i.e., they learn to "behave" in certain ways), and with situationally appropriate practice and use, the behavior becomes second nature. (See, for example, DeKeyser, 2007, p. 3.)

Outside of skill theory we find another group of scholars, who may not ascribe to any particular learning theory but believe that both explicit and implicit processes (or learning) are at work in SLA. Among these are Schmidt (2001, and elsewhere) who has suggested that for acquisition to occur, learners must notice linguistic features in the input (see **noticing**). Under this scenario, some kind of conscious awareness is necessary as learners attend to input in order for them to acquire the full gamut of linguistic features that can propel them toward successful (e.g., native-like or near-native) acquisition. However, Schmidt does allow that some aspects of language may "sneak by" conscious processing, particularly if these aspects are easy and transparent in terms of meaning and function. Thus, he allows for both explicit and implicit learning to occur, partly determined by the nature of the linguistic item that the learner encounters in the input.

Assessment

We have been necessarily simplistic in our presentation of the issues surrounding the roles of explicit and implicit learning in SLA. Assuming that we had the time and space to review all relevant essays and empirical studies to date, our assessment of the issues would come down to this: SLA has to be largely implicit in nature, that is, involve implicit learning, but this does not mean that learners—especially adults—do not attempt to engage explicit learning in some way. Our reason for this conclusion is that we are primarily concerned with competence, that is, the linguistic system that winds up in the learner's head. Our understanding is that competence is not just information about what is possible in a language, stuff that can be articulated by lots of pedagogical rules and thus learned explicitly (although, many observable things about language are almost impossible to describe, and thus can't be learned explicitly as rules). Competence is also about what is impossible in a language. If we imagine the learner of English as L2 trying to learn *wh*-question formation, we might conclude that he or she learns how to form questions explicitly. The rules about putting *wh*-words at the beginning of sentences are fairly easy to learn, fairly easy to see in the input. Yet, research has repeatedly shown that learners know much more than the basics of learning to say *Who did John see?* Research has demonstrated that these learners also come to know that *Who did John believe that the guy saw?* is fine but **Who did John meet the guy* *who saw?* is not. If we further imagine that the learner does not have *wh*-movement in the first language (as would be in the case of Chinese speakers learning English), we are forced to ask how that learner came upon this knowledge. The learner did not get rules about this in a classroom so he or she didn't learn it explicitly that way. And because ungrammatical sentences don't appear in the input, the learner can't scan the input explicitly and learn about restrictions on *wh*-movement that way. So, how did learning of constraints on *wh*-questions occur?

SLA research is chock-full of examples of how learners come to know much more than what they were taught, practiced, or even exposed to (see **poverty of the stimulus**). The conclusion of many scholars is that this knowledge is the result of the interaction of Universal Grammar with data from the environment: that is, *input*. Because Universal Grammar operates outside of awareness, only implicit learning can be involved. This would suggest that any aspects of language that are the result of the interaction of Universal Grammar with the input data would have to be acquired via implicit learning— and that would mean most linguistic knowledge.

Does this kind of perspective rule out explicit learning altogether? Surely not. We do know that adult learners actively try to learn such things as verb endings, nominal inflections, rules, and more generally, "how to say it right." And they do this very consciously. What is not clear, however, is how explicit learning of this nature interfaces (if at all) with what happens when Universal Grammar encounters data from the input. The default position would be that it doesn't. But because of the somewhat positive effects of instruction (see **Does instruction make a difference?**), it is not clear that explicit learning does not interface in some way. For the time being, this question is open.

Question 6: What are the roles of input and output in SLA?

Two major constructs within SLA research are **input** and **output**. As we know, input refers to language that learners are exposed to, that is, language couched in communicative contexts that learners either hear or read. Output refers to language that learners produce for the purpose of communication and can be both written and oral, although the latter is more widely researched within the context of SLA. Some debate has ensued over the years regarding the relative roles of each vis-à-vis the development of formal features of language over time. The question is basically this: What role does each play in the development of the formal features (i.e., grammar) of the learner's language? Although most people agree that input is necessary for acquisition, what is less clear is the role that output plays. Is it necessary? Is it beneficial? In either case, what is it supposed to do in terms of aiding the acquisition of formal features? To address these questions, we begin with the role of input.

Input

In the vast majority of theories and approaches to SLA, input is a critical variable as it is a major data source for the language learner. That is, the learner goes about constructing some kind of grammar (see also **competence, mental representation of language**) on the basis of the exemplars in the input. This is true of linguistic theories and cognitive theories (with the exception of skill-based theories which we address later). However, the theories differ in terms of what they believe the learner's grammar to be and the *internal* mechanisms that interact with input data to create a grammar. For example, **Universal Grammar** does not deny the fundamental role of input. But it clearly says that learners come to the task with innate **principles** regarding language that are not necessarily visible in the input. Thus, acquisition is the result of the interaction of data from the environment (input) and these principles (or better, the mechanisms that make use of these principles). As White (2007) puts it, "Universal principles and language specific parameter settings must be triggered by input from the language being learned. In our examples, learners acquiring an L2 with *wh*-movement will require input to motivate the +*wh* value of the parameter. However, once they have established that the L2 involves *wh*-movement, they will not require input to determine [constraints on that movement]; these come for free, so to speak" (p. 50).

On the other side of things is the connectionist perspective (see **connectionism**) that does not impute the learner with any innate knowledge. Instead, the learner is like a human computer that processes and tallies linguistic information in the input. From this processing and tallying, something that looks like grammar emerges over time. Under this scenario, everything the learner needs is contained in the input data; there is no innate "knowledge system" that interacts with the data. Within connectionism, then, input takes on even a slightly more important role as there are no special internal mechanisms that contain pre-existing linguistic information such as Universal Grammar. N. Ellis (2007) puts it this way: "As with other statistical estimations, a large and representative sample of language is required for the learner to abstract a rational model that is a good fit with the language data" (p. 88).

Again, if one reviews major theories and research paradigms within SLA, we see input as a central construct. Even in instructed SLA, input is the primary database on which learners build linguistic systems, hence the term **input enhancement** to describe current models of pedagogical intervention regarding formal features of language (see, for example, Wong, 2005).

Output

In the mid-1980s, Merrill Swain launched her now famous Comprehensible Output Hypothesis in which she claimed that learner production was required for successful language acquisition. She said,

> Comprehensible output ... is a necessary mechanism of acquisition independent of the role of comprehensible input. Its role is, at

minimum, to provide opportunities for contextualized, meaningful use, to test out hypotheses about the target language, and to move the learner from purely semantic analysis of the language to a syntactic analysis of it. (1985, p. 252)

By semantic analysis, she meant reliance on words and real-world information, for example, to get meaning (e.g., reliance on adverbials such as *yesterday* for reference to past tense) and by syntactic analysis she meant actual detection of the formal properties of language that help to convey meaning (e.g., reliance on verb inflections for getting tense). Swain's claim launched a debate in SLA that still exists today. The positions are that output is necessary (Swain's original claim), output is not necessary, or output may be beneficial. There is no research that demonstrates that output is necessary, and even Swain has softened her claim a bit since 1985. So, we will look at the second and third positions.

That output plays little to no role in acquisition was championed by Steven Krashen in the 1980s and thereafter. His major claim was that if the Output Hypothesis were correct, then the learner would have to test out in production every single feature of language during acquisition, something that is impossible. And if those working within Universal Grammar are correct about how acquisition proceeds, then a good deal of underlying competence cannot come from learner production: It can only come from input interacting with the principles and parameters embodied in Universal Grammar.

A different position is not that output is necessary but that interaction with other speakers (thus implying output in some way because learners have to speak in order to interact) is useful for acquisition. First staked out by Long (1981) (but see also Wagner-Gough & Hatch, 1975), the idea of modified interactions between non-natives and natives emerged. What Long argued was that natives modified their own speech based on interactions with less proficient speakers, and that these modifications were a direct result of natives' perceptions of the output of learners. He also claimed that these modifications in native speech (input to the learners) could be beneficial for acquisition. Thus, learner output triggered useful input modifications (i.e., learner output triggered better input from other speakers). This eventually became known as the **Interaction Hypothesis,** and since the early 1980s, a good deal of research has focused on interactions with non-natives to examine what kinds of modifications are made during conversations and how this might impact learner development (Gass, 1997, 2003; Mackey & Philp, 1998, and many others). We can consider this interaction position a weaker claim about output: It is not that production of output causes changes in learner development, as Swain claimed in 1985, but rather that learner output causes changes in the input learners receive. In addition, a major claim of those who support a role for interaction in acquisition is that it may produce **feedback** to learners that they are doing something wrong (see also **negative evidence**). This feedback could act as a signal that pushes learners to "scan the input" subsequently to "fix the problem" in their competence. In this way, interaction and negative evidence might heighten learner attention. Thus, there is an *indirect* causal link between output and acquisition, with input appearing again as a major and critical intervening factor.

Since the 1980s, Swain has adjusted her hypothesis slightly and now speaks of the "potential" of output to push the development of the learner's linguistic system. For example, she says "I have hypothesized that, under certain conditions, output *promotes* noticing [i.e., Schmidt's type of noticing]" (1998, p. 66, emphasis added). Later, she makes the following statement: "A second way in which producing language *may* serve the language learning process is through hypothesis formation and testing" (p. 67, emphasis added). Finally, she states that output (interaction) promotes metatalk—that is, learners talking out loud about language itself—and says, "by encouraging metatalk among second and foreign language students, we *may* be helping students to make use of second language acquisition processes" (p. 69, emphasis added). Thus, the point to underscore here is that Swain has moved from output being "necessary" to a weaker position in which output "promotes" or "may" enhance particular aspects of acquisition. What is also clear is that Swain is largely concerned with educational contexts: It is not clear what her position would be on learners who acquire language largely without instruction.

Other perspectives

It is worth mentioning at least one other perspective and that is the perspective based on skill acquisition. Skill refers to *ability to do* rather than underlying competence or mental representation. Within such perspectives, output would be indispensable for the development of, say, oral language ability—in particular, the ability to communicate fluently (i.e., rapidly and accurately). In other words, one can't learn to speak unless one engages in speaking behaviors. However, such perspectives ignore the construct of underlying competence. (See, for example, DeKesyer, 2015, as well as **Adaptive Control of Thought model** and **skills** under Key Terms in this volume.) So, output is necessary to develop the skills associated with making meaning.

Assessment

Although most scholars accept that input is indispensable for acquisition, there is less agreement that output is indispensable. Instead, scholars seem to converge on the idea that output—especially as part of interaction—may enhance acquisition, and there is research to support this on a number of fronts. However, the research has yet to convincingly demonstrate that output and interaction assist in the development of formal features of the language related to **syntax** (cf., Izumi, 2002, as well as Mackey, 1999)—and there is no evidence that it plays any significant role in the properties of language governed by Universal Grammar.

There is evidence that interaction may facilitate the acquisition of lexical items (words) and their meanings, and there is also evidence that it may promote acquisition of certain transparent surface features of language such as certain verb and noun inflections. To illustrate this, we offer here a typical example from interactional research:

> NNS: There's a basen of flowers on the bookshelf.
> NS: A basin?
> NNS: Base.
> NS: A base?
> NNS: A base.
> NS: Oh, a vase.
> NNS: Vase.
>
> (Mackey, Gass, & McDonough, 2000)

In this exchange, we see that communication is hampered by the non-native's use of *basen*. The native speaker attempts to clarify the intent of the non-native, and through negotiation we see that the native comes to understand that *vase* was the intended word. In the final line, the non-native realizes the problem and uses the correct word with the correct pronunciation. In this case, interaction seemed to assist in lexical acquisition and pronunciation. It is difficult to find reported research in which interaction helps with, for example, syntax. So, while we can link interaction to the development of skill (speaking) and to the development of lexicon and surface features of language, we cannot at this time link it to the development of competence or a mental representation of language.

Because one of the major claims within interaction and output-oriented research is that interaction provides learners with negative evidence (feedback), we end here with a citation from Susan Gass: "It is likely that there are limitations to what can and cannot be learned through the provision of negative evidence provided through conversation. One possibility is that surface-level phenomena can be learned, but not abstractions [i.e., syntactic phenomena] ... Negative evidence can probably not apply to long stretches of speech, given memory limitations ... But it may be effective with low-level phenomena such as pronunciation or basic meanings of lexical items" (Gass, 2003, p. 248).

Question 7: What are individual differences and how do they affect acquisition?

Even though SLA is clearly marked with universal tendencies (e.g., **developmental sequences, acquisition orders, Universal Grammar**), it is clear that SLA learners are not all alike nor do they attain similar degrees of knowledge or proficiency over time. It is the study of individual differences that attempts to address variation in outcome over time. The origins of individual differences as a field of study are found in classroom-based research conducted in the late 1950s, in which researchers wanted to know why some people were better students of second languages compared to others. It was during that time that the concept of "language aptitude" was born. At about the same time, another possible influence on acquisition surfaced: motivation for acquisition. Research on motivation emerged largely from concern for Canadian language policy and why some learners were more successful at acquiring and using English or French in a country with two official languages. Since the 1960s and 1970s, the field of individual differences has evolved to become a complex field studying a variety of factors and subfactors. We will focus on four major areas of inquiry: aptitude, motivation, learning styles, and learning strategies.

Aptitude

Broadly defined, aptitude refers to cognitive abilities that learners bring to the task of acquisition. These abilities can be anything from the perception and encoding of sounds to **working memory** to grammatical sensitivity (e.g., pattern recognition ability) and others. Scholars have differed on the various components of aptitude as well as how to measure them, but aptitude continues to be a variable referred to by scholars, such as Robert DeKeyser, Peter Robinson, and Peter Skehan, and others working in cognitive approaches to SLA. For example, DeKeyser (2000) tested Hungarian L1 speakers of English L2 who lived in the Pittsburgh area. He found a strong positive correlation between their scores on the aptitude test and their scores on a test of the acquisition of various aspects of English morphology and syntax. However, this correlation was only positive for those who arrived after the age of 17. Prior to that age, the correlation between aptitude and acquisition scores was not significant. His conclusion, among others, is that the aspects of aptitude he measured are good predictors of success in SLA and also point to explicit processes in adult acquisition.

Robinson (2001a, and elsewhere) has devoted considerable attention to the role of aptitude in SLA, both in and out of the classroom. His contemporary approach abandons isolated aspects of aptitude and instead focuses on *aptitude complexes*, and he has offered the Aptitude Complex Hypothesis that claims that learning draws on different combinations of cognitive abilities (aspects of aptitude) depending on the conditions of instructional exposure. In short, different learners with different aptitude clusters will respond to different instructional treatments differentially. Thus, the idea of a "uniform" trait called aptitude that is invariant and context-independent does not fit into Robinson's thinking.

As Dörnyei (2005) points out, research on aptitude has yielded conflicting findings on its role in SLA success, which is why the concept of aptitude has evolved over the years. He points out, however, that with more contemporary approaches to aptitude, such as Robinson's, the role of aptitude and its interaction with situational variables (e.g., types of instruction, types of tasks) are more likely to be illuminated.

Motivation

Motivation is another individual difference that has received a good deal of attention and has also undergone evolution as a construct. Basically, motivation refers to a willingness to learn or do something. However, within SLA we have seen motivation move from a static construct related to sociopsychological variables (e.g., how the learner perceives the target language and culture and the degree to which the learner wishes to interact with the latter) to more cognitive-oriented constructs (e.g., the mental self of learners), to constructs related to contemporary psychology on self-esteem, self-regulation, and other advances in research on human personality. Ultimately, all are related to *desire*. The reason for such shifts in scholarly attention is that researchers are trying to uncover the sources of motivation vis-à-vis learner internal factors. It is widely held that motivation, no matter where it comes from or how it works, is somehow related to successful acquisition, much as it is related to successful dieting or successful completion of a book. In short, motivated people stick with tasks. This is important in SLA because SLA is such a protracted process; it takes years for someone to reach advanced levels of ability with language.

Learning styles

We have defined learning styles under Key Terms but briefly stated, learning styles—sometimes referred to as *cognitive styles*—refer to someone's overall preferences for learning and processing information from the environment. Some people like concreteness, for example, while others don't mind abstractness. In Ehrman and Leaver's (2003) concept of learning styles, learners basically come down to two types: ectenic and synoptic. Ectenic learners prefer or require conscious control over their learning; synoptic learners leave more to unconscious processes. However, various constructs for learning styles have been suggested (e.g., Kolb, 1984; Riding, 1991; Oxford, 1993; Skehan, 1998, to name some in addition to that of Ehrman & Leaver).

Research on learning styles in SLA has been largely restricted to classroom contexts (cf., e.g., the research on aptitude, especially that of DeKeyser's mentioned earlier). The issues that people have addressed are centered largely on whether classroom practices and teachers' styles match or fit with students' learning styles. Oxford (1999, and elsewhere) has referred to "style wars" (a play on the hit movie series *Star Wars*) in which she describes mismatches between teacher orientations and learner orientations. Such mismatches can result in less-than-optimal learning environments for students of languages.

Learning strategies

Learning strategies refer to any conscious strategies learners use to acquire language and can be anything as mundane as underlining new words in texts to more social strategies in which learners actively seek out speakers of the L1 with whom to "practice." The central concerns in SLA research on learning strategies are (1) to what extent strategies correlate with successful learning; (2) which learners (or what kinds of learners) use which strategies; (3) whether learners can be taught strategies in order to maximize their learning; and, to be sure, (4) what the strategies are (i.e., what taxonomy of strategies do we want to measure and how do we measure them?). As Dörnyei (2005) suggests, though, there is a question as to whether strategies are "real things" and more importantly to what extent they are part of the more abstract notion of individual differences. While individual differences are traits such as talent (aptitude), motivation, or cognitive orientation, learning strategies are actions. As Dörnyei states, "[And] let's face it: actions and thoughts are not individual differences" (p. 162). It seems that strategies per se have begun to fall out of favor in SLA research and instead researchers—influenced by trends in educational psychology research— have turned attention to more general constructs such as "self-regulation" in learning. Finally, it should be clear that strategies research has largely, if not exclusively, focused on classroom learners.

Assessment

The main question that research on individual differences seemingly addresses is: What is the relationship, if any, between individual differences and ultimate attainment or success? First, we begin with an assessment made by Dörnyei and Skehan (2003) in their overview of research on individual differences: "An assessment of individual differences research has to portray a mixed picture" (p. 621). On the one hand, they argue, research on learning styles and learning strategies is problematic. The main problem, it seems, is the lack of theoretical underpinnings for most of the taxonomies and research, and thus the promise of the research has not been realized. We would concur, adding that a major issue for all individual differences research is how it relates to SLA more generally. Just what does research on learning styles and strategies have to say about staged development, acquisition orders, and the roles of Universal Grammar, processing mechanisms, and other internal "stuff" responsible for how language actually makes its way into the learner's developing system? After all, no matter one's learning style and no matter one's strategy, language has to be processed and stored by internal mechanisms. How do learning styles and strategies relate to these mechanisms? It's not clear they do. At the same time, it seems that from an *educational* perspective, learning styles and strategies may be relevant to how *happy* students are about their experiences in classrooms and thus how successful they are under *the conditions that classroom learning imposes.* This is not a trivial matter because so many people begin language acquisition in classrooms, but there is a limit to the importance of individual differences in regard to classroom contexts: No learner of a language ever gets to be advanced or native-like solely because of the early stages of classroom learning. Ultimately, the learner leaves the classroom as he or she begins to interact with L2 speakers, maybe marrying into the culture, reading on his or her own, taking a job in which the L2 is required, watching movies—in short, by engaging in a host of social and interactive activities. All of these activities and situations are not classroom bound and most likely have little to do with the kinds of styles and strategies traditionally looked at for classroom learners. So, the question remains open as to their relationship to ultimate attainment and the outcomes of SLA in the long run.

While we are neutral on the research on motivation and it seems self-evident that some kind of motivation is necessary for language acquisition, we agree with Dörnyei and Skehan that aptitude provides an interesting avenue of research that may help to illuminate issues related to ultimate attainment (see the Key Question **Can L2 learners become native-like?**). Again, one of the central questions of SLA research is to what extent it is similar to or different from L1 acquisition, and a second question is why L2 learners vary so much in their success compared with L1 learners. Aptitude may shed some light on these matters. Although it hasn't happened yet, it may be possible to link aptitude to such things as language processing (i.e., the processing of linguistic data during the act of comprehension), something we know to be a key component of acquisition. It may well be that various components of aptitude relate to certain aspects of processing and people may vary individually on the processing of input. We thus think that in addition to the strands of research related to aptitude currently under way, research on aptitude and language processing may be useful for understanding ultimate attainment.

Question 8: Does instruction make a difference?

Since the 1970s, scholars have debated to what extent instruction makes a difference in acquisition of the formal properties of language. By formal properties, we mean morphological and syntactic aspects of language such as verb forms, word order, rules on question formation, and nominal inflections (see **formal instruction**). Research in this domain is not concerned with, say, vocabulary acquisition, the acquisition of reading skills, and other aspects of language use and skill. There are four possible positions: (1) Instruction makes no difference; (2) Instruction is constrained; (3) Instruction is beneficial; (4) Instruction is necessary.

Instruction makes no difference

In the Acquisition–Learning Hypothesis of the Monitor Theory, Krashen (1982, and elsewhere) distinguishes between conscious learning and unconscious acquisition of an L2 and argues that these two processes are autonomous and unrelated. Of the two, he argues that acquisition is the more important one, the process responsible ultimately for language use (see **acquisition/acquisition versus learning, Monitory Theory**). According to Krashen (1982), formal instruction has a very limited role in SLA since the learned knowledge that is the result of instruction does not help learners in the acquisition of the target language. Krashen claims that formal instruction contributes to the learning of explicit knowledge and is unrelated to acquisition. In addition, he views the learned system as having a fragile and peripheral role in acquisition as learned knowledge cannot turn into or influence the unconscious acquisition of an L2. According to Krashen, there is no interface between these two systems.

Evidence for instruction making no difference emerges from studies conducted to investigate the effects of formal instruction on the route of acquisition and accuracy. By "route," we mean **acquisition orders** and **developmental sequences**. The former refers to the order in which particular **morphemes** such as plural -s, past tense -ed, and third-person -s are acquired over time. Developmental sequences refer to the stages that learners traverse in acquiring one particular feature of language. According to the "makes-no-difference" position, instruction is unable to alter acquisitional sequences; learners cannot acquire linguistic features out of order nor can they skip developmental sequences. Because acquisition orders and developmental sequences appear to be immutable, instruction is seen to have no role in the acquisition of formal features of language.

Other researchers (e.g., Cook, 1991) have also argued that instruction is not necessary as learners have access to **Universal Grammar** principles. Acquisition of an L2 occurs through the interaction between these universal **principles** and input. Thus, learners reset **parameters** not because they are taught, but because the available evidence in the input leads them to do so. Others, such as Truscott (2004), question the overall impact of instruction on the acquisition of formal features. In reviewing the research to date, Truscott says that (1) assessment tasks used in instructional research bias toward explicit learning (i.e., they measure conscious or explicit knowledge), and (2) the observed statistical effects of instruction research are so minimal that one could consider the effects equivalent to no effects at all on acquisition (in Krashen's sense) itself. In other words, the gains made from instruction are minimal at best.

In addition, few long-term studies on the effects of instruction have surfaced in the literature. Most studies on the effects of instruction are short-term: The researcher provides a treatment and then assesses learners after treatment (comparing the results to pretreatment assessment). However, post-treatment measures usually occur immediately after treatment or shortly thereafter. What would the research reveal if another measurement were taken six months later? A year later? In the several studies in which such delayed post-tests were administered, the effects of instruction were no longer evident. Only in VanPatten and Fernández (2004) did the effects of instruction show up eight months after treatment—however, not without visible decline.

Instruction is constrained

Pienemann (1998) has also advanced a series of hypotheses concerning the effects of instruction on SLA. He has argued that instruction will not enable learners to acquire any developmental features out of sequence because **processability** constrains acquisition and thus any instructional efforts. In addition, instruction will enable learners to acquire particular features provided that the processing operations required to produce those features that precede it in the acquisitional sequence have already been acquired. For example, here is the developmental sequence for ESL question formation.

- Stage 1 = SVO (He live here?)
- Stage 2 = wh– + SVO (Where he is?)
- Stage 3 = Copula inversion (Where is he?)
- Stage 4 = AUX (Where has he been?)

    (SVO = subject-verb-object; AUX = Auxiliary)

According to Pienemann, each stage implies certain output processing procedures that the learner has acquired. However, the stages are hierarchical in order and cannot be skipped. Learners follow a very rigid route in the acquisition of grammatical structures. Structures become learnable only when the previous steps on the acquisitional path have been acquired. Thus, a learner at stage 2 cannot be taught to make the output processing procedures for stage 4, for example.

However, in Pienemann's view, instruction can promote language acquisition in that if the learner is at stage 2 and has successfully acquired the ability to produce the structure at that stage, the learner can be taught to produce the structure in stage 3. Therefore, according to Pienemann, instruction can facilitate the SLA process if it coincides with the point at which the learner is ready to acquire the next stage. As such, instruction can improve the speed of acquisition. What is more, Pienemann also claims that instruction can affect the frequency of rule application and the different contexts in which the rule has to be applied. That is, learners may not be able to skip stages because of acquisition, but instruction at the right time may help learners better apply rules in their output.

Because instruction cannot alter developmental sequences in any real way but it can help learners in the application of particular rules when they are ready to use them, Pienemann would claim that instruction is not completely useless; instead, instruction is constrained.

Instruction is beneficial

In direct challenge to Krashen's position, Long (1983a) questioned the relative effects of instruction in SLA. Long reviewed a series of studies in which classroom only, naturalistic exposure only, and classroom plus naturalistic exposure were compared. He concluded that when these studies are taken in the aggregate, instruction is beneficial for adults (intermediate and advance stages) as well as for children. Instruction is beneficial in both acquisition-rich environments (i.e., contexts in which learners are exposed to the target language outside the classroom context) and acquisition-poor environments (i.e., contexts in which learners are exposed to the target language only in a classroom context). Such benefits emerge despite the way they are measured. Long concluded that instruction and a combination of instruction and naturalistic exposure were more beneficial than naturalistic exposure alone, as instruction seems to have an effect on the rate and success of SLA.

Another scholar who provides a series of arguments in favor of instruction is Richard Schmidt. Schmidt (1990), for example, has suggested that conscious attention to form is the *sine qua non* for acquisition to take place. According to Schmidt, it is increasingly evident that instruction might have a facilitative role by enabling learners to notice linguistic features in the input. In his well-known **Noticing**

Hypothesis, Schmidt has argued that in order to acquire a language it is necessary for learners to pay conscious attention to forms/structures of the targeted language. It is necessary for learners to notice forms in the input otherwise learners might just process input for meaning and fail to process and to acquire specific linguistic features. Many features and characteristics of the target language might influence and determine whether learners are able to notice a form in the input (e.g., frequency, perceptual saliency, and communicative value of a given form/structure). From this position it would follow that instruction would be beneficial as it would direct learners' attention to linguistic features.

Finally, Norris and Ortega (2000) reviewed over forty published studies on the effects of instruction, conducting a meta-analysis of the research to date. Their conclusion was that overall instruction seems to make a difference, no matter what kind of instruction is in question. They do, however, caution the reader to consider that not all assessment tasks and research designs used in the research are created equal, and thus the claim that any and all instruction would be equally useful or actually result in acquisition is not valid.

What needs to be clear from these positions and variations on them is that all scholars agree that the route of acquisition cannot be altered. That is, instruction cannot alter acquisition orders or developmental sequences. Instead, those who argue that instruction is beneficial are basically arguing that either instruction can speed up the processes used by learners as they traverse acquisitional routes or instruction will help learners get further along.

Instruction is necessary

A final position on the role of instruction is that it is necessary for the acquisition of formal features of language. The idea here is that learners' linguistic systems will fossilize without instruction. That is, their linguistic systems will cease to develop and exhibit a variety of non-native-like features without explicit help. (See **fossilization**.)

This position was somewhat popular in the 1980s, especially among foreign language educators in the United States (e.g., Higgs & Clifford, 1982), but has since fallen to the wayside in mainstream SLA research. First, non-nativeness is a widely accepted phenomenon (see **Can L2 learners become native-like?**); learners just don't seem to become native-like in a variety of domains. Second, the concept of instruction being necessary is not operationalizable in L2 research. How would someone prove that instruction is necessary, especially given that most L2 learners are not native-like anyway? One would have to find learners who were native-like and only became like that because of instruction. Because of all the other intervening variables (e.g., immersion, input and interaction, personality traits), it would be impossible to demonstrate the actual effects of instruction. In short, the idea that instruction is necessary or learners can't learn without it is untenable.

Assessment

A solid review of the literature on instructional effects would lead the readers to the following conclusions:

- instruction cannot alter the route of acquisition (i.e., acquisition orders and developmental sequences);
- instruction is not necessary, but instruction may be beneficial; research is investigating the conditions under which this would be so.

Learners bring to the task of acquisition a variety of internal mechanisms and traits that effectively override most instructional efforts. However, the more researchers learn about what learners do with input and how they do it, the closer they come to understanding the possibilities of instructional effects. To this end, the question about the role of instruction has begun to shift in research. When the debate on the role of instruction first surfaced in the late 1970s and early 1980s, instruction consisted largely of grammar-only types of activities such as mechanical drills, fill in the blank, and various other form-only exercises. Meaning and input were clearly excluded.

Since the 1990s, however, researchers began to seriously examine the issue of how learners interact with input asking questions, such as, "Why do they skip over some things in the input?" and "What makes some features harder to process than others?" Such questions drove researchers to examine the effects not of instruction more generally but of particular kinds of instructional interventions: those that were both input-oriented and meaning-based. These interventions include such things as text enhancement, processing instruction, input flood, and recasts (see **input enhancement** as well as **focus on form**). It is not clear whether these more acquisition-driven approaches to instructional intervention actually affect SLA in any significant way, but it is clear that the field has shifted from the more global "Does instruction make a difference?" to more specific "Does manipulating input make a difference?"

Question 9: What constraints are there on acquisition?

As we know from research, acquisition is not instantaneous and involves such things as acquisition orders, developmental sequences, and other stage-like learning. These orders and sequences are relatively fixed and immutable, meaning they can't be altered in any significant way (e.g., learners don't skip stages and go from A to Z without passing through other stages first). At the same time, we see that acquisition is largely impervious to instructional effects in that instruction does not seem to alter acquisition orders or developmental sequences. Because of these observations, we can think of acquisition as being constrained. That is, learners must be bringing something to the task of acquisition that constrains the shape of acquisition. What are these constraints? Here, we briefly describe some perspectives that suggest how acquisition might be constrained. As is the case of the rest of these sections on Key Questions, our presentation is not exhaustive, but should provide a mechanism by which novice readers can begin to seek additional readings and to explore this question in greater breadth and depth.

Linguistic constraints

In at least one theory of acquisition, the development of formal features of language may be constrained by universal properties of language. That is, languages themselves are constrained in certain ways and because languages are constrained, acquisition of them is constrained as well. Two kinds of linguistic constraints have been studied in SLA: those based on **Universal Grammar** and those based on **typological universals**. Let's take typological universals first.

Typological universals are those aspects of language that are derived from the study of a large sampling of languages and exist as implicational statements; that is, if X is present in a language, then Y is present as well. For example, if languages have object relative clauses (*That's the man who I saw last night*), then they will have subject relative clauses (*That's the man who saw me last night*). If a language has voicing contrasts for sounds in syllable final position (e.g., *kid* vs. *kit*), then that language has voicing contrasts in syllable initial position (e.g., *dip* vs. *tip*). Note that these statements turned around do not hold. For example, voicing in initial position does not necessarily imply voicing in final position. Out of such statements comes the notion of **markedness**. Briefly stated, markedness refers to how typical something is relative to something else. Something less typical is more marked than something more typical. The term also refers to the implicational statements we just saw: The thing that implies something else is more marked than the thing implied, or the thing implied is less marked than the thing implying it. In the case of voicing, voiced consonants in final position imply voiced consonants in initial position and thus voiced consonants in final position are more marked, or voiced consonants in initial position are less marked.

How do typological universals and markedness affect acquisition? It has been shown that more marked things are more difficult to acquire. They either appear later in acquisition than less marked things or are more difficult to master. Thus, voicing with initial consonants is easier to acquire than voicing in final position. Subject relative clauses are easier to acquire than object relative clauses. What is meant by easier? Again, the more marked item may emerge later and show evidence of difficulty through more "errors." Thus, markedness may constrain acquisition in that unmarked aspects of language ought to emerge before marked aspects.

Within Universal Grammar, the idea is that language is composed of abstract principles and that these principles constrain the way in which acquisition happens. Thus, learners may actually be "barred" from making some errors because Universal Grammar just doesn't allow the options the errors would imply. For example, one such principle is the Structure Dependence Principle, which states, "All syntactic operations are structure dependent." This principle keeps learners from thinking that syntactic operations happen on words or on the order of elements in a sentence. Instead, words are part of syntactic structures such as phrases, which are the foci of syntactic operations. Thus, if a learner hears in English, *John will come tomorrow* and *Will John come tomorrow?* that learner could assume that yes/no questions are formed either by (1) moving the second word to the front or (2) by simple subject-verb inversion. Note the errors that would result: **Eats John chocolate?* from *John eats chocolate* and **Of boxes presents arrived?* from *Boxes of presents arrived.* Such errors do not occur in either first or second language acquisition. This is because Structure Dependence requires that operations happen on phrases and not individual words.

Modals such as *will* are part of a phrase that is different from other kinds of main verbs (which are part of another phrase), and something like subject-verb inversion must consider that subjects can be phrases (*boxes of presents*). Thus, learners come to the task "knowing" certain things about what languages can and cannot do and these things are the principles of Universal Grammar. Universal Grammar, then, constrains the "hypotheses" that learners can make and constrains their linguistic development in certain ways (see, for example, Schwartz, 1998, and White, 2003).

Processing constraints

Not all researchers ascribe to linguistic approaches to acquisition and believe there are cognitive (i.e., mind-related but not linguistic) constraints on acquisition. A prominent position here would be that acquisition is constrained by processing issues. William O'Grady is a leading proponent of this position. His basic idea is that the more difficult the processing operation is for a feature or structure, the more difficult it is to acquire and he refers to this as *computational complexity*. As a simple illustration, let's look at *wh*-questions (see O'Grady, 2003, p. 50). Research has shown that there is asymmetry in the acquisition of subject *wh*-questions (*Who met Mary?*) and object *wh*-questions (*Who did Mary meet?*), with subject questions being easier than object questions. O'Grady would claim that this is due to computational complexity and structural distance. Assuming that the *wh*-element must move from a position to occupy the position it does in standard questions, subject *wh*-elements do not hop as many syntactic boundaries as do object elements. The readers can see this if we sketch out the syntactic boundaries (S = sentence, VP = verb phrase, [= a syntactic phrase or boundary, __ = origin of the *wh*-element):

Who [$_S$__[$_{VP}$ met Mary]]?
Who did [$_S$ Mary [$_{VP}$ meet____]]?

In the first sentence, the subject *wh*-question, the *who* only has to move across one boundary, but in the object question, the *who* moves out of the verb phrase and crosses that boundary as well as the S boundary to land in initial position. (Again, we note here that our annotations are not the way syntacticians would annotate these sentences; we are simplifying for the novice readers.) According to O'Grady, it is the multiple boundary crossings that make object *wh*-questions more difficult than subject *wh*-questions. O'Grady would claim, then, that computational complexity is a constraint on acquisition, making some aspects of language more difficult than other aspects of language.

In a similar vein, Manfred Pienemann has claimed that output processing constrains acquisition. In short, the way that learners can string together elements to produce a sentence is constrained by processing procedures, with some being simpler than others. In his Processability Theory (see **processability**), he has developed a hierarchy of processing procedures with the simplest being *lemma access* (retrieving words from the lexicon), the hardest procedure being the exchange of grammatical information across a clause boundary (e.g., having a grammatical feature in an embedded clause be dependent on something that happens in the main clause), and the exchange of grammatical information within or between phrases in a sentence falling in-between (e.g., agreement between nouns and adjectives, agreement between subjects and verbs within a sentence). In total, Pienemann has proposed six major processing procedures. These procedures constrain acquisition in the following way. First, some procedures are acquired before others; thus, the aspects of language production governed by those procedures will appear before those governed by procedures acquired later. Second, the procedures exist in a hierarchical and implicational order. The acquisition of a particular procedure can only occur if the procedures "below it" have been acquired. Thus, procedures higher up in Pienemann's hierarchy imply that the learner has acquired the procedures below it, but not the other way around. By existing in a hierarchical fashion, these procedures severely constrain the order in which elements of language can appear in learner output over time.

Other constraints

In the constraints briefly outlined above—linguistic and processing constraints—fairly elaborate theories have been discussed. However, it is clear that acquisition can be constrained in a number of ways that are not part of elaborate theories. For example, we could make the following claims regarding various kinds of constraints.

- *Access to input*: Clearly, acquisition is constrained by the quantity and quality of input. For example, classroom environments tend not to offer the same kind and amount of input as "the outside world." At the same time, the outside world may not offer the more complex input that classrooms sometimes offer via texts and classroom discourse that is planned or more elaborate than everyday conversation. Thus, context may constrain acquisition because it constrains access to the amount and type of input learners get.

- *Access to interaction*: If the **Interaction Hypothesis** is correct (see also **What are the roles of input and output in SLA?**), then contexts may restrict or constrain acquisition by limiting learners access to native speakers. The clearest example would be the student living abroad with a family and attending classes versus the socioeconomically disadvantaged immigrant who winds up in a linguistic ghetto with other immigrants. The former has greater access to native speakers and to interaction, while the latter may spend more time speaking in his or her L1 with peers and only use the L2 for the most functional purposes (depending on employment and other matters).

- *L1 transfer*: For those who ascribe to a significant role for L1 influence in SLA, the type of L1 may be a significant constraint on acquisition of the formal features of the L2. In the Key Question **Can L2 learners become native-like?** we caught a glimpse of Patty, a long-time learner/speaker of English L2 with Chinese as L1. We saw how the phonological rules of her L1 constrained her acquisition of the phonological properties of English (i.e., syllable structure), and how this in turn constrained her ability to consistently and correctly supply past tense verb endings in speech.

Clearly, we could list other constraints. The point here is that SLA is complex and a variety of linguistic, psycholinguistic, and contextual factors interact that shape and constrain the course of acquisition.

As we see it, linguistic and psycholinguistic (processing) factors play the largest role in constraining how linguistic systems develop. Other factors contribute but ultimately do not dictate, for example, why X is learned before Y. In short, we are saying that there are two kinds of constraints: those most likely involved with the course of development (e.g., how language unfolds over time such as in the case of **developmental sequences**) and those involved with how far learners get (e.g., **ultimate attainment**).

And this is the stuff of SLA research.

Key Theories and Frameworks in Second Language Acquisition

In this section, we present nine contemporary theories, frameworks, and models that dominate discussion about second language acquisition. For more detailed discussion of theories and frameworks, the reader is referred to the volumes by VanPatten and Williams (2015), Mitchell, Myles, and Marsden (2012), and García Mayo, Gutierrez Mangado, and Martínez Adrián (2014). Before beginning, we need to offer a few definitions and clarifications.

In the sciences and social sciences, the construct "theory" has a particular meaning. A theory is a set of statements about naturally occurring phenomena that attempt to explain why these phenomena occur the way they do. So, the primary purpose of a theory is to explain the world around us. A secondary purpose is to make predictions; that is, a good theory allows us to make hypotheses about what ought to happen given X or Y conditions. Thus, a theory and a hypothesis are not the same thing. In addition, hypotheses can be formulated without a theory. Someone could have an idea about something independent of a theory and in the sciences we would call this a stand-alone hypothesis. So the reader should not confuse a theory with a hypothesis.

What is more, theories are also distinguished from frameworks and models. These latter constructs refer to compilations of ideas and constructs that are bigger than theories. They may subsume some theories but their intent is less to explain and predict and are generally more descriptive in nature. They can describe what happens in some detail and in some cases make relationships between different things, but they may not be able to explain why something happens the way it does.

Unfortunately in the field of SLA, people often confuse theory, hypothesis, framework, and model, conflating them and assuming they are all on the same "level." Some are called theories when in actuality they are frameworks or models, and some called models function more like theories. We invite you to keep this in mind as you read these brief introductions to some of the major approaches to second language acquisition.

Universal Grammar and linguistic theory

The basics

Those working within the theory of Universal Grammar and current linguistic theory see language as **mental representation**. That is, it is an abstract and complex system residing in the mind/brain of a human. This position contrasts with those who view language only as observable behavior (i.e., speech or signing). Thus, within this theory it is important to account for both what people accept as possible or grammatical in their language and what they reject as possible or grammatical. For example, an English speaker would accept as a possible sentence *Who do you wanna invite to the party?* but would reject as not possible *Who do you wanna bring wine to the party?* (but *Who do you want to bring wine to the party?* is fine). Thus, the speaker accepts a contraction in one instance but rejects it in another. Current linguistic theory, then, is an attempt to account for what is called **mental representation** of language. A major construct within the theory is Universal Grammar, an innate component that is species specific: only humans possess human grammar. Universal Grammar consists of an inventory of features from which languages may select principles that regulate all human languages and basic syntactic operations. Languages are said to vary because they select different features and these features have different consequences in different languages, for example. To illustrate, Spanish selects for T (Tense) whereas Mandarin Chinese does not. This has a series of consequences in how verbs and sentences "behave" in the two languages.

Another basic aspect of this theory is what is called the **poverty of the stimulus** problem. The POS is based on the observation that people come to know more about language than what they have been exposed to. How, for example, do people know that *Who do you wanna bring wine to the party?* is not a good sentence in English when their only exposure is to what is possible in English? That is, people only hear actual sentences; nobody tells them what is impossible. Yet, on the basis of possible sentences, somehow people arrive at what is impossible. On the flip side, people can know when a sentence is possible in a language even when they have not encountered that particular sentence before or perhaps even a particular structure. People can project beyond a limited experience with language to "know" that something is possible in a language even though they have not experienced it themselves. As one example, if a Japanese child hears obligatory object-verb (OV) order in Japanese early on—which of course that child does—then the child is able to project or "assume" that all phrases in Japanese follow the same order. That is that the head (in this case, the verb) comes after the complement (the object). That child would assume that prepositional phrases would be complement + head, that clauses would be complement + complementizer, and so on.

It should be clear from this brief overview that Universal

Grammar and linguistic theory are concerned with how language is represented in the mind/brain. When applied to the L2 context, the main question asked is whether L2 learners come to have intuitions (underlying mental representation) about language similar to those of native speakers. A related question is whether or not Universal Grammar is operative in second language acquisition as it is in first language acquisition.

The claims

There are a number of claims made by those working within current linguistic theory. Here are some of the major accepted claims.

- *All human languages are constrained by Universal Grammar.* A human language cannot have properties that are not "sanctioned" by the information contained in Universal Grammar. Applied to the second language context, at any given point in time, a learner's **interlanguage** cannot have properties that are not sanctioned by Universal Grammar.

- *The poverty of the stimulus problem exists in the L2 context as well as the L1.* Just as in first language acquisition, second language learners project beyond the data they are exposed to and come to know what is possible and impossible in a given language even though they may not have direct experience with a particular structure.

- *Although Universal Grammar constrains second language acquisition, it does not guarantee native-likeness.* When those working within linguistic theory claim that interlanguages are constrained by Universal Grammar, they do not mean to imply that L2 learners will achieve a mental representation equivalent to that of a native speaker. Again, the basic claim is that the interlanguage will be constrained and must adhere to properties of human language. No guarantees about anything else are suggested.

Researchers within this framework dispute other claims, such as the role of the first language in the formation of interlanguage, and whether or not native-likeness is a possibility. Because these are disputed, we do not include them here.

Conclusion

The application of linguistic theory to second language acquisition has enjoyed a rich and bountiful research agenda since the mid-1980s, especially in the United States and Canada. One of its strengths has been a clear conceptualization of the nature of language, allowing researchers to make clear predictions or hypotheses that can subsequently be tested regarding the mental representation of L2 learners. Missing from the theory is what is called a transitional theory. This means that while those working within linguistic theory can account for representation, the theory has no mechanism by which learners' interlanguages change over time. Many scholars are associated with the application of linguistic theory to the L2 context including, but not limited to, Lydia White, Bonnie Schwartz, Silvina Montrul, Anna Vainikka, Martha young-Scholten, Rex Sprouse, Juana Liceras, Roger Hawkins, and Donna Lardiere.

Emergentism and usage-based theories

The basics

Emergentism is a theory within cognitive psychology that attempts to account for human learning and knowledge. Central to the theory is that all human learning uses the same general architecture for knowledge and performance development be it language, tennis, or assembly-line work. In contrast to linguistic theory that posits a **Universal Grammar** that is unique to language and is responsible for the nature of language, emergentism would claim there is nothing special about language. What is more, the theory says that all learning and representation (knowledge) in the mind/brain is sensitive to frequency. So, those things that are more frequent in the environment or those things with which a person has more frequent experience are more likely to be learned before others. At the same time, more frequent things are likely to have more robust representations in the mind/brain. Emergentism is aligned with what are called usage-based theories because such theories rely on people's experience with their environment and how this is indicated in their performance. Performance is central to Emergentism in that observable behaviors are taken to be indicators of what exists in representation and how robustly it is represented.

Applied to language, emergentism would suggest that something like sentence structure is a result of frequencies of occurrence in the **input** that people are exposed to. For example, a basic noun phrase "emerges" over time as people confront something like "the" in the input. Their internal processors will notice that this word is often followed by things like "man," "dog," "house," and so on. Thus, they will have initial and strong associations (contingency relationships) in their mind/brain for "the" followed by these and similar words. They may also encounter that "the" is followed by words such as "red," "big," "enormous," and so on, and that these words are almost always followed by words such as "house," "man," "dogs," "one," and so on. In short, the various configurations of noun phrases are built up due to exposure to language with some configurations—or better yet, the associations between words that make up phrases—having stronger and more robust representations in the mind/brain because they are more frequent. As the reader might surmise, a central idea within emergentism is that the human mind/brain is a statistical tabulator par excellence, and although other factors may come into play in how important a piece of linguistic data is, human knowledge and performance with that knowledge is a direct result of experience with the environment. There is nothing special in the mind/brain that constrains or regulates language.

The claims

As with all theories we present in this section, emergentism makes a number of claims and here we will only list several of the more important ones.

- *Language learning is an implicit statistical learning process.* As we saw earlier, frequency in the input is an important factor in learning. Also important to this claim is recency and context. Things that are more recent and are more relevant to a particular context are those that "come to mind" when we are performing with language.
- *Language and its properties emerge over time.* As stated before, emergentists do not ascribe to something like Universal Grammar that is an innate mechanism constraining language and thus language acquisition. Instead, emergentists believe that all properties of language we can describe, as complex and abstract as they may seem, are all the result of simple cognitive-learning mechanisms interacting with data from the environment.

As with many other theories, emergentism makes no claims about how far learners get in language or that they will ever become native-like. Because it recognizes a role for the L1 in inhibiting the establishment of associations, emergentists would claim that by definition, L2 learning would be more difficult than L1 learning.

Conclusion

Emergentism (and its predecessor connectionism) arrived on the L2 scene in the late 1980s. Since then, it has received attention by theorists but as of yet, it has not yielded as great an amount of empirical research as other frameworks and theories. Some of the research has not used L2 learners but instead computer simulations of what L2 learning would look like. As a psychological theory, emergentism has replaced

behaviorism as a major way of thinking about learning. Unlike linguistic theory, emergentism does contain a transition theory—that is, a theory of how learning progresses over time. Emergentism does have problems, however, in accounting for the **poverty of the stimulus** problem. Within the theory, there is no real way to explain how people come to know more than what they are exposed to. Because the theory relies heavily on frequency in the input and general learning architecture, it cannot explain why people know that certain kinds of sentence permutations are impossible. Scholars associated with emergentism include Nick Ellis, William O'Grady, and Brian MacWhinney.

The Declarative/Procedural Model

The basics

The Declarative/Procedural Model (DPM) is unlike other theories in that its roots lie in neuroscience and the structure of the brain.

Whereas almost all other theories examine some kind of performance (e.g., **grammaticality judgments, truth-value tasks,** reading times, spoken language, conversations), the DPM uses the results of brain activity (e.g., **event-related potentials/ERPs, fMRIs, PET or positive emission topography**) to make claims about language processing, and by inference, language learning. Fundamental to the model is that there are two memory systems served by different parts of the brain. One is declarative memory and the other is procedural memory (not to be confused or equated with how these terms are used in skill theory, which is reviewed elsewhere in this section). Declarative memory is entrenched in one set of neural structures and is largely responsible for what may be called "idiosyncratic" aspects of knowledge. This is the kind of knowledge that is unpredictable. Procedural knowledge is served by a different network of neural structures and, although not as well researched as declarative knowledge, is understood to be used for implicit learning of statistical relationships among elements in the environment including sequencing, sets of rules, categories of things, among others. Although independent, the two systems may overlap in the types of things they attempt to learn, as we will see in a moment.

Applied to language, the DPM would suggest that such things as vocabulary and stock phrases are learned via declarative memory, as these are unpredictable and unique. On the other hand, procedural memory is expected to be more important for grammatical aspects of language as, under the theory, these are rule-oriented aspects of language that are predictable regardless of vocabulary. However, in the L2 context, non-child learners may make initial use of declarative memory for rule learning while, in the background, procedural memory hums along to do its work on the same. In this way, there is some overlap.

The claims

The DPM makes a number of interesting claims and predictions about second language acquisition, especially comparing it to first language acquisition. Following are some of the more important claims.

- *Both L1 and L2 learners will rely on declarative knowledge for the learning, storage, and retrieval of idiosyncratic information.* This knowledge involves lexical items, fixed phrases, idioms, irregular **morphology**, and similar items. For example, both L1 and L2 learners use declarative knowledge to learn irregular past tense verb forms such as *went, took, saw,* and *ate.* Both L1 and L2 learners would use declarative knowledge to learn that "cat" stands for a particular kind of animal, that "love" is a particular kind of emotion, and so on.

- *Both L1 and L2 learners will rely on procedural knowledge for the implicit learning, storage, and retrieval of rule-oriented information.* What this claim means is that in both L1 and L2 situations, learners will rely on procedural knowledge to acquire agreement patterns among nouns, determiners, and adjectives in languages like Spanish, that lexical verbs cannot invert with subjects in English but auxiliaries and modals can, and so on. But the next claim points out some differences.

- *Although both L1 and L2 acquisition are served by the same mechanisms, there will be marked differences in outcomes between the two.* In both L1 and L2 learning, the use of procedural knowledge is both slow and gradual. L1 learners have much more time on task during acquisition. L2 learners have less so, and the older the onset of acquisition, the less time on task there is. Thus, in the L2 context, the DPM would say that L2 learners might rely more on declarative knowledge, especially in the initial stages, to work with regular (predictable) grammatical information. Given enough time, procedural knowledge would "replace" declarative knowledge (i.e., it is working in the background in its slow and gradual manner). However, what is also true is that as a general phenomenon, procedural memory declines over time so that the later the onset of L2 learning, the less efficient procedural memory becomes. But, those working within the DPM also note that the context of learning plays an important role. The more the L2 learning context pushes learners to use procedural memory (e.g., immersion contexts, input-rich environments, non-explicit learning conditions), the more the procedural memory is likely to be engaged.

Conclusion

The DPM is a relative newcomer on the L2 scene compared to other theories and frameworks. Nonetheless, it is providing evidence for the claims reviewed earlier and is serving as a useful tool to underscore both fundamental similarity and fundamental difference between L1 and L2 acquisition. Because the research is costly and time-consuming (i.e., the use of ERPs, fMRIs, and other techniques is not easy or cheap and must be conducted in specialized laboratories), the quantity of research using this framework will likely not be as great as that from other theories and frameworks. The names most associated with the DPM are Michael Ullman and Kara Morgan Short, although many others work in the neuroscientific domain of second language acquisition with an indirect connection to the DPM. These scholars include Lee Osterhout, Peter Indefrey, Michel Paradis, and Darren Tanner, to name a few.

Complexity Theory/Dynamic Systems

The basics

Within the framework of Complexity Theory and Dynamic Systems is the idea that complexity (in any domain, not just language) arises as a result of the interaction of various individuals or components. Order, as it were, seems to emerge out of nowhere. What is more, this complexity or order is not reducible to the action of one component. An oft-cited example is bird flocking. When one sees several hundred birds fly and swoop in some seemingly grouped fashion, this flock seems to simply emerge when one bird takes off, and one cannot understand that "synchronism" of all the birds in flight by studying any single bird in isolation. Another facet of complexity is that even though order emerges from seemingly nowhere, that order isn't necessarily static (hence the term *dynamic system*). Complexity is adaptive and may change in response to external stimuli or the environment. Finally, complexity is non-linear. Changes are not mere additions to a system; they can have both quantitative and qualitative effects. Complexity Theory, then, is not a theory of any particular thing. It is not a theory that attempts to account for any one thing. It is better seen as a lens through which to look at various—and often quite disparate situations—and see how the sum is greater (and, of course, more complex) than the parts.

Complexity Theory has been applied to language and more specifically to language development. In so doing, it focuses on processes involved in the creation of a linguistic system and less on the product (e.g., mental representation, performance on a given task). If we imagine a child, for example, undergoing first language acquisition, we might say that the first signs of a sentence might be two-word utterances: 'no ball,' 'doggy gone.' But this stage emerged from something else (e.g., babbling, isolated words) and something else will emerge from this stage. In fact, we see that children learning a first language experience an "explosion" of language growth around the age of 3 years, and at first blush it would seem that this comes almost out of nowhere, much like a flock of birds. All of a sudden children are producing full sentences, there may be tense marking on verbs, there are clear lexical and functional phrases, and so on. In short, order emerged from something, and yet that order is not static. We know from research that children are not done learning language at the age of 3 or 3.5 or 4 or 4.5, and so on. Complexity Theory asks how this system arose, not by looking at any one aspect of language but by looking at everything from internal architecture to input to social context and so on. And even within these isolable areas there is complexity.

Such a view is taken on second language acquisition by those interested in complexity and dynamic systems. For them, one can look at L2 development in the same way one looks at L1 development, regardless of how native-like or non-native-like the learner sounds. To be sure, there is overlap with other perspectives, especially emergentism or usage-based approaches, sociocultural approaches, and others. In fact, some scholars working within complexity and dynamic systems see the approach as a broad framework that can envelope other theories and approaches that are focused on more narrow aspects of development.

The claims

Unlike other theories, Complexity Theory is not used to make predictions about language acquisition or development other than to highlight the complexity involved. However, there are several major claims that fall out of complexity and dynamic systems when referencing the L2 context.

- *Learning is not just about taking in data.* Embodied in this claim is that although a complexity theorist would certainly underscore the role of input in language development, that person would further say that the actual system is more complex than an inventory of features and rules, for example. Important is how learners use linguistic knowledge and how it is influenced by the context of use—context being defined as the setting and persons involved in an interaction.

- *Stages and linearity are external perspectives as learners' systems are constantly in flux.* Although we might say that learners are in an early stage of acquisition of negation (let's say, the subject + 'no' + phrase stage as in 'I no drink beer'), this is at best an idealistic rendering of what learners do. Variability is common and to be expected, and because context influences language development, what gets strengthened and what gets weakened within the system may depend on who learners interact with and the environments they find themselves in.

- *Components are constantly interacting within the learner's system.* Although we may often think of syntax, phonology, lexicon, semantics, pragmatics, and so on, as separate entities and linguists may certainly study each in its own right, Complexity Theory would say that to understand development would involve seeing how all these components interact in the meaning-making process. A syntactic stage of development, for example, cannot be understood without looking at the words available to the learners, the morphology available to the learners, and so on, all couched within the context of "What are the learners trying to say and to whom?"

Conclusion

Complexity Theory and Dynamic Systems are in their infancy when applied to L2 research, having just made their way into L2 thinking in the early 2000s. It is not yet clear what impact the approach will have on the field. Because the theory is more of an encompassing framework than a theory about anything specific, it might best be used as a way of aggregating various predictions and findings from other theories and approaches to get a better sense of the immensity that is the acquisition of something like language—especially when language is viewed in its broadest sense as a linguistic, cognitive, and social "thing." Scholars associated with Complexity Theory and Dynamic Systems are Diane Larsen-Freeman, Kees de Bot, Wander Lowie, Marjolin Verspoor, among others.

Input processing

The basics

Within the model of input processing is the basic idea that learners bring processing strategies for making **form-meaning connections** to the task of comprehension. That is, as learners are attempting to comprehend what they hear, they must somehow tag and encode linguistic features in the input for use by the internal mechanisms responsible for developing **mental representation**. It is obvious that acquisition is not instantaneous (i.e., nothing is acquired immediately upon exposure in input); thus learners must somehow be "filtering" input as they attempt to make sense out of what someone is saying to them. Research in input processing attempts to understand what this filtering mechanism is. To be sure, **input processing** refers not to **noticing** but to how learners do (or do not) link meaning to a piece of linguistic data—be it a word, a phrase, or a piece of a word (e.g., an inflection). Input processing is particularly concerned with those strategies that constrain the processing of linguistic form. For example, when learners encounter case marking on German articles in the input, what keeps them processing that case marking? When learners of English encounter past tense *-ed* in the input, what keeps them from processing this verbal inflection?

The claims

The most widely known model for input processing has been developed by Bill VanPatten. In that model, learners' processing strategies are couched in terms of principles that guide processing. Following are four of the major principles in the model. Each of these principles has corollaries or "subprinciples" that refine and explicate them.

- *Learners process content words in the input before anything else.* Called the Primacy of Content Words, this principle claims that L2 learners come to the task of acquisition knowing that words exist and seek these as the key elements to the meaning of an utterance.

- *Learners will process lexical items for meaning before grammatical forms when both encode the same meaning.* Here the idea is that when redundancy exists in language, lexical items are processed prior to grammatical form as a natural consequence of the Primacy of Content Words. This is called the Lexical Preference Principle.

- *Learners tend to process the first noun or pronoun they encounter in the sentence as subject and/or agent.* Regardless of learners' first language, this principle is posited as a universal tendency among learners. The idea is that word order serves as a major first cue to who did what to whom even when the word order leads to a wrong sentence interpretation (as we will see below). This is called the

First-noun Principle.

• *Learners tend to process items in sentence initial position before those in sentence final position and those in sentence medial position.* This is the only principle that deals with what is called **salience** in the input. It is referred to as the Sentence Location Principle.

To illustrate, let's look at the First-noun Principle. This kind of strategy works fine for languages that are rigidly subject-verb-object or subject-object-verb, but many languages are not so rigid. Thus, learners make errors in comprehending object-verb-subject sentences and deliver incorrect linguistic information about sentence structure to their **developing system**. So, learners of German, for example, do fine with this principle when it comes to basic SVO sentences such as *Die Frau hört den Mann* "The woman hears the man" but will incorrectly process its OVS version *Den Mann hört die Frau* as "The man hears the woman", missing completely the accusative case marking on the masculine article (*der Mann* = nominative, *den Mann* = accusative). Thus, the First-noun Principle mitigates against the early processing of case endings in the input, as learners rely on word order and not case as a cue to who did what to whom.

Conclusion

The model of input processing has garnered wide attention in the field and is mostly known for the instructional intervention derived from it called **processing instruction**. In fact, more research has been conducted in processing instruction than in input processing itself. The model is useful in that it melds with a variety of other theories of representation. For example, both linguistic theory and emergentism can link to input processing without a clash of underlying assumptions. Nonetheless, the theory downplays the role of the L1 in acquisition, which is not the position taken by most theories of representation. What is more, some recent research suggests that although the principles hold overall, they may need to be attenuated as additional factors may interact with them. As stated, Bill VanPatten is the name most associated with input processing, but other scholars have addressed input processing, albeit in different ways. These scholars include Michael Sharwood Smith, John Truscott, William O'Grady, and Susanne Carroll.

The Interaction Hypothesis

The basics

This framework was developed in the early 1980s with the view that comprehensible input is a key factor in second language. The research associated with this framework focused on how input can be made comprehensible. **Interaction** refers to conversations between learners and other interlocutors, and the Interaction Hypothesis focuses on how such interactions might affect acquisition by positing that interactions play a central role in second language acquisition processes. They may do so in essentially two ways: (1) by modifying input, (2) by providing **feedback** related to the linking of meaning and form. Input modification occurs when the interlocutor perceives that the learner does not understand what is being said, and restates something by simplifying, exemplifying, or otherwise altering the original statement. Feedback occurs when the interlocutor uses particular devices to inform the learner about something he or she has said. These include such things as "Do you mean…?", "I'm sorry. I don't understand.", and "OK. I get it." According to the Interaction Hypothesis, both input modifications and **feedback** can bring something in the input into the learner's focal attention at a given moment, offering an opportunity to perceive and process some piece of language the learner might miss otherwise. Following is an interaction that occurred in a men's locker room after a tennis match. Bob is a native speaker and Tom is the non-native (of Chinese L1 background). Dave, Tom's tennis partner, was absent that day and a substitute played for him.

Bob: So where's Dave?

Tom: He vacation.

Bob: He's on vacation?

Tom: Yes, on vacation.

In this interaction, Tom produced a non-native sentence "He vacation." Bob responded with what is called a confirmation check. Using rising intonation, he wanted to see if he understood Tom correctly: "He's on vacation?" We can deduce from the interchange that this confirmation check brought the preposition "on" into Tom's focal attention, but not the contracted copular verb 's on the end of "he" which is why Tom repeats the preposition in his response to the confirmation check. In this episode, the confirmation check is a type of "conversational feedback" to the learner, but note that is natural to conversations as such things also exist among native speaker interactions. Imagine the above scenario with the following fictitious counterpart between two native speaking adults in the same context:

Fred: So where's Dave?

Harry: He's on vacation.

Bob: He's on vacation?

Harry: Yep, on vacation.

The confirmation check plays the exact same conversational purpose in each interchange. However, for a language learner, it may serve as an additional prompt to bring something into focal awareness or attention.

The claims

The Interaction Hypothesis makes a number of claims in terms of the role of input, interactional modifications, feedback, and output in second language acquisition.

- *Input plays a crucial role in second language acquisition.* Like all mainstream SLA models and theories, the data for learners reside in the communicative language they are exposed to.

- *Input is crucial but it is not sufficient. Interaction also plays a key role.* Through interactions, learners may be led to notice things they wouldn't notice otherwise, and this noticing can affect acquisition. How learners are led to notice things can happen in several ways, including the following: input modifications—the other speaker adjusts his or her speech due to perceived difficulties in learner comprehension (see caretaker speech); feedback—the other speaker indicates in some way that the learner has produced something non-native-like.

- *Output is necessary for the development of language.* Output modifications through negotiation of meaning help learners to notice important aspects of the target language.

- *Negative feedback obtained during negotiation of meaning might facilitate the acquisition of vocabulary, morphology, syntax, and pronunciation.* When the learner does not understand the other interlocutor, interactions that elicit negative feedback can have a facilitative role in acquisition. Feedback is seen a natural part of the conversation and not as error correction.

Conclusion

One of the main assumptions of this theoretical framework is that native speakers and non-native speakers can work actively together to achieve mutual understanding. Negotiations involve both linguistic and interactional modifications, and facilitate acquisition because they connect input, learner's abilities, attention, and production in a productive way. More research needs to be conducted to determine the extent to which such conversational and interactional exchanges actually result in acquisition. A number of factors (developmental stages, extent to which acquisition is engaged in meaning negotiation, amount and type of information, the amount of effort native and non-native speakers make in constructing discourse) might attenuate the effects the usefulness of modified input. What is more, to date the evidence for interaction affecting the acquisition of morphosyntactic features has been scant, with the research more clearly showing effects for vocabulary and some aspects of pronunciation. Scholars most associated with interaction include Susan Gass, Alison Mackey, Michael Long, and Teresa Pica, among others.

Processability Theory

The basics

Processability Theory's main concern is the constraints on learner production of formal features during real-time communication. An important aspect of Processability Theory is that L2 grammar develops in conjunction with processing prerequisites. Relying on Lexical Functional Grammar, Processability Theory is built on the idea that grammatical information needs to be exchanged between elements during output processing (e.g., the grammatical information that a subject is singular has to be exchanged with the verb to make sure it's in the correct form). What this means is that in a sentence such as *The boy speaks English well* learners would need to develop a number of procedures to string together elements of the sentence (e.g., *The* and *boy*) and matching the subject and the verb in the sentence (e.g., *The boy* and *speaks*). At the same time, elements in a sentence may be syntactically close to each other or syntactically far from each other, with the grammatical information that needs to be shared having to travel shorter or longer syntactic distances (or no distance at all).

The theory consists of two psycholinguistic dimensions: the developmental dimension and the variational dimension. As far as the developmental dimension is concerned, the basic idea of this theoretical framework is that language processing for speech production is incremental. Output processing procedures emerge over time and in a set order or stage-like fashion. Learners cannot skip any procedure or stage and any given stage assumes the stages prior to it. The procedures/stages are the following (greatly simplified for exposition here):

Stage 1: lemma access. The learner retrieves individual lexical items from the lexicon. Example: cat, house, man.

Stage 2: category procedure. The learner adds grammatical information that does not need to agree with anything else in the sentence or discourse. Example: I ate (past tense of eat).

Stage 3: phrasal procedure. The learner can exchange grammatical information within a phrase such as a noun phrase. Example: two boys (plurality is exchanged between the numeral and the noun).

Stage 4: S-procedure. The learner can exchange grammatical information across phrasal boundaries in a single clause. Example: The boy speaks English well (third-person singular is exchanged between the noun phrase and the verb phrase).

Stage 5: clause procedure. The learner can exchange information between a matrix clause and an embedded clause. Example: I wonder where he is (the learner knows that inversion is not normally possible in an indirect question that is embedded).

While we provide these examples in English, the task for the learner is to build the language-specific procedures needed to handle a specific second language. The outcomes may be different, but the universal procedures are always ordered in the same sequence.

The variational dimension of Processability Theory accounts for the existence of possible learner strategies for a given structure before they have acquired a particular processing procedure. For example, different learners may opt for different solutions when they lack the processing procedure for inversion in yes/no questions in English. Although the standard might be *Why did she eat that?*, learners may come up with variations such as *Why she eat that?* and *She ate that. Why?* because they do not yet have the procedure allowing them to invert subject and auxiliary verb. In some cases, learners might even avoid producing such questions.

The claims

The main claims of the Processability Theory in second language acquisition are:

- *Language acquisition consists of staged development with some variation within stages.* L2 learners can only produce linguistic structures for which they have acquired the necessary processing procedures. If a learner is at stage 3, he or she cannot produce—in a creative fashion—grammatical structures that require the procedures at stage 5, for example. However, learners might display individual variation with regard to the extent they apply developmental rules.
- *Teaching of formal structures is constrained.* Instruction cannot cause learners to skip developmental stages. For instruction to be beneficial, a learner's interlanguage must close to the point when this structure would be acquired anyway.

Conclusion

Processability Theory has a history spanning more than twenty years. The theory provides a detailed account of speech production and focuses on the developmental problem in language production. In fact, it is the only theory with an articulated account of how grammatical properties emerge in speech over time. Because the theory focuses on how and why development is constrained, it is one of the few theories that offer predictive power regarding the limitations of instruction (see, for example, the **Key Question "Does Instruction Make a Difference?"**). However, most of the research to date has focused on demonstrating the applicability of the theory cross-linguistically with very different languages (e.g., English, German, Spanish, Swedish, Japanese) and only a few published studies have specifically tested whether instruction can override the constraints imposed by processability. At the same time, because some of the studies on the applicability of the theory to various languages have used classroom-based learners, by implication the effects of instruction are tested. The theory is most closely associated with Manfred Pienemann.

Sociocultural Theory

The basics

Sociocultural Theory, based on the work of the Russian psychologist Vygotsky, argues that the development of human cognitive functions derives from social interactions and that through participation in social activities individuals are drawn into the use of these functions. The theory focuses not only on how adults and peers influence individual learning, but also on how cultural beliefs and attitudes impact how instruction and learning take place. The central constructs of the theory are: mediation; the zone of proximal development (ZPD); and verbal thought. Language learning is a socially mediated process and language is a cultural artifact that mediates social and psychological activities. Mediation refers to the idea that humans possess certain cultural tools, such as language, literacy, numeracy, and others, that they purposefully use to control and interact with their environment. The ZPD is a difficult concept to articulate and is often subject to misinterpretation, but to summarize here, the ZPD refers to the distance between a learner's current ability to independently solve problems and the level of potential development present when guided by more capable persons. According to Vygotsky, learning occurs in this zone and it is achieved through the cooperation of experts and novices working together. Applied to language, learning concerns the development of language function and mental function, along with the combination of language and thought. Generally speaking, acquisition includes the process in which the low level external or social speech develops into the highest level inner speech or verbal thought.

The claims

Sociocultural Theory makes a number of basic claims as far as social interaction, participants, and cultural context is concerned.

- *All learning or development takes place as people participate in culturally formed settings.* These settings include schools, family life, peer groups, work places, and so on. Socioculturalists claim that the most important cognitive activities in which people engage are shaped by these environments. Thus, all learning is situated and context-bound. Social interaction plays a crucial role in the process of cognitive development. In this context, social learning precedes development.

- *The highly knowledgeable participant can create good learning conditions for the novice learner.* The more knowledgeable participant (somebody who has a higher understanding or ability) plays a fundamental role in helping the less knowledgeable learner in language development.

- *Learners use tools such as speech and writing to mediate their social environments.* These tools mediate between individuals and the situations in which they find themselves. At the same time, these tools have certain limits, such that people use them only in certain ways.

Conclusion

Sociocultural Theory appeared on the scene in SLA research in the 1990s, and has had particular influence in educational circles and schools of education but less so in linguistic and psycholinguistic circles, possibly because of its underlying belief in explicit learning. The theorists associated with this theory support the view that learning occurs effectively when students interact with others, especially those who are more advanced. One of the main criticisms of Vygotsky's sociocultural perspective is the assumption that his theory is relevant to all cultures. Some of the major names associated with Sociocultural Theory are James Lantolf, Steven Thorne, Amy Ohta, and Richard Donato.

Skill Acquisition Theory

The basics

Skill Acquisition Theory (a derivative of Adaptive Control of Thought) is a theory in cognitive psychology centered on three stages of development: cognitive (or declarative), associative (or procedural), and autonomous (or automatic). The three stages are distinguished by major differences in the nature of knowledge, usage, and behavior. Learners can gain some **declarative knowledge** ("knowledge that") through observation or analysis without being required to use any skill at the initial learning stage. The second stage is when the learning is visible as behavior or **procedural knowledge** ("knowledge how"). Thus, declarative knowledge is transformed into procedural knowledge. This proceduralization of knowledge is not particularly difficult or time-consuming providing that the relevant declarative knowledge is available to the learner. This is achieved by engaging in the target behavior while relying on declarative knowledge (paying attention to something while practicing). Once the procedural knowledge has been realized, continued practice reinforces the skill. This practice is called **automatization**. As a general rule, the more the learner practices the skill, the more automatic the skill becomes.

Another important concept of Skill Acquisition Theory is the role of explicit or implicit learning in acquiring rules. This is very much dependent on the complexity of the rule. Simple rules can be learned explicitly, while more "complex" ones may be better acquired implicitly. According to Skill Acquisition Theory, the gradual automatizing of a rule essentially means that a rule becomes implicitly acquired. Therefore, practice leading to automatization is not always at odds with implicit learning.

Also important to the theory is the idea of appropriate practice. That is, for someone to get control over a skill and automate a behavior, that person must engage in the very skill he or she wishes to acquire. One does not learn to cook by eating. One learns to cook by actually cooking over and over again.

Applied to the second language context, the implications should be clear. Learners first learn "rules" about language explicitly. They have declarative knowledge about language and must engage in appropriate practice. For example, if a skill they wish to acquire is speaking, then learners must engage in speaking (not rote practice, not repetition, not classic "drills"). Practice for speaking, then, would mean events in which learners are attempting to communicate information. The process is slow, but as learners engage more and more in such appropriate practice, the skill becomes fine-tuned and more and more automatic. That is, the learner becomes more fluent with the language and more error-free.

The claims

The main claims of Skill Acquisition Theory are:

- *Learning of a wide variety of skills shows a remarkable similarity in development from initial representation of knowledge through initial changes in behavior to eventual fluent, spontaneous, and highly skilled behavior.* Skills are automatized only after they have first been under controlled processing. Controlled processing leads to automatic processing.

- *Subskills involved in the complex task of language learning must be practiced, automatized, and integrated into organized internal representations.* The internal representations of language are constantly restructured as proficiency develops.

Conclusion

Skill Acquisition Theory assumes that learners use the same cognitive processes for the learning of all skills through a three-staged development (declarative knowledge turns smoothly into procedural knowledge and then to automated performance through consistent and appropriate "practice"). However, one of the limitations outlined by some critics is that Skill Acquisition Theory assumptions only apply to highly motivated and high-aptitude adult learners engaged in the acquisition of simple structures at fairly early stages of learning in classroom contexts. The theory is most closely associated with Robert DeKeyser.

Key Terms in Second Language Acquisition

Accessibility Hierarchy 可及性等级

Noun Phrase Accessibility Hierarchy 名词短语可及性等级

One important issue in SLA research is to establish how L2 learners acquire certain linguistic features. We know that learners might follow a particular order in the acquisition of some features (see **acquisition orders, morpheme studies**). We also know that the acquisition of question formation, negation, and other sentential syntax follows specific and predictable acquisitional stages (see **developmental sequences**).

Another well-researched area of studies has attempted to establish a universal order of acquisition of relative clause structure. The Accessibility Hierarchy attempts to characterize the various types of relative clause construction among different languages. Researchers have argued that the accessibility of a noun phrase (NP) for relativization depends on its grammatical role (e.g., subject or object). The Noun Phrase Accessibility Hierarchy indicates that the easiest relative clause construction is when the relative pronoun is the subject of the relative clause. A specific hierarchy is proposed:

Subject (Ex: The player who played at the match …)

Direct object (Ex: The player who we saw …)

Indirect object (Ex: The player whom I spoke to …)

Object of preposition (Ex: The player who we talked about …)

Genitive (Ex: The player whose son played …)

Object of comparison (Ex: The player who I am taller than …)

The above sentences show that the focus of attention in the Noun Phrase Accessibility Hierarchy is on the grammatical role (function) of the relative pronoun no matter the role taken by the head noun in the main clause. However, relativization is not the only problem L2 learners are facing in learning relative clauses (see **markedness** as well as **typological universals**).

Research investigating the Accessibility Hierarchy has suggested that universal principles are at the center of acquisition processes in different languages. Researchers associated with this research are Edward Keenan, Bernard Comrie, and in the L2 context Susan Gass, Fred Eckman, and others.

Acculturation model 文化适应模式

The acculturation model claims that the process of acculturation (adapting to a new culture) is directly linked to acquisition. There are social and psychological factors that have a direct effect on the success L2 learners have in acquiring a second language. According to the model, success depends on the extent to which learners adapt fully to target language culture. Two major factors are identified in acculturation: social distance and psychological distance.

Social distance factors refer to those involving the relationship between the internal characteristics of a language group and the ability for the learner to become closer (socially) to that target language group. Among these factors are the social dominance of the language group, the ability for the individual to integrate into the group, the cohesiveness and size of the group, the attitude of both the group and the individual toward each other, and the length of the exposure between the two.

Psychological distance factors refer to the extent to which individual learners cope psychologically with learning an L2. Among these factors are anxiety, motivation, and self-confidence.

Because the model focuses on relative success of learners (i.e., how far along learners get in acquisition), it does not provide any explanation or insight into the internal processes responsible for the acquisition of an L2. That is, it does not attempt to explain why there are **developmental sequences** or **acquisition orders**, for example, and what causes them. Although both social and psychological factors remain important in acquisition (see, for example, **individual differences**), the acculturation model lost favor by the early 1980s as research increasingly turned its attention toward linguistic and psycholinguistic approaches to explaining acquisition phenomena. The scholar most associated with acculturation is John Schumann.

Acquisition 习得　　acquisition versus learning 习得与学得

Acquisition is a general term in SLA research used to mean the internalization of a linguistic system. However, in the 1970s, Steven Krashen made a distinction between learning and acquisition. For him, learning referred to the conscious effort at learning rules from books and teachers. When learners receive information such as "You need to add an -s to verbs that refer to someone else. This is called third-person -s." and then practice this rule, Krashen would consider this learning. Learning results in a particular kind of knowledge system, an "explicit" system.

Distinct from learning is acquisition. According to Krashen, acquisition involves processes by which learners internalize language from exposure to **input** (basically, samples of language they hear or read in communicative contexts). To acquire third-person -s, learners would need to hear lots of third-person verbs in context, as part of the communication of information. In a certain sense, Krashen likens acquisition for L2 learners to acquisition for L1 learners: namely, acquisition happens because of exposure to input, not because anyone teaches the learner a rule or because he or she practices it. Unlike learning, acquisition for an L2 learner results in an implicit (unconscious) linguistic system, just as it would for the L1 learner.

For Krashen, acquisition is more fundamental. His claim is that learning is limited in terms of what learners can do with explicit information, that ultimately communication involves tapping into the acquired linguistic system and not the learned linguistic system. The learned system can be used for monitoring (editing one's production) under certain conditions (see **Monitor Theory**). What is more, under this scenario, learning and acquisition are separate processes that result in separate systems that do not interact. Most importantly, learning cannot become acquisition. That is, one doesn't learn rules and, because of practice, acquire them. Acquisition happens in one and only one way for Krashen: by exposure to input in communicative settings. A variety of classroom approaches were either based on Krashen's ideas or found support in them (e.g., the Natural Approach, immersion).

Krashen's learning–acquisition distinction caused considerable debate in the field, as did his Monitor Theory, of which the distinction is a part. Scholars argued over whether such a distinction truly existed, or, if it did, whether or not there could be an interface between the two processes as well as the two resulting linguistic systems. However, it is safe to say that today, regardless of the processes involved (learning vs. acquisition), scholars accept that learners develop an implicit mental representation of language, which subsumes Krashen's acquired system (see **competence**, **mental representation of language**). At the same time, they accept that learners may also have explicit knowledge, which subsumes Krashen's learned knowledge about language. The notable exception are scholars who work within skill theory, who do believe in the practicing of rules as part of skill development. As we said at the outset, acquisition is now used as a cover term for what happens to learners regardless of context and regardless of whether they explicitly practice rules or not. Thus, the field is called *second language acquisition* and not, for example, *second language acquisition and learning.* Scholars associated with the debate in the late 1970s and early 1980s over learning and acquisition include Kevin Gregg, Steven Krashen, Barry McLaughlin, and Tracy Terrell. The learning–acquisition distinction was reformulated by Bonnie Schwartz in the late 1980s and early 1990s.

Acquisition orders 习得顺序

The language produced by L2 learners seems to suggest that learners from different language backgrounds acquire different morphological features in a fixed and predicted order over time. Evidence for this claim was provided by the morpheme studies, which investigated the order of acquisition of grammatical features such as articles and other morphological features (see **morphemes/morpheme studies**). The morpheme studies have shown that learners of English tend to learn verbal morphemes in the following order:

1. *-ing*
2. regular past tense
3. irregular past tense
4. third-person present tense *-s*.

Therefore, we might conclude that learners from different L1s would develop their accuracy in using these morphemes following this predictable and universal order of acquisition. These findings were important in suggesting that L2 learners use internal strategies to organize and process language, and these strategies are not influenced by external factors. Scholars associated with this research include Heidi Dulay and

Marina Burt, Steven Krashen, Diane Larsen-Freeman, and many others. (See also the Key Question **What does development look like?**)

Adaptive Control of Thought model 思维适应性控制模型

See **Skill Acquisition Theory** in the **Key Theories and Frameworks in Second Language Acquisition** section.

Affective (filter, activities, and so on) 情感（过滤，活动等）

Affective is an adjective derived from *affect*, which refers to moods, personal states of being, attitudes, feelings, opinions, and so on. In Krashen's **Monitor Theory**, there exists the construct *affective filter*. The affective filter is a metaphor that the theory uses to talk about why language (**input**) enters or doesn't enter the head of the learner.

The theory would say that learners with "high affective filters" block out language due to attitudes, emotions, and so on, while those with "low affective filters" do not. Affective activities are those used in classrooms that invite learners to express beliefs, feelings, emotions, and so on. Thus, any use of affective refers to the "personal" side of things in acquisition.

Applied linguistics 应用语言学

Applied linguistics is a fuzzy term and can mean different things to different people. In its original conception (1960s), applied linguistics was a term used to refer to language teaching and the application of linguistics to classroom matters. Contrastive analysis (see **Contrastive Analysis Hypothesis**) was a form of applied linguistics. People used the then current theory of language to describe linguistic learning problems, and then fashioned teaching methods and materials around this information. Later, the term became something that meant the application of linguistics to just about any endeavor that might use it (e.g., analysis of acquisition disorders). However, its contemporary usage has evolved even further, and people use it to refer to any endeavor that is language related at all, whether linguistics is involved or not. For example, papers presented at such conferences as the American Association of Applied Linguistics and the British Association of Applied Linguistics sometimes contain no references to any kind of linguistics and linguistics are not even implied in what the researchers are presenting (e.g., papers on motivation). One current definition of applied linguistics, then, would be something like this: scholarship on real-world issues related to language.

Aptitude 语言学能

Aptitude can be defined as a learner's propensity to learn an L2 and is one of the many factors researched in the field of **individual differences**. Under classic scenarios of aptitude (e.g., prior to the 1970s), there were four main factors associated with such a propensity:

- the ability for a learner to handle and memorize new sounds in an L2;
- the ability for a learner to recognize grammatical function of words in an L2;
- the ability for the learner to extrapolate grammatical rules from L2 samples;
- the ability for the learner to memorize new words in an L2.

Since the 1970s, the concept of aptitude has evolved. What has transpired is that researchers in aptitude have tended to focus on specific aptitude-related constructs to see how they interact with acquisition. Such constructs include **working memory**, certain features of phonological encoding (i.e., turning external sound into internal **mental representation of language**), L1-based skills, and **noticing**, among others. Some researchers, however, have attempted to identify clusters of factors that may be at work and that may cluster differentially depending on proficiency level. The names most associated with classic aptitude research are John Carroll and Paul Pimsleur. Contemporary leading researchers in aptitude include Peter Robinson, Peter Skehan, Richard Sparks, and Leonore Ganschow.

Aspect 体

Aspect is a linguistic term referring to how people view and report events, regardless of tense. With **tense**, for example, a person can easily report whether something is past, present, or future (the major categories of tense or temporal reference). Aspect, however, crosses tense boundaries. A person can report any event as one that is in progress (e.g., "John is eating") or not (e.g., "John eats three meals a day"). This is an aspectual difference and, again, refers to how the person chooses to report the event or what "aspect" of the event the person is reporting. In principle, events have beginnings, middles, and ends; when we speak, we implicitly or explicitly make references to these points, especially in the past. For example, we can report the middle of an event, that is, one in progress at a particular point in time, by saying "John was eating (when I checked in on him at 3:00)." We can also implicitly refer to the end point by suggesting the event was over at a particular point as in "John ate for one hour." In English, to refer to the beginning point of eating, we have to use a different verb, as in "John began to eat at 2:00." In addition, we can talk about repeated actions in the past, such as "John ate everyday at 3:00" or "John used to eat everyday at 3:00." Languages other than English can encode all these differences through verb endings or other means without using different verbs. Spanish, for example, can use *comía* to mean either "he was eating" or "he used to eat/ate" (repeatedly), and can use *comió* to mean "he ate" and 'he began to eat.'

The acquisition of both aspect and tense has received considerable research in SLA. Research reveals a complicated interaction between learner-internal factors (e.g., linguistic factors and universals related to aspect across languages) and external factors (e.g., discourse, input, instruction). Noted scholars in this subarea include Kathleen Bardovi-Harlig, Yashi Shirai, Roger Andersen, and M. Rafael Salaberry, among others.

Attention 注意力

Attention is a cognitive process involving the ability to select and focus on particular stimuli from the environment while ignoring others. For example, while driving, a person selects and focuses on traffic, stoplights, crosswalks, and so on, while tending to ignore the sky, birds chirping in a tree, and the license plates on most other cars. In SLA, the stimuli would be linguistic items in the input. Three constructs of attention are generally discussed in the literature: capacity, selection, and effort.

Capacity refers to learners' ability to allocate attention to the processing of the information they receive. It is well established that attention involves a limited capacity; that is, people are exposed to a large number of stimuli and the brain cannot process all of them at the same time (see **working memory**). However, capacity may be modal and context-dependent. That is, people may be able to eat and watch TV at the same time because these activities require different kinds of attention (e.g., eating does not require the audio modality). However, people find it difficult to carry on a full conversation on the phone while watching TV (i.e., because both tap into the attention required for listening).

The second construct within attention is selection. Assuming that there is a limited capacity to attend to stimuli, the attentional system must select from incoming information/stimuli. Detection is the process involved in selecting and registering data in working memory.

The third construct is effort. The degree of effortful attention needed depends on the capacity demands of the task learners have to accomplish. A task differs in the modes of processing information. Automatic processing of information would require little attentional efforts for L2 learners, whereas controlled processing of information will require lots of attention and would proceed slowly.

Attention is a construct that has attracted the interest of second language researchers, and it plays a major role in some hypotheses about L2 acquisition (e.g., **noticing**). The general idea of some of these hypotheses is that

(1) learners must actively attend to linguistic stimuli in order to learn; and

(2) attention may affect what learners can detect in the input at any given time. That is, some scholars have looked at the possibility that learners "selectively attend" to stimuli in the input. Scholars associated with the application of attention to understanding SLA include Richard Schmidt, Richard Tomlin and Victor Villa, Susan Gass, Peter Robinson, and Ronald P. Leow.

Automatization 自动化

Automatization refers to the increasing ability for someone to perform a particular task in a fluent and error-free manner. Applied to the second language context, it generally refers to the ability to produce or comprehend language in real time with few non-native like structures. A learner who, for example, consistently produces the correct past tense form with *–ed* when required is said to have "automatized" the regular past tense. See also **Skill Acquisition Theory** in the section **Key Theories and Frameworks in Second Language Acquisition**.

Awareness 意识

Awareness refers to consciousness, that is, the degree to which people are conscious of what they are doing or learning. Three main criteria to describe awareness have been identified. Individuals are considered aware of a given experience if they can: (1) show that a change (cognitive or behavioral) has taken place as a result of that experience, (2) report that they are aware of what they are experiencing (e.g., they report noticing linguistic features in the input), and (3) describe their experience (e.g., verbalize an underlying rule of the L2).

Scholars disagree about the role of awareness in SLA (see the Key Question **What are the roles of explicit and implicit learning in SLA?**). Some scholars have held that acquisition is mainly an unconscious process, and conscious learning has only a **monitoring** function. These scholars have argued against the key role of awareness in language acquisition as the acquisition of a second language can happen without awareness. Others have argued that awareness at the level of noticing is a necessary condition for acquisition (see also **noticing**). Three levels of awareness have been identified: perception (we might perceive a stimulus but not be aware); noticing (we are able to bring a stimulus into our focal attention); and understanding (we are able to analyze and compare a language feature with what we have already stored in our memory). Key scholars who have addressed issues related to awareness in SLA include Peter Robinson, Richard Schmidt, Richard Tomlin and Victor Villa, and Ronald P. Leow.

Avoidance 回避

Avoidance behavior occurs when L2 learners attempt to avoid using structures in their production that are difficult as a result of (perceived) differences or similarities between their L1 and the target L2. Although avoidance is a complex phenomenon to describe, scholars in SLA have attempted to address the complexity of this phenomenon by identifying three main types of avoidance:

- when L2 learners know that the structure of the target language is complex as they have a minimum idea of what the structure is like;
- when L2 learners know the structure well but they find it difficult to be used in a particular context (e.g., in conversation);
- when L2 learners know what to say and how to say it, but they don't say it.

It is understood that the phenomenon of avoidance is influenced by a number of factors: the extent of learners' existing knowledge; learners' attitude toward their first and second languages; and their L1 knowledge. The source of avoidance is not clear. One view argues that it is due to differences between L1 and L2. Another view argues that the source of avoidance is due to similarities between L1 and L2. A third position holds that it is due to the complexity of the target L2 structures in question. Among scholars associated with this concept are Eric Kellerman and Jacquelyn Schachter.

Behaviorism 行为主义

The theory of behaviorism was a predominant framework for explaining human and animal learning (behavior) prior to the 1970s. It attempted to explain learning without reference to thinking or mental processes. Essentially, it claimed that as an organism interacts with its environment, its behavior is conditioned. Dogs that get bitten by spiders will avoid spiders in the future (negative reinforcement). Dogs that stick their paws out to shake and get a treat for doing so will stick their paws out later when told to shake (positive reinforcement). We are of course simplifying here.

Behaviorism was applied to language learning in the 1940s and 1950s. At the heart of the application is the belief that language is a set of patterns or habits. Child L1 acquirers learned language by imitating the language they heard and receiving positive reinforcement from the environment (e.g., getting what they want, receiving praise, getting people to interact with them). In the L2 context, learners were to be trained to repress L1 habits and acquire good L2 habits. Behavior was modified over time when learners were rewarded for responding correctly. Errors were a sign of failure that should be corrected immediately. The pedagogical and practical implications of behaviorism resulted in the audio-lingual method (ALM). The ALM was an approach to language teaching based on mechanical and pattern language practice called "drills" (e.g., repetition and substitution/transformation drills). L2 learners had to repeat, manipulate, or transform a particular form or structure in order to complete the drill.

Research on both first and second language acquisition (as well as general linguistics under Chomsky) undermined the behaviorist view, and by the late 1960s, behaviorist approaches to first language acquisition were on their way out in favor of the idea that children bring something internal to the task of language acquisition. By the late 1970s, the same view took hold in SLA. In both L1 and L2 contexts, research on **acquisition/morpheme orders** and **developmental sequences** suggested that language acquisition had some internal non-environmental schedule. Learners produced language that was not a mere reflection or imitation of what they heard, and they also came to know more about language than what was contained in the data they were exposed to (see **poverty of the stimulus**). Scholars associated with behaviorism are B. F. Skinner (first language) and Robert Lado, among others (for second language).

Bilingual 双语者　　bilingualism 双语现象

Bilingualism refers to the knowledge and use of two or more languages by an individual or a community. There are, in principle, two types of bilinguals: early and late. Early bilinguals are those who learn more than one language prior to the age of 4, that is, prior to the (relatively) complete acquisition of another language. (Children are said to have native-like competence in most formal areas of language by the age of 5.) Early bilingualism may be complete or not; that is, early bilinguals may possess strong knowledge and skills in two languages or may possess strong knowledge and skills in only one language. Early bilinguals may or may not belong to a larger speech community in which two languages are spoken. A child born in Barcelona may grow up speaking Spanish and Catalan where both languages are spoken in the community. A child born in Lubbock, Texas, with Spanish-speaking parents may learn Spanish at home, but English would be the language spoken in the larger community. *Heritage speakers* is another term for these latter early bilinguals.

Late bilinguals are those who acquire a second language after a first language is already in place, although in practice late bilingualism refers to people who acquire a second language after childhood. Thus, SLA is a type of bilingualism. It does not matter whether a late bilingual receives instruction or not, and like early bilinguals, late bilinguals may possess strong knowledge/skills in two languages or not. In both early and late bilingualism, however, most people are dominant in one language. Even if a person seems relatively fluent in two languages, most likely that person will exhibit dominance in one language in either overt or subtle ways. For example, the person may have a larger vocabulary in one language as opposed to another, or greater facility with rhetoric and discourse. A person may be better with language A in one kind of context (e.g., science) but better with language B in another context (e.g., interpersonal communication).

Scholars have studied and analyzed the benefits of being bilingual and have identified three main types of advantages: communicative, cultural, and cognitive. Overall, bilinguals seem to have superior metalinguistic ability compared with monolinguals. Research has also shown that bilinguals, especially early bilinguals, may have superior memory retention as age progresses. There are many scholars associated with bilingualism.

Caretaker speech 照看语　　modified input 修饰过的输入

Caretaker speech refers to the language adults use to talk to children. The speech that children are exposed to is generally simpler than the speech used between adults. It involves, for instance, the use of a slower rate of speech, less complex syntax, repetition, and paraphrasing (e.g.,

"Do you see the ball? Of course you see the ball! Where's the ball? Where's the ball? Go find the ball."). Researchers believe that adults make such adjustments in order to make themselves more comprehensible to children, and some researchers also believe that these modifications have an important role in helping children learn a language.

Adapted speech has also been researched in the acquisition of an L2 and is generally referred to as modified input. It is defined as the language used by native speakers (and instructors) to L2 learners to facilitate comprehension. Among those characteristics of modified input are (1) slower rate, (2) increased use of high frequency vocabulary, (3) simplified syntax (e.g., short sentences, repetition, fewer clauses), (4) discourse adjustments (e.g., clearer connections between pronouns and their antecedents), and (5) alterations in prosody (e.g., increased acoustic stress on content words), among others. As in the case of L1 acquisition, some L2 researchers believe that modified input may be beneficial for SLA. A particular type of modified input, foreigner talk, has been identified, and that modified input is used by natives with L2 learners they perceive to be of low language abilities, especially if they are perceived to be of a lower socioeconomic class. A characteristic of foreigner talk not found in caretaker speech for children or modified input more generally for L2 learners is that foreigner talk can and often contains ungrammatical language as native speakers attempt to "mimic" what they think non-natives produce (e.g., "You likee soupee?" "No likee soupee?"). Modified input was of greater interest in the 1970s and 1980s compared with the present day, and scholars associated with caretaker speech in L1 include Ann Peters, Catherine Snow, and Elinor Ochs, while those associated with modified input in L2 situations include Evelyn Hatch, Teresa Pica, Susan Gass, Steven Krashen, and Charles Ferguson, among others.

Cognitive style 认知方式

See **learning styles**.

Cognitive theory 认知理论

In general learning, cognitive theory is one in which psychologists attempt to understand how humans create and use knowledge. As such, it is not domain specific. That is, for cognitivists, there are no special places in the mind for language, math, or any other knowledge system (which stands in stark contrast to those who work in contemporary linguistic theory; see, for example, **Universal Grammar**). Cognitive researchers are thus interested in learning processes, and a good deal of cognitive research centers on learning styles, understanding (i.e., how people make sense of something), aptitude, information processing, and other areas. Within cognitive theory, all learning (no matter the object of that learning) utilizes the same general principles for human understanding and learning. Thus, language learning would utilize the same mechanisms for learning as would, say, history learning and chess learning.

Applied to SLA, cognitive theory views language acquisition as the formation of a knowledge system that L2 learners must eventually tap for speaking and understanding. However, unlike linguists and psycholinguists, scholars within a cognitive theory approach would be more interested in the learning factors that affect acquisition such as how learners come to understand the nature of a particular feature and what strategies learners go about to master a concept. Under the umbrella of cognitive theory, then, would fall **individual differences** such as aptitude, motivation, and memory. A related area of interest would be **restructuring**, that is, how the learning of new information causes changes in the already existing knowledge. Skill theory (see **skill/s**), with its concern for how people develop fluency and accuracy with anything (typing, chess playing, speaking), is a particular branch within cognitive theory. In fact, some psychologists would prefer to speak of cognitive theories or even cognitive approaches. Within SLA, noted scholars taking cognitive approaches to study language acquisition include Robert DeKeyser, Peter Robinson, Peter Skehan, Jan Hulstijn, Rod Ellis, Nick Ellis, Richard Schmidt, Zoltán Dörnyei, and others.

Communication strategies 交际策略

When L2 learners are faced with the task of communicating some kind of meaning but do not have the linguistic resources to express what they mean, they employ communication strategies. An agreed upon taxonomy of communication strategies has eluded L2 researchers, but some examples of communication strategies include paraphrasing (i.e., using a word for another related word, such as "horse" for "stallion"), avoidance, circumlocution, direct translation from the L1, switching to the L1 (such as inserting an L1 word hoping the other person might understand), and simply asking the interlocutor for help. Research on communication strategies and how they affect both interaction and acquisition reached its zenith in the 1980s, and since then, one rarely finds research on the topic. Scholars who have researched communication strategies include Elaine Tarone, Claus Faerch, Gabriele Kasper, and Ellen Bialystok.

Communicative competence 交际能力

Communicative competence refers to the underlying knowledge involved in language use. Whereas **competence** and **mental representation of language** refer only to formal properties of language (**morphology, lexicon, syntax**, etc.), communicative competence refers to the knowledge that guides a speaker's choice. Thus, it includes knowledge related to the context of language use as well as the purpose of language use. The notion of communicative competence has evolved since it was first proposed in the early 1970s. Currently scholars may group subcompetences in different ways, but some accepted components of communicative competence include the following:

- *Grammatical Competence*: knowledge of the linguistic forms and structure of language (i.e., the formal properties of language including the lexicon);

- *Discourse Competence*: knowledge of cohesion and coherence; that is, knowledge about how sentences combine in either written form or spoken form to create meaning beyond the sentence level (see **discourse**);

- *Pragmatic Competence*: knowledge of how language is used to express particular kinds of meaning as well as the ability to make and understand jokes, irony, and other aspects of communication (see **pragmatics**);

- *Sociolinguistic Competence*: knowledge of appropriate use of language (e.g., what to say in what context as well as what not to say, how to speak in one context as opposed to another, see **sociolinguistics**);

- *Strategic Competence*: knowledge of how to express meaning when your resources don't provide the means (e.g., what to say in a situation you haven't encountered before, what to do when you don't understand a word or don't know which word to use, see **communication strategies**).

The idea behind communicative competence is that although linguistic or grammatical competence is important, when people interact or write/read, they rely on much more than grammatical competence to express, interpret, and negotiate meaning. In part, the development of communicative competence as a construct in the early 1970s was a direct response to the prevailing emphasis on formal features of language within linguistics. Some language researchers felt that linguistic competence alone could not capture how language was *used* in various contexts.

As SLA research progressed in the 1970s, how L2 learners communicated with limited L2 ability became a matter of interest. And because tests of speaking ability in a second language needed to include more than just information about formal accuracy (e.g., whether a learner could successfully accomplish a given communicative task in a given context), researchers interested in L2 assessment increasingly turned their attention to models of communicative competence to talk about testing. At the same time, language teaching and curriculum development became increasingly concerned with the development of communicative ability, moving away from the more narrow focus of the structural syllabus that had dominated language teaching until then. Within SLA, names associated with communicative competence in theory, assessment, and practice include Sandra Savignon, Michael Canale, Merrill Swain, Dell Hymes, Lyle Bachman, and Adrian Palmer.

Competence 语言能力

Within Chomskyan linguistics, competence is the implicit and abstract knowledge of a language possessed by native speakers. We say implicit because speakers generally are unaware of this knowledge and, even if aware, cannot articulate its contents. We say abstract because it does not consist of rules such as "verbs must agree with their subjects," but instead, of other syntactic operations that yield sentences that can be described as having verbs that agree with their subjects. What is more, competence contains information that not only generates grammatical sentences, but also informs speakers of what is impossible in their languages. For example, the native speaker of English has competence that allows the sentences *John thinks Mary brought what?* and *What does John think Mary brought?* At the same time, that competence allows the sentence *John wonders who brought Mary what* but disallows the sentence *What does John wonder who brought Mary?*

As another example, the simple definition of "subject of a sentence" eludes the average person. A subject is not the "doer of the action," as verbs such as *seem* do not have "doers" but entities that experience something (e.g., *What did John do? He ate.* But not *What did John do?*

He seemed sad.). A subject is not the thing that comes before the verb in English as demonstrated by *John comes to class* and *Here comes John.* In short, the notion of "subject of a sentence" is an abstract and implicit notion, and yet, every English speaker intuitively knows what a subject is, or would not be able to make well-formed sentences in English.

Again, competence is not a list or set of rules and grammatical forms, but instead a complex interaction of abstract constraints and principles of language that makes sentences look the way they look to us. Competence is often contrasted with *performance*. Performance refers to how people use language in concrete situations. For example, whether or not people contract *want to* to *wanna* in *Do you wanna go?* is a performance matter as *Do you want to go?* is equally possible. Both are allowed by competence, but people may use one or the other in concrete situations. However, no one would say *Who do you wanna tell Bill he's fired?* under any circumstance because competence bars contraction of *want to* in this particular instance.

Competence has become a central concern of scholars applying linguistic theory to SLA. One of the main concerns is to what extent learner competence resembles or can resemble native speaker competence, and how to measure it. (See also **mental representation of language** and **interlanguage**, as well as **grammar**.)

Competition Model 竞争模型

The Competition Model is a model of language comprehension that its proponents have attempted to relate to acquisition. According to the model, languages possess cues that listeners may attend to in order to comprehend sentences. For example, if a listener wants to know what the subject of a sentence is, there might be the following cues he or she could attend to: word order, subject-verb agreement, animacy (e.g., does the verb require an animate being to perform the action), case marking, and others. The model claims that such cues vary from language to language in terms of strength. For example, in English, word order is a strong cue for subject status, in Spanish, subject-verb agreement is a stronger cue. Cue strength is based on three constructs: availability, reliability, and conflict validity. Availability refers to how present or frequent the cue is. In English, word order is a readily available cue for what a subject is; however, subject-verb agreement is not (i.e., only in the present tense and with third-person singular do we see person-number marking on verbs). Reliability refers to how often the cue leads to the correct sentence interpretation. In English, word order almost always leads to correct interpretation of what the subject is as English is rigidly subject-verb-object. Conflict validity refers to how valid a cue is for correct sentence interpretation when it is in conflict with another. In a language like Hebrew, case marking has high conflict validity because Hebrew sentences can be either subject-verb-object or object-verb-subject (or possibly other combinations). If people normally expect subjects to appear before verbs, then object-verb order is in conflict with case marking, but case marking would win out because it is more reliable (i.e., subjects are always marked one way and objects are always marked another). This is not the case in German. Although German consistently marks articles for case, the markings themselves are not always unique. Masculine definite articles are either *der* for subject or *den* for object. But for feminine, the article is always *die*. Thus, when case marking is in conflict with word order in German (German allows object-verb-subject and requires certain orders in embedded clauses and other constructions), case marking has high conflict validity only for masculine nouns indicating subject and object.

In language acquisition, cues that are available, highly reliable, and have high conflict validity will be acquired before those that do not possess the same characteristics. What is more, the Competition Model claims that L2 learners will transfer the cue strengths of their L1 to the L2 in the initial stages of acquisition. The Competition Model has been subsumed under **connectionism** in recent years, but research on the Competition Model made important contributions to SLA research in the 1990s. The name most associated with the model is Brian MacWhinney.

Connectionism 联结主义

Connectionism is a nonlinguistic, psychology-oriented approach to learning that is now subsumed under the broader term *usage-based theories* or *emergentism*. See the section **Key Theories and Frameworks in Second Language Acquisition**.

Consciousness raising 意识提升

Consciousness raising refers to a pedagogical technique during which L2 learners are asked to solve a grammatical problem of a targeted language. The main goal of consciousness raising is to develop learners' conscious representation of the rules that govern the use of particular language forms while it provides them with the opportunity to engage in meaningful interaction and negotiation of meaning. During consciousness raising tasks, learners develop explicit knowledge about how the target language works. They are encouraged to discover the rules as they are provided with data related to the grammatical feature in focus and they are asked to arrive at an explicit understanding of that feature (problem-solving task). Research in instructed second language acquisition has provided mixed results about the effectiveness of this technique. It seems that it might be effective as a type of **negative evidence** technique. Names most associated with research measuring the effects of consciousness raising are Rod Ellis and Sandra Fotos.

Contrastive Analysis Hypothesis 对比分析假说

The Contrastive Analysis Hypothesis was a prevalent hypothesis prior to the 1980s that predicted acquisition difficulties. In essence, the hypothesis claimed that where there were similarities between an L1 and an L2, acquisition would be easier compared with situations in which there were differences between the L1 and the L2. Two main versions of this hypothesis were developed: the weak position and the strong position. The strong position claimed that all L2 errors could be predicted by analyzing the differences between the L1 and the target language. The main cause for difficulty and error in language learning was to be found in L1–L2 differences. In other words, the real and only "problem" in acquisition was **transfer**. Positive transfer involved similarities or sameness and negative transfer involved differences. During the 1970s, the Contrastive Analysis Hypothesis began to fall out of favor as research showed that many L2 "errors" were not a result of transfer. These errors either looked like those that children learning the L1 would make (although we don't really call what children do "errors"), or their source was ambiguous (see **error analysis**). In addition, research also found that similarities across languages led to errors that could persist; that is, when the function of structures in two languages were similar but not the same, learners showed evidence of transfer resulting in errors that persisted over time. Finally, some of the errors predicted by the Contrastive Analysis Hypothesis did not occur in the speech analyzed by researchers. Therefore, the second position—the weak position—was formulated. This position emphasized the importance of analyzing learners' recurring errors as only some could be traceable to transfer.

One of the underlying problems of the Contrastive Analysis Hypothesis is that it was intimately tied to a theory of learning called **behaviorism** that emphasized learning as habit formation. Contrastive analysts worked with a theory of language in which rules were viewed as habits. As research appeared that showed language not to be habits, in conjunction with research on SLA that showed that not all errors were attributable to L1 transfer or interference, contrastive analysis declined as a field of inquiry and its accompanying hypothesis fell out of favor. The scholars most associated with the Contrastive Analysis Hypothesis are Robert Lado, Charles Fries, Robert Stockwell, and Donald Bowen.

Creative Construction Hypothesis 创造性建构假说

The Creative Construction Hypothesis emerged from the open criticism toward behaviorism and particularly the **Contrastive Analysis Hypothesis**, along with the early research on SLA in the 1970s. Under creative construction, SLA is considered to be very much like L1 acquisition in that SLA is a process in which learners make unconscious hypotheses on the basis of the input they get from the environment. Creative construction viewed acquisition as a learner-internal driven process, guided by innate mechanisms that are impermeable to outside influences such as instruction and corrective feedback. Very often, creative construction is viewed as the "L1 = L2 Hypothesis"—namely, that L1 acquisition and SLA are basically the same in terms of how acquisition happens.

The major evidence for creative construction consisted of the **morpheme studies**, in which learners of different L1 backgrounds seemed to acquire features of language in the same order (discounting the strong transfer hypothesis). Additional important research centered on **developmental sequences**, which revealed that learners with different L1 backgrounds tended to traverse the same stages of acquisition of a given structure (e.g., negation, question formation) over time. Thus, major features of the Creative Construction Hypothesis were: (1) L1 transfer is negligible; and (2) there is universality in acquisition sequences.

As an account of acquisition, creative construction was subsumed under **Monitor Theory**, and by the late 1980s had all but disappeared from the active discourse on SLA as other theories and accounts began to surface. The names associated with the Creative Construction

Hypothesis are Heidi Dulay and Marina Burt, and to a certain extent, Steven Krashen.

Critical Period Hypothesis 关键期假说

The main concept of the Critical Period Hypothesis (CPH) is that there is a limited time period for language acquisition. One version of this hypothesis claims that children must learn their first language by puberty or will not be able to learn the language afterwards. Another version of the CPH maintains that learning will be more difficult after puberty. The main question addressed by scholars is whether or not there is a critical period and when it ends. Scholars have made a distinction between two critical periods for language. From birth to about age 2, children need exposure to language in order to develop the brain structures necessary for language acquisition. Until about the age of 16, children can still acquire a language, but without native-like competence.

In the L2 context, there is debate about whether there is a critical period for learning an L2; that is, the question is whether or not people can acquire native-like competence and ability in L2 if learning begins after a certain age. (See **Is there a critical period?** in the Key Questions section.)

Declarative 陈述性　　procedural knowledge 程序性知识

Within cognitive- and skill- oriented accounts of SLA, declarative knowledge refers to information (e.g., facts and rules). It is knowledge *that*, as in Lubbock is in Texas, or they speak Spanish and Catalan in Barcelona. People gain declarative knowledge through instruction, reading, observation, or even attempting to do something. Procedural knowledge is knowledge of *how* to do something, as in when to shift gears in a car. Procedural knowledge is sometimes described as consisting of "action pairs": if X, then do Y. Procedural knowledge can only be obtained through completing appropriate tasks. Within skill theory, people are said to progress from a stage of declarative knowledge to a stage of procedural knowledge (and then beyond). Note that having procedural knowledge does not imply that someone can execute a task rapidly and without error. Speed and accuracy are the result of a subsequent stage of skill development (see **skill/s**).

Applied to SLA, declarative knowledge would be information about grammar and lexicon. For example, a person might know that in English we can contract *want* and *to* to form *wanna* or that in Italian there are two verbs used to form the past tense: *essere* and *avere*. Procedural knowledge would be the ability to apply the knowledge under certain conditions. For example, if the verb is *mangiare*, use *avere* to form the past tense. In SLA, the name most associated with skill theory and the roles of declarative and procedural knowledge is Robert DeKeyser. (See also the related terms **explicit/implicit knowledge** as well as **Skill Acquisition Theory** in the section **Key Theories and Frameworks in Second Language Acquisition**.)

Descriptive grammar 描写语法

See **grammar**.

Detection 觉察

Detection is one of the three components of **attention** and refers to the cognitive registration of stimuli in working memory. Detection is required for processing and learning of new information. The scholars most associated with the model of attention that posits detection are Richard Tomlin and Victor Villa.

Developing system 发展中的体系
approximative system 渐进体系

Developing or approximative system is a term used for L2 learners' mental representations at any given time during acquisition. That is, a learner's developing system is that learner's internal and unconscious representation of the language (including, for example, components related to **syntax, morphology, phonology, lexicon,** and **pragmatics**). The term *developing* is used because the system is dynamic and changing, with the idea that the learner is attempting to converge on a linguistic system resembling that of a native speaker (but see the Key Question **Can L2 learners become native-like?**). Thus, the developing systems of beginners will not look like the developing systems of advanced learners. Another term used for the developing system is **interlanguage**.

Developmental sequences 发展顺序
stages of development 发展阶段

Developmental sequences are stages or steps that learners traverse as they acquire a particular structure. They are different from **acquisition orders.** Whereas acquisition orders reflect the relative order of *different* structures over time (e.g., various verb and noun inflections, articles), developmental sequences reflect the acquisition of a *single* structure. For example, how do learners acquire negation? How do they acquire question formation? What stages do they exhibit as they undergo acquisition? Research in the late 1970s and 1980s determined that learners did indeed follow certain stages in their acquisition of L2 structures. In the case of negation, the developmental sequences or stages look like the following:

Stage 1: *no* + X: negator placed outside the "sentence"
No drink beer.
No have time.

Stage 2: Sentences appear with subjects, and the negator is placed inside the sentence before the verb. *Don't* may appear as an invariant form (see **formulaic sequences/chunks**) that alternates with or replaces *no*.

I no drink beer/I don't drink beer (but also He don't drink beer).
I no have time/I don't have time.

Stage 3: Appearance of modals with *not*.
I can't do this.
He won't come.

Stage 4: Analysis of *do* as auxiliary with *not*. Native-like negation.
I don't know.
He doesn't understand.

Developmental sequences have been found for a number of structures and in a number of languages. (See also the Key Question **What does development look like?**) Key people who established developmental sequences are Henning Wode, Courtney Cazden, John Schumann, Jurgen Meisel, Harald Clahsen, Manfred Pienemann, and many others.

Discourse 话语 discourse analysis 话语分析

Discourse refers to units of language that go beyond the sentence. Thus, a discourse can be a short interaction, an entire conversation, a written paragraph, a speech, and so on. Interactions and conversations are referred to as *unplanned* or *spontaneous* discourse, whereas such things as speeches, paragraphs, and book chapters are called *planned* discourse. The idea behind discourse is coherence; that is, within a discourse, multiple sentences or propositions logically follow each other. Scholars engaged in discourse analysis focus on how this coherence is achieved as well as what the differences are between planned and unplanned discourse. (See also **pragmatics** and **communicative competence**.)

Emergentism 涌现论

See the section **Key Theories and Frameworks in Second Language Acquisition**.

Error 语误　　error analysis 语误分析

Error analysis is a research tool characterized by a set of procedures for identifying, describing, and explaining L2 learners' errors. Error analysis emerged as a reaction to the **Contrastive Analysis Hypothesis** and the associated theory of **behaviorism**. Much of the early work in error analysis focused on determining whether SLA was the result of L1 **transfer** or creative construction (i.e., something similar to the processes L1 learners used to acquire language—see **Creative Construction Hypothesis**). What early error analysis showed was that not all errors could be attributed to L1 influence and that L2 learners were active creators of linguistic systems. These results were used to argue against behaviorism and the Contrastive Analysis Hypothesis. The first scholar who called for error analysis was S. Pit Corder, back in the late 1960s, and indeed the 1970s were marked by a good deal of error analysis research. But with the push for the application of theories from linguistics, psychology, and other disciplines, error analysis eventually disappeared as a major thrust of research. In addition to S. Pit Corder, other names associated with error analysis during the 1970s are Marina Burt, Heidi Dulay, ElaineTarone, Jack Richards, and Jacquelyn Schachter.

Event-related potentials/ERPs 事件相关电位

Event-related potentials—commonly referred to in research as ERPs—are mappings of electrical activity in the brain as a result of cognitive activity. Normally, an array of electrodes is affixed to a person's head. The person is then asked to perform a task. In second language research, this task might be to judge a sentence, to read a sentence and then answer a question, or to decide if a word is a possible word or not, to give a few examples. As the person performs the task, the device affixed to the head records brain activity and delivers it to a computer whereby the information is recorded and converted into data readable by the experimenter. ERPs are generally used in **neurolinguistic** approaches to second language research.

Explicit knowledge 显性知识
implicit knowledge 隐性知识

In cognitive psychology, researchers often make the distinction between explicit knowledge and implicit knowledge. Explicit knowledge is generally referred to as conscious knowledge, or knowledge a person is aware of and normally can articulate. For example, a native speaker might have explicit knowledge of spelling as in the mnemonic device "I before E except after C, and except like EIGH as in 'neighbor' and 'weigh.'" Implicit knowledge is unconscious in nature. It exists outside of awareness and most people may not know they have implicit knowledge except under reflection and introspection. For example, a native speaker may have implicit knowledge that *want to* cannot contract to *wanna* when a noun has been removed from between the two as in *Who do you want to tell John he's fired?* which cannot be *Who do you wanna tell John he's fired?* (The *who* originates as the object of *want* and head of the *to* phrase, that is, *You want who to tell John he's fired?*).

In SLA, the concepts of explicit and implicit knowledge have been applied the same way as in cognitive psychology, with a major debate focusing on what the relationship is between explicit and implicit knowledge of language. While all scholars agree that ultimately learners must develop an implicit system, the debate centers on the role of explicit knowledge and how the implicit system comes to be. Do learners begin with explicit knowledge that is converted to implicit knowledge? Or, is implicit knowledge developed via unconscious processes and **processing**? Is there some kind of interface between explicit and implicit knowledge and, if so, what is the nature of that interface? In other words, the debate in SLA is centered on explicit and implicit *learning*. (See also **declarative knowledge** as well as the Key Question **What are the roles of explicit and implicit learning in SLA?**)

Feedback 反馈

Feedback refers to the response that learners receive regarding the language they produce. Feedback can take one of two forms: explicit or implicit. Explicit feedback involves such things as overt correction (e.g., *No. Say* bakes, *not* bake) or even comments about what the learner generally does (e.g., *I notice that when you try to say … you often …*). Implicit feedback occurs during communicative interactions and can take the form of **recasts**—for example, when the learner's interlocutor rephrases what the learner says without making any explicit statements. This recast can function like a confirmation check (e.g., Did I understand you correctly?), as in the following interchange between Bob, a native speaker, and Tom, a non-native speaker:

> Bob: So where's Dave?
> Tom: He vacation.
> Bob: He's on vacation? [confirmation check]
> Tom: Yes, on vacation.

Bob's confirmation check and recast of what Tom said act as implicit feedback. Bob neither says "You said it wrong" nor tells Tom explicitly that he did something wrong. Bob's sole intent was to confirm what he heard. Yet, this confirmation could serve as feedback, and in this case it did. Tom picked up on the preposition *on*.

Negative evidence is another term used to refer to feedback and has tended to replace "feedback" as the preferred term in the literature, largely because of the term **positive evidence** (i.e., **input**). Positive evidence consists of the samples of language learners hear or read as part of communication, whereas negative evidence is the feedback they receive about what they do incorrectly.

A major question in SLA is to what extent feedback of any kind is either useful or necessary for language acquisition. (See, for example, **interaction**.)

fMRIs 功能性核磁共振成像

fMRI stands for functional magnetic resonance imaging. Like **ERPs**, fMRIs are used in **neurolinguistic** approaches to second language research. Unlike ERPs, fMRIs do not measure electrical activity in the brain but oxygenation of blood or blood flow. A person is positioned with a machine that scans the brain using a magnetic field and radio pulses. As in other neurolinguistic approaches, the person performs a task—often listening through special headphones—such as reacting to grammatical and ungrammatical sentences. The machine maps the blood flow and converts it into a readable color image for the researcher.

Focus on form 重形式教学　　focus on forms 全形式教学

In the subfield of instructed SLA, many researchers have focused their attention on the Key Question **Does instruction make a difference?** What this question refers to is whether explicit intervention by teachers or other speakers regarding the formal properties of language (e.g., grammar) aids acquisition. Does providing rules help? Does providing feedback help? What kind of practice is useful for promoting the growth of grammar? These questions are examples of researchers' interests in this subfield. In the early 1990s, a distinction was made in instructed SLA between focus on form and focus on form*s*. Focus on form generally refers to any intervention in which simultaneous attention is brought to both meaning and how that meaning is encoded. Normally, this would happen in a communicative context as in the case of **recasts**. In a recast situation, a learner produces something non-native-like during a conversation, and the interlocutor responds by recasting what the learner says in a native-like way as part of that interlocutor's indication that he or she understood the learner. Thus, the main focus is on meaning with only a brief sidestep to formal features of language as the conversation continues (cf., overt error correction in which a teacher stops and corrects a learner explicitly as part of practice).

Focus on forms is generally defined as an explicit or overt focus on the formal properties with either little or no attention to meaning. Teachers who drill students repetitively engage in focus on forms. Activities such as fill in the blank, in which the learner does not have to pay attention to what the sentence means in order to complete the sentence, are focus on forms exercises. The distinction between focus on form and focus on forms originated with Michael Long, although other researchers, such as Catherine Doughty and Jessica Williams, have produced scholarship related to focus on form and forms. (See also **input enhancement**.)

Foreigner talk 母语者与外国人谈话时所用的话语

See **caretaker speech**.

Form-meaning connections 形式—意义联结
form-function connections 形式—功能联结

A form-meaning connection refers to the correspondence between the formal properties of language and the meaning they encode. For example, the word *cat* (phonologically symbolized by /kæt/) is a lexical form. It corresponds to the meaning of "feline" (with the various connotations associated with it: animate, four-legged, paws, claws, fur, whiskers, carnivore, etc.). As another example, the verbal ending *-ed* in English is a grammatical form that encodes the meaning "pastness" (or "not present"). Past versus present is a semantic (meaning) distinction, and that meaning is encoded on the ends of verbs in English and other languages. So, form can be grammatical or lexical, while meaning refers to some real-world concept that is part of the semantic component of the learner's mind. Forms, of course, can have multiple meanings or functions: The lexical form *do* can be a main verb with various meanings such as "make" (e.g., *John did the cake. Isn't it pretty?*) or it can be an auxiliary with no meaning and the sole function of carrying tense and person-number features (e.g., *Did John bake the cake?*). (See also **semantics**.)

A form-function connection refers to the grammatical function that a form plays in sentence interpretation or sentence meaning. For example, the form *that* functions as either a determiner (demonstrative) as in *Hand me that pair of scissors, will you?* or a clause marker/clause head as in *The book that I read wasn't good.* Thus, as in the case of meanings, forms can have multiple functions.

Form-meaning/function connections are important concepts in a variety of theories and models of both linguistics and SLA, such as **connectionism**, **functional approaches**, and **input processing**.

Formal instruction 语言形式教学 / 课堂教学

Formal instruction is a term that refers to any activity or curriculum in which a language learner engages in focused work on the properties of language itself. The use of the term *formal* refers to the idea of grammatical *form*, as linguists often talk about the "formal features of language," such as **morphology**, **syntax**, and **phonology**. Classrooms, for example, tend to be environments where formal instruction happens, even in many classrooms that are called "communicative." In such classes, even though the primary focus is on meaning and meaning-making, elements of language may be isolated while teachers or materials draw learners' attention to them. Thus, it is very difficult to find purely formal and purely communicative classrooms. There tends to be some kind of formal instruction in communicative classrooms, and in formal instruction classrooms there is attention paid toward using language to make meaning at some point. In the Key Question **Does instruction make a difference?**, the actual question is does *formal* instruction make a difference on the acquisition of *formal* features over time?

Formulaic sequences 程式语   chunks 语块

Formulaic sequences or chunks are phrases or whole utterances that learners internalize as a whole, without analysis of the individual parts. For example, we know that *don't* consists of *do* + *not*. A learner may hear and pick up *don't* and not know that it is a contraction consisting of an auxiliary verb and a negator. The learner thinks it is one word and stores it as such in the mental lexicon. It exists as a chunk. Chunks (or formulaic sequences) can be whole utterances such as *How do you do?*, which a learner might pick up and know to use in certain social encounters, but doesn't know what all the internal parts of the chunk are.

Other kinds of chunks/formulaic sequences include "incomplete" phrases that learners pick up and use in combination with other words and phrases to make a sentence. For example, if a learner hears *Do you wanna …?* enough, that learner might extract it as a chunk and become able to create a variety of sentences. That is, the learner has *Doyouwanna* and uses it productively. That learner may not know that there is a do, a pronoun, and contracted verb altogether in that sequence.

Note that native speakers, too, can work with chunks and formulaic sequences. Children often show evidence of this, especially when they learn certain social routines. The difference is that native speakers also know that chunks can be broken up. Thus, a native speaker may have the chunk *Doyouwanna*, but also has *do*, *you*, and *want to*, as well as *wanna*, as separate items in the lexicon.

Fossilization 石化／僵化

Fossilization is a concept that refers to the end-state of SLA, specifically to an end-state that is not native-like. By end-state, we mean that point at which the learner's **mental representation of language, developing system**, or **interlanguage** (all are related constructs) ceases to develop. Theoretically, the term can be applied to subsystems within the learner's mental representation; that is, the phonological component can fossilize while the syntactic and semantic components continue to develop.

Most research on fossilization in SLA has focused on the formal properties of language (e.g., syntax, morphology), and a number of debates regarding fossilization have emerged and/or persisted in SLA scholarship. Among them is whether or not fossilization exists and how to determine if it does (e.g., how long does a researcher have to wait to see if the learner's system shows no signs of continued development? one year? five years? twenty years?). Some researchers prefer the term *stabilization*, which suggests a plateau in learning but not necessarily a complete cessation in development. Another important debate concerns the source or cause of fossilization, assuming it exists. Do learners' linguistic systems fossilize because of learner traits such as motivation and aptitude? Is fossilization partly dependent on L1–L2 differences? What is the relationship between fossilization and the **Critical Period Hypothesis**, if any? The name most associated with fossilization is Larry Selinker, who coined the term in 1972. Researchers focusing on fossilization as a construct include ZhaoHong Han, Donna Lardiere, and others. Fossilization is closely related to the Key Question **Can L2 learners become native-like?**

Frequency in the input 输入频率

Frequency in the **input**—sometimes referred to simply as frequency— refers to the relative frequency of formal features in the language that people hear or read. For example, *the* is a highly frequent grammatical form in English whereas the past participle *swum* is much less frequent. Subject relative clauses, as in *He is the president who invaded Iraq*, are more frequent than object of preposition relative clauses, as in *He is the president on whom Congress turned its watchful eye*.

Frequency is a construct that has been investigated to explain **acquisition orders** and the results of **morpheme studies** (e.g., one position is that -*ing* is more frequent than third-person -*s* in the input, which is why L2 learners of English get -*ing* first when it comes to verbal suffixes) and is a central construct in **connectionism**. Most researchers, of course, believe that frequency is only one of a number of factors that can explain acquisition orders—or the acquisition of anything for that matter. Scholars for whom frequency has taken a central role in their thinking about SLA include Nick Ellis, Diane Larsen-Freeman, and Brian MacWhinney, among others.

Functional approaches 功能流派

Among the various theories and approaches to understanding SLA are the functional approaches. As a group, they depart from the purely formal approaches of syntactic theory (see **mental representation of language**, **Universal Grammar**, **syntax**) in that functional approaches view language as a means to communicate. They thus attempt to relate function to form and form to function. According to functionalists, meaning and function influence both language structure and language acquisition.

In the L2 context, functional approaches have been very popular in Europe and elsewhere, but less so in the United States. A good example of a functional approach to SLA research can be found in much of the literature on the acquisition of **tense** and **aspect**. What a researcher might ask is, "How do people express tense (past, present, future) in their speech?," with the expression of temporality being the function and the linguistic devices people use as the form. In SLA, learners might begin to express the function of temporality through adverbs and not verb inflections with "Last night John study very much." In this case, the adverb is the only form the learner uses to express temporality. In terms of acquisition, what the functionalist would want to know is how the learner's expression of temporality changes over time and what the interplay is between all the linguistic resources available to him or her at any given point in time during acquisition. Some scholars working within functional approaches to SLA include Kathleen Bardovi-Harlig, Roger Andersen, Wolfgang Klein, Carol Pfaff, and others.

Fundamental Difference Hypothesis 根本差异假说

The Fundamental Difference Hypothesis (FDH) claims that first language acquisition and adult second language acquisition are fundamentally different in a number of ways. The FDH is predicated upon a number of observations about SLA, among which we highlight the following:

- Children always achieve complete grammatical knowledge of their native language, whereas adult L2 learners seem to rarely achieve full target language competence (see **fossilization** as well as the Key Question **Can L2 learners become native-like?**).
- Unlike first language acquisition, which is uniformly successful across children (i.e., all native speakers converge on the same mental representation regarding the formal properties of language), adult L2 learners show considerable variation in their language-learning success. In other words, L2 learners vary as to how far they get with an L2 and to what degree they approximate what native speakers know about language and can do with it.
- First language acquisition is constrained and guided by innate mechanisms (e.g., **Universal Grammar**) and is not really influenced by external factors. SLA, especially with adults, seems to be influenced by (1) L1 **transfer**, (2) **individual differences**, and (3) social-communicative contexts of learning, among other factors.

Proponents of the FDH take the above observations (and others) to mean that at their core, L1 and L2 acquisition cannot be the same and thus are different. In particular, the FDH claims that whereas child L1 acquisition is guided by innate mechanisms, adult SLA is guided by general cognitive-learning or problem-solving principles and not by any innate linguistic knowledge. Thus, implicit in the FDH is that there is probably a critical period for language acquisition, after which such things as Universal Grammar and other language-specific mechanisms are no longer available for learning language. The originator of the hypothesis, and the name most associated with the FDH, is Robert Bley-Vroman.

Grammar 语法

Grammar is a term with varied meanings depending on who uses the term and the context in which it is used. Common meanings and uses of grammar are as follows.

- *Instructional Settings*: grammar is generally used to refer to the rules and formal features of language that learners must master as part of coursework. Thus, grammar would include such things as verbal paradigms in the Romance languages, case marking on articles in German, use of particles (e.g., subject and object indicators) in Japanese, the difference between the use of *-ing* and *will* in English to express future events, among other examples. This kind of grammar is often called *pedagogical grammar*.
- *Linguistics*: grammar is often used to refer to the **mental representation of language** that native speakers possess regarding the formal aspects of language. As such, it is the information about what a native speaker's competence allows and disallows. For example, the grammar of English speakers disallows null subjects in simple declarative sentences (e.g., **Is on the table*, where *it* is required), whereas the grammars of Spanish and Italian speakers allow null subjects (e.g., *Está en la mesa*, where the equivalent of *it* is not expressed in the sentence). Grammar in this sense refers to abstract features of language and how they are manifested in the actual language (e.g., there are certain abstract features in language that allow or disallow the use of null subjects).

Within linguistics, scholars also make the distinction between a descriptive grammar and a prescriptive grammar. A descriptive grammar refers to how people actually use language. Within the descriptive grammar of English would be *ain't* as a negative and how it is used in particular ways (e.g., *I ain't got none* sounds fine but *I ain't have any* sounds awful). A prescriptive grammar is used by teachers, parents, and others to impose "good language use" on others. In a prescriptive grammar, the use of *ain't* would be admonished. Very often, when we hear someone say that another person has "bad grammar," the reference is to prescriptive norms and not descriptive grammars.

To be sure, there is some overlap in whether a particular aspect of language comes from a pedagogical grammar, a descriptive grammar, or a prescriptive grammar. In general, descriptive grammars are broader because people's competences permit them to say things that textbooks and prescriptive grammarians would say is wrong. As one final example, within a descriptive grammar, English speakers might use both *who* and *whom* as objects of a verb, *Who/Whom did you see?*, whereas a prescriptive grammar might suggest that only *whom* is grammatical after a verb.

Grammaticality judgments 语法判断

Grammaticality judgments refer to tests of underlying competence or **mental representation of language**. In a typical grammaticality judgment test, a person is asked to read or listen to a sentence and then indicate whether the sentence is grammatical or not. In terms of actual design, researchers use a variety of terms to ask their participants to determine if a sentence is grammatical or not, such as *good/bad, acceptable/unacceptable, possible/impossible*, among others. In some cases, researchers use a Likert scale, on which the participant indicates the degree of grammaticality or acceptability of a sentence:

Acceptable				Unacceptable
1	2	3	4	5

Grammaticality judgment tests are important tools for those researchers interested in learners' underlying competence. This is so because such judgments help researchers to see what learners deem to be ungrammatical. Learners' speech only shows us what they deem to be grammatical (even if it is not grammatical by native standards). For example, a learner could produce hundreds of well-formed *wh*-questions in English, but if we want to know if that learner's mental representation disallows such things as *Who did Mary meet the man who saw?* (contrast with *Mary met the man who saw who?*) we have to test them. Grammaticality judgment tests serve this purpose. Most grammaticality judgments occur as off-line tests (see **on-line/off-line tasks**).

i + 1 高出学习者目前二语水平一个级别的输入

i + 1 is a construct within **Monitor Theory**. According to the tenets of the theory, learners acquire language by being exposed to language that contains structures just beyond (i.e., + 1) their current level of development. As a construct, *i* + 1 has intuitive appeal, but unfortunately is not operationalizable as a research construct—meaning a researcher cannot create an experiment saying "Here's the learner's *i* and now I'm going to give that learner language containing + 1 to see if he/she learns the + 1." The problem, of course, is in establishing what *i* is and also what *i* + 1 would be. *i* + 1 fell away as a major construct within SLA as Monitor Theory's appeal began to wane.

Incidental learning 附带学习

Incidental learning refers to picking up aspects of language as a by-product when a person's attention is not on learning those aspects per se. Incidental learning is said to be at the heart of vocabulary learning, for example. A reader's primary attention is on extracting meaning from a passage. As a new word is encountered, the reader may deduce it from context; thus, the learning of that word is a by-product of reading. Research on native vocabulary acquisition suggests that most speakers' vocabularies are a result of incidental learning.

Incidental learning contrasts with intentional learning in which a person purposely sets out to learn something. Intentional vocabulary learning might include, for example, studying the dictionary or thesaurus; the person's intent is to learn new words, not to read for meaning.

Incidental learning is not the same thing as implicit learning; however, *intentional* learning can be equated with explicit learning (for these terms, see the Key Question **What are the roles of explicit and implicit learning in SLA?**). Implicit learning suggests the learner is not consciously aware of learning something, whereas with incidental learning the person may or may not be aware of picking up something new. To take the example of reading and vocabulary learning, a person may consciously focus on a new word in a passage and deduce its meaning while reading. Such an action would suggest some kind of awareness.

The bulk of work in incidental learning in SLA has centered on vocabulary acquisition, with prominent scholars such as Jan Hulstijn, James Coady, and Bhatia Laufer at the forefront. Little empirical work has surfaced on incidental acquisition of syntax and morphology.

Individual differences 个体差异

Every learner brings a set of personality and psycho-emotive characteristics to the task of learning something. Those characteristics have the potential to influence learning, specifically how learners explicitly go about learning as well as how quickly they learn and how far they get in their learning. What are these characteristics? Some include the following:

- **aptitude** or particular talents or abilities related to the learning in question (e.g., an aptitude for music, an aptitude for math, an aptitude for language);
- **motivation** (e.g., willingness to do something and the source of that willingness);
- **learning styles** (e.g., some people like to see things written down; some people are fine with abstraction, while others need things to be concretely presented; some people tolerate ambiguity more than others; some people like interaction in order to learn, while others less so);
- **learning strategies** (e.g., repeating things over and over in one's head to memorize them).

A number of scholars have been interested in how individual differences affect SLA and have asked questions such as "What is the relationship between motivation and success in SLA?," "What kind of motivation correlates with success in SLA?," and "How do differences in working memory affect acquisition?" (see the Key Question **What are individual differences and how do they affect acquisition?**). A noted authority on individual differences in SLA is Zoltán Dörnyei, and in related key terms (e.g., **motivation, learning styles**) the reader will find other names.

Innatist position 先天论

The innatist position refers to the view that children bring a biologically endowed abstract knowledge to the task of learning a first language, and this abstract knowledge constrains the shape of the target linguistic system they learn. This innate knowledge allows them to discover the underlying rules of a language system and minimizes guessing and hypothesis formation. (See also **Universal Grammar** and **nativism**.)

Although the innatist position is almost universally accepted by child language acquisitionists, in SLA research a major question has been whether innate knowledge that children have for L1 acquisition is still available for L2 acquisition, and to what extent adult SLA is similar to child L1 acquisition. (See the Key Questions **Can L2 learners become native-like?** and **Is there a critical period?**)

Noam Chomsky is the linguist who first proposed the innatist position back in the 1960s and has continued to support it. Steven Pinker does as well. In SLA, major figures associated with the innatist position (i.e., that L2 learners have access to Universal Grammar) include Lydia White, Bonnie Schwartz, Rex Sprouse, and others, while those who reject an innatist position include Robert DeKeyser, James Lantolf, and others associated with cognitive and psychological or sociocultural approaches. Nick Ellis and William O'Grady are scholars who reject innate linguistic knowledge as a component of acquisition but accept other kinds of innate architecture that constrain or direct language learning.

Input 输入

Input consists of language that L2 learners are exposed to in a communicative context. That is, it is language that learners hear or read that they process for its message or meaning. As such, it is distinct from language that, say, instructors might provide as models or examples of how to do something. It is distinct from language that learners process purely for its formal features. It is also distinct from **output**, language that learners produce.

Different kinds of input have been discussed over the years, including comprehensible input (i.e., language that learners can readily understand for its meaning) and **modified input** (i.e., language that is adjusted so that learners can better comprehend the speaker's meaning). Some have referred to input as *primary linguistic data*. The reason for this is that all current linguistic and psycholinguistic theories of acquisition believe that input is the data source for acquisition as opposed to, say, practice, grammar explanations, **feedback**, and **negative**

evidence. Thus, learners' developing linguistic systems are a result of input interacting with learners' internal mechanisms used for processing and storing language. The fundamental role of input in acquisition emerged as a consequence of the rejection of **behaviorism** in the 1970s.

Input enhancement 输入强化

Input enhancement is a term that refers to directing learners' attention to formal features of language while also maintaining a focus on meaning. As such, input enhancement is a pedagogical tool meant to assist learners' development regarding formal properties of language. Input enhancement is an externally conducted activity; that is, it is teachers and/or materials that enhance input. It is not an activity that originates from within the learner.

Input enhancement entails any effort to make formal features of the language more salient to learners and comes in two varieties: positive and negative. Positive input enhancement involves manipulating input in certain ways to make formal features more obvious to learners. Such manipulations include louder voice or increased acoustic stress on something while the teacher is talking; bolding or highlighting particular features (among other manipulations) would be used in written input. Negative input enhancement is basically **feedback**: The teacher draws a learner's attention to an incorrect production in order to signal that the learner has violated target norms. There is a relationship between input enhancement and **focus on form**, as both involve simultaneous attention to form and meaning in the input.

A major assumption of input enhancement is that learners must attend to formal features in the input. In particular, they must pick up and process linguistic examples that their internal mechanisms can subsequently use as data for the **developing system**. The originator of the term *input enhancement* is Michael Sharwood Smith. Another scholar who has written extensively on input enhancement is Wynne

Wong. Given the close relationship between **focus on form** and input enhancement, however, there are dozens of researchers who have looked at the effects of input enhancement.

Input Hypothesis 输入假说

The Input Hypothesis is a component of **Monitor Theory**. The Input Hypothesis claims that learners acquire language in only one way: by exposure to **input**. In other words, it is only through consistent attempts to comprehend language directed at them that learners acquire language. In its strongest form, the Input Hypothesis rejects any significant role for **formal instruction** (i.e., a focus on grammar in the classroom) and for **negative evidence** (i.e., certain kinds of feedback on learners' non-native-like production). That is, the strong version of the Input Hypothesis would claim that *only* exposure to input can cause acquisition to happen. In a weaker form of the Input Hypothesis, formal instruction and/or negative evidence might be beneficial, but not necessary (see, for example, **input enhancement**).

Because Monitor Theory fell out of favor by the late 1980s, the Input Hypothesis figures little in contemporary research. However, it is fair to say that all major linguistic and psycholinguistic theories of SLA in use today assume *some* version of the Input Hypothesis; that is, these theories assume that input contains the data necessary for acquisition and that acquisition is partially a by-product of comprehension. Steven Krashen is the scholar who originated the Input Hypothesis.

Input processing 输入加工

Input processing refers to how learners connect meaning and function with formal features of language in the input and the strategies or mechanisms that guide and direct how learners do this. The idea behind input processing is this: Acquisition is input-dependent. Learners get data during the act of comprehension. Comprehension involves extracting meaning from the input. However, acquisition is about the development of the formal properties of language. So, how do learners get linguistic data from the input while they are attempting to comprehend language? What is more, we know that acquisition is not instantaneous; something must be "filtering" data from the environment. This is the focus of input processing research. For example, L2 learners of English are exposed to third-person -*s* from the earliest stages of acquisition, yet we know this is a difficult feature for them to acquire. Why is this? One approach is to suggest that somehow the data from verb forms in English is just not making it past the first round of processing during comprehension. Something internal to the learner ignores these formal features such that they do not get picked up by the processing devices in the learner's head.

The name most widely associated with input processing is Bill VanPatten and his model is covered in the section **Key Theories and Frameworks in Second Language Acquisition**. Other scholars have also addressed input processing, albeit in different ways from VanPatten. These scholars include Michael Sharwood Smith, John Truscott, William O'Grady, and Susanne Carroll.

Intake 吸收

Intake is a term that has been used in different ways by different scholars and theories. It was originally coined by S. Pit Corder in 1967 to be distinct from the term **input**. Input is the language that learners are exposed to. It was Corder's intention to distinguish what learners are exposed to from what they actually "take in." He thus suggested the term *intake*.

The reason the term has been used differently by different scholars is that the notion of "take in" itself is not clear. For example, for Corder, the term meant what the learner actually processes and acquires, that is, becomes part of his or her competence. In other models, intake refers only to linguistic data that is processed from the input and held in **working memory**, but not yet acquired. That is, the data are taken into working memory, but may or may not be processed further and/ or can be rejected by other mechanisms responsible for the storage of linguistic data and its relationship to the learner's competence. In still other models, intake can refer to a process and not a product. In such cases, intake is defined as the process of assimilating linguistic data or the mental activity that mediates between the input "out there" and the competence "inside the learner's head." For various perspectives on intake, the reader is referred to S. Pit Corder, Susan Gass, and Bill VanPatten, among others.

Interaction 互动   Interaction Hypothesis 互动假说

See **Interaction Hypothesis** in the section Key Theories and Frameworks.

Interlanguage 中介语

Interlanguage is a term coined by Larry Selinker in 1972 and was intended to describe the competence of L2 learners and the source of that competence. As originally conceived, the idea was that learners possessed a special competence (or language) that was independent of the L1 and also of the L2, even though it might show influences from both. Interlanguage development is guided by three basic concepts: (1) L1 **transfer**; (2) **overgeneralization** from L2 patterns; and (3) **fossilization**. According to the original tenets of interlanguage, the vast majority of L2 learners (95 percent) have an interlanguage. That is, they do not have and normally do not obtain a native-like competence.

Since the early 1970s, other terms have arisen that are used instead of interlanguage, or as a synonym for it, including the **developing system**, approximative systems, learner language, idiosyncratic dialects, and others. All have in common that what a learner knows at a given time is rule-governed and systematic. Thus, it behaves like any other natural language. Larry Selinker remains the quintessential figure associated with the term *interlanguage*.

L1 = L2 Hypothesis 一语二语等同假说

See **Creative Construction Hypothesis.**

Language Acquisition Device 语言习得机制

The Language Acquisition Device (LAD) is an older term coined by Noam Chomsky in the 1960s to describe an innate or biological endowment for language and language acquisition. According to Chomsky, children cannot possibly acquire a first language by mimicking, hypothesis testing, or generalizing from input data because such strategies would lead them down the wrong paths (e.g., wrong hypotheses) and cause delays in acquisition. What is more, Chomsky noted that the language to which children are exposed does not contain all the data they need to wind up with native-like competence (see **poverty of the stimulus**). Yet, children are known to be rather successful at language acquisition with most parts of the formal properties of language in place prior to school age. To account for the phenomenon of rapid and successful acquisition, Chomsky said that children have a LAD that guides and constrains acquisition, a device that removes a lot of guess work. Since the 1960s, Chomsky has refined his ideas and no longer speaks of LAD, but instead refers to **Universal Grammar**, an innate knowledge source that governs the shape of natural languages. (See also **innatist position** and **nativism**.)

Learning strategies 学习策略

The definition of learning strategies is not straightforward. However, a compilation of the definitions offered by major scholars in the field suggests that learning strategies are efforts by learners to enhance or assist their language-learning experience. Elements attributed to these strategies or efforts include the following:

- they involve choice on the part of the learner;
- they involve conscious selection; that is, the learner is aware of deciding to use a strategy;
- they are goal-directed (i.e., they are purposeful in nature and geared toward task completion);
- they are effortful.

Learning strategies are distinguished from communication strategies that center on how learners compensate for incomplete competence during interactions in the L2.

There is a vast literature on learning strategies that has focused on such topics as a taxonomy of strategies (i.e., a classification of strategies); which strategies are used by which learners (e.g., more proficient learners appear to use a wider range of strategies in a greater number of situations than do less proficient learners); which strategies are used for what kinds of tasks; how strategies relate to successful learning; to what extent learners can be trained in strategy use, and others. As examples of strategy types, here are five: (1) *metacognitive* strategies for organizing, focusing, and evaluating one's own learning; (2) *affective* strategies for handling emotions or attitudes; (3) *social* strategies for cooperating with others in the learning process; (4) *cognitive* strategies for linking new information with existing schemata and for analyzing and classifying it; and (5) *memory* strategies for entering new information into memory storage and for retrieving it when needed. Again, categorization and definitions of strategies vary from scholar to scholar. In addition, most research on L2 strategies focuses on classroom learners and classroom success, and it is not clear how learning strategies relate to SLA more generally. Major researchers in L2 strategies include Andrew Cohen, Rebecca Oxford, J. Michael O'Malley, Anna Chamot, and others.

Learning styles 学习风格

Learning styles refer to the different ways in which learners perceive, absorb, process, and recall new information and skills. As such, they are preferences about how people go about learning and acquiring new information. They are sometimes referred to as *cognitive styles*, although some scholars do not equate the two. Unlike **learning strategies** that may be specific to tasks (e.g., always underlining new words), learning styles encompass broad traits concerning learning. For example, one distinction made in at least one model related to learning styles is concrete versus abstract thinking. Concrete thinkers are oriented toward experiences and specific human situations and generally emphasize feeling over thinking. Abstract conceptualizers are oriented toward logic, ideas, and concepts. Another difference in learning styles that has been researched is field dependence versus field independence. Field dependent people are said to have difficulty seeing the details of the field in front of them. They take in the whole. This kind of person might have difficulty finding something small dropped on a floor, such as a pin or a pill. Field independent people are the opposite and can more easily see details or subtle differences. They could more quickly find the pin on the floor. Of course, all of these contrasts are ideals, and most people fall on a scale rather than to one extreme or another. In addition, people are composed of various orientations involving different kinds of oppositions. In the two cases, a person could be measured on both concreteness and abstractness, as well as field dependence/independence, and along with other traits about learning or cognitive style, this information would tell us something about how this person processes the world around him or her.

A number of scholars have researched the *what* of learning styles (i.e., their classification and what they mean), the *how* of assessment (i.e., what measures to use in order to determine people's learning styles), and the relationship between learning styles and outcomes (success) in SLA.

In the case of outcomes, most research is related to classroom success. It is thus tied to educational concerns rather than to, say, immersion environments, immigrant situations, and other kinds of acquisitional contexts. Some names associated with learning styles are Andrew Cohen, Rebecca Oxford, Madeline Ehrman, Betty Lou Leaver, and Peter Skehan.

Lexicon 词库

Lexicon is the word linguists use to refer to the mental dictionary we all carry around in our heads. As such, it is composed of all the words we know and each person has his or her own mental lexicon. Words in the mental lexicon are quite complex in that they carry more than just **meaning**. For example, the word *cat* would exist in the mental lexicon as something like this (with N = noun and V = verb):

/kæt/: [+N, –V], [+animate], [+mammal], [+feline], and so on

Verbs are more complicated because they have certain underlying semantic notions that must be indexed with the verb, as these notions have syntactic consequences. These semantic notions are called *thematic roles*. The verb *eat*, for example, must include the thematic role of the eater, with an optional eatee (or the thing eaten). The first we call an *agent* and the second we call a *theme*. (In the case of the agent and theme of *eat*, the syntactic consequences are which roles become the subject and the object when the verb actually appears in a sentence.) In the mental lexicon, then, we would find *eat* with the following minimal information:

/īt/: [–N, +V], [required thematic roles: agent], [optional thematic roles: theme], (plus the semantic notions that make up *eat*)

The verb *die* would have a different thematic role because the underlying thematic role in this case is an experiencer: one experiences death, one is not an agent of *die* the same way one is an agent of *eat*. Contrast this with *commit suicide* in which the person actually does bring about the act of dying. Thus, *die* would look something like this in the mental lexicon:

/day/: [–N, +V], [required thematic roles: experiencer], [optional thematic roles: none], (plus the semantic notions that make up *die*)

In short, the mental lexicon is made up of words, their meanings, the sounds that make up words, required and optional semantic and grammatical information, as well as other things. In addition, it is believed by most researchers of the mental lexicon that words have links to each other. Thus, *eat* is linked to *eater*, to *eaten*, to *ate*, to *food*, to *edible*, and so on—and all of these are linked to each other. These links are what are sometimes responsible for slips of the tongue, such as when someone says, "Pass me the knife—I mean, the fork."

Markedness 标记性

Markedness is a linguistic concept related to how common or typical a feature is. Generally speaking, something that is more common or ubiquitous is considered less marked or unmarked, while something less common or less natural is considered marked or more marked.

In addition, something unmarked or less marked may be considered the default form of the feature. Markedness can be used to make cross-linguistic comparisons (what happens around the world with languages) or what happens within a single language. Some examples follow.

In the world's languages, there are relative clauses such as *Tom is the man who studied SLA*, with *who studied SLA* as the relative clause. There are various types of relative clauses depending on the relationship of the relative marker (e.g., *who, that*) to the verb:

- subject relative clause: Tom is the man *who studied SLA*;
- object relative clause: SLA is the subject *that Tom studied*;

- indirect object relative clause: Tom is the guy *who I gave the SLA book to*;
- object of preposition clause: Tom is the guy *who I studied SLA with;*
- genitive clause: Tom is the guy *whose SLA book I borrowed*;
- object of comparison clause: Tom is the guy *who I am taller than.*

According to surveys of world languages, subject relative clauses are the most common and are the least marked. Object of comparisons are the least common and are the most marked.

Other features of language that exist in binary opposition to each other are often considered to exist in a marked relationship. For example, masculine gender is less marked/unmarked relative to feminine or neuter gender. In sound systems, voiceless consonants such as *s, t,* and *k* are considered less marked/unmarked compared to their voiced counterparts *z, d,* and *g.* And, as one final example, in semantics, the term *lion* is considered unmarked and can refer to any kind of lion (it is the default form of the word) while *lioness* can only refer to female lions. This is so because *lioness* entails the addition of a suffix to *lion.* Note that other derivatives and phrases are based on *lion* and not *lioness*: *lion-like, pride of lions,* and so on.

Markedness has been shown to be relevant to both L1 and L2 acquisition. In general, learners have more difficulty with more marked elements of language in an L2 (regardless of whether the same elements exist in their L1 or not). Returning to the example of relative clauses, research has shown that subject and object relative clauses are easier to acquire compared to genitive and object of prepositions. By "easier to acquire" what is normally meant is that the less marked clauses appear sooner in learner output and learners make fewer errors with them. More marked items may take longer to appear: Learners may make more errors with them, or the marked items may simply not appear at all (depending on the structure or feature in question). Four names associated with markedness are Susan Gass, Fred Eckman, Eric

Kellerman, and Helmut Zobl.

Meaning 意义

The term *meaning* is slippery, at best, and can be used to denote a variety of concepts. It can be especially slippery when used in the context of **form-meaning connections**. Meaning can refer to "basic meaning" such as *cat* referring to a four-legged feline (e.g., we all know what a cat is) or it can refer to more elaborated information as would be included in a semantic inventory, such as *cat* includes [+animate], [+mammal], [+four-legged], [+predator], and so on, with each of these entailing additional meanings ([+mammal] would entail [+fur/hair], [+warm blooded], [+live birth], etc.).

In terms of grammatical inflections (**morphology/morphological inflections**), meaning may be more or less transparent and/or more or less concrete depending on the inflection. For example, the *-s* on the end of dogs is pretty clear: It means "more than one." However, the absence of *-s* on dogs does not always mean "just one." In the sentence *Dog is man's best friend*, the intended meaning is not a particular dog or even one dog, but dogs as a species. Looking at a more complex example, what does *have* mean when used as an auxiliary such as *I've done it*? As an auxiliary, it implies some sort of perfectivity (i.e., an action completed prior to a particular point in time), but what makes it different from *I did it*, which also implies perfectivity? A speaker of English has a great intuitive grasp of the meaning and function of *have done* compared with the simple past tense form *did*, but it may elude his or her ability to articulate it.

Meaning is also wrapped up in what is called **pragmatics**. In short, pragmatics refers to what a speaker intends to mean, not what the words themselves represent. For example, the modal *will* may mean "future" in its prototypical use as in *I'll get to it later*. But it can also be used as a directive (command) such as *You will do it now*.

One of the central jobs of the language learner is to map meaning onto form (language) over time. However, not all grammatical devices carry meaning. Relative clause markers in English, for example, don't. In *The letter that I sent you was special*, there is no semantically based meaning for *that* as there is for *cat*, plural *-s*, or modal *will*, for example. It has a grammatical function, but no reference to "stuff out there in the real world" such as pastness, number, or person. (See also **semantics**.)

Mental representation of language 语言的心理表征

Mental representation refers to the underlying, abstract, and implicit (unconscious) linguistic system that exists in a speaker's head. It is a synonym for **competence**. **Explicit knowledge** and **metalinguistic knowledge** are not part of mental representation as defined here. Both L1 and L2 speakers have mental representations of language, although there is debate as to the degree to which L2 learners can arrive at a mental representation that is the same as that of native speakers. (See the Key Question **Can L2 learners become native-like?**)

Metalinguistic knowledge 元语言学知识

In addition to having a **mental representation of language** that is abstract and implicit, speakers of a language may also have what is called metalinguistic knowledge. This knowledge is essentially conscious knowledge about language itself, usually manifested as the ability to talk about language. Let's suppose an English speaker says, "English is a very rigid language in terms of word order. English likes for sentences to be subject-verb-object and it is almost impossible to find any other word order." That person is exhibiting some kind of metalinguistic knowledge because of his or her ability to use terms like *subject, object, rigid word order*, and so on. Scholars of language such as linguists and L2 researchers are quintessential possessors of metalinguistic knowledge as they are able to do such things as define the nature of subjects, contrast languages on various features, and talk about a wide range of language-related matters using language about language. Classroom L2 learners often develop rudimentary levels of metalinguistic knowledge because of the pedagogical rules they learn or because of the information about how language works that is provided to them by instructors and textbooks.

Modified input 修饰过的输入

See **caretaker speech**.

MoGul 模块的在线生长和语言使用

MOGUL is the acronym for Modular Online Growth and Use of Language. Used as a framework for both first and second language acquisition, MOGUL brings together linguistic, psycholinguistic, and cognitive perspectives on language under one umbrella. Essential to the framework is that language acquisition is a by-product of **processing** or **parsing**. Also important to the framework are the roles of **frequency** and how it affects the nature of the information stored as "language." In this sense, it shares some features of **usage-based theories** (see the section **Key Theories and Frameworks in Second Language Acquisition**), but it departs significantly from these because MOGUL incorporates the idea of specialized modules for information processing, one of which is dedicated to language. Thus, MOGUL is also committed to the basic tenets of approaches that make use of **Universal Grammar**. The scholars associated with MOGUL are Michael Sharwood Smith and John Truscott.

Monitor/monitoring 监控   Monitor Theory 监控理论

The construct of the monitor is related to Steven Krashen's Monitor Theory. In this theory, he posits five important constructs:

- the acquisition–learning distinction;

- the Input Hypothesis;
- $i + 1$;
- the monitor;
- the affective filter.

Each of these is reviewed elsewhere in this section, so we will focus on the monitor only. According to Krashen, L2 learners can develop two separate and autonomous linguistic systems. One is the acquired system, consisting of unconscious rules related to language (see **acquisition, competence, mental representation of language**). The other is the learned system, consisting of conscious, explicitly learned rules about the language. Although Krashen posits the acquired system as central to language knowledge and performance, he does attribute a secondary—but much less important role—to the explicit conscious system. He claims that this system can be called upon under certain circumstances to monitor one's output; that is, to edit what one says (or writes) given the following conditions: (1) the learner has to know the rule to apply; and (2) the learner must have time to apply the conscious rule. Krashen claims that under normal spontaneous speaking conditions, learners do not have the time to monitor their output. Thus, the monitor is very limited in its usefulness. Because learners are focused on getting meaning across—and they may be under time constraints—the monitor is generally not engaged. The monitor may show up more in writing, especially planned and carefully constructed writing for which there is time to apply consciously learned rules.

Although Monitor Theory as a whole has fallen out of favor with SLA researchers, the concept of monitoring continues to be important in research design, especially in how we assess learner's underlying mental representation. If tests and assessment tasks are supposed to provide information about what exists in the mental representation—that is, the acquired system—those tests and tasks must be formulated in such a way as to disallow or minimize monitoring. Tests that allow monitoring most likely do not offer an accurate picture of what exists in the learner's unconscious and implicit system. This is especially important in that SLA researchers are increasingly distanced from the idea that learned conscious knowledge can "turn into" acquired knowledge (see **acquisition versus learning**). The name most associated with the monitor and Monitor Theory is Steven Krashen.

Morphemes 语素
morpheme studies 语素（习得顺序）研究

A morpheme is the smallest unit of language that carries any kind of meaning. Any simple word is a morpheme, such as *dog*, *cat*, and *window*. However, when pluralized in English, we add -*s*, which means "more than one." Thus, dogs consists of two morphemes, the root word *dog* and the plural marker -*s*. Each carries its own meaning, and combined they make up the meaning "more than one dog." Here are some other examples:

- runner = two morphemes: run + -er (the one who does the action);
- distrust = two morphemes: dis (lack of) + trust;
- review = two morphemes: re (do again) + view;
- anti-Americanism = four morphemes: anti (against) + America + n (pertaining to or one of) + ism (belief system).

Morphemes can be either free or bound. Bound morphemes attach to words, such as plural -*s*. Free morphemes do not attach. All simple words are free morphemes, as are function words like *the* and *an*. (See **morphology/morphological inflection**.)

In the early 1970s, SLA researchers took interest in the acquisition of English morphemes. Work in the 1960s on child L1 acquisition in English studied fourteen morphemes and found that children, regardless of the homes they were raised in, acquired these morphemes in the same order. L2 researchers wanted to know whether this was true for English L2 and whether or not the L2 order(s) matched the L1 order.

They studied morphemes such as plural -*s*, third-person -*s*, possessive -*s*, contracted copular -*s* (*he's coming*), past tense regular -*ed*, and progressive -*ing*, among others. By the late 1980s, dozens of morpheme studies had been conducted using a variety of techniques. It is fair to say that, overall, the results suggest that L2 learners, regardless of their L1s, acquire these English morphemes in a predictable order. These are now referred to as **acquisition orders**. However, why an order exists the way it does and just what these orders reflect are still unclear. Also, there has been some controversy about what the morpheme studies overlook, such as underlying meaning attributed to some morphemes by learners. The names most associated with morpheme studies and acquisition orders are Heidi Dulay, Marina Burt, Steven Krashen, and Diane Larsen-Freeman from the 1970s. However, as mentioned, there are dozens of studies that have examined various aspects of morpheme acquisition and acquisition orders. (See **What does development look like?**)

Morphology 形态学

morphological inflection 屈折形态学

Morphology is a branch of linguistics that studies how words are formed, including the pieces and parts of words and what they mean or what function they serve. As such, the term is related to the concept of **morpheme**. There are basically two subareas within morphology: derivational morphology and inflectional morphology. Derivational morphology focuses on how new words are made from other words. These new words always involve either a change in meaning or a change in syntactic function. For example, from *honest* we get the "derived" word *dishonest*. This derivation results in a change of meaning: *dishonest* is the opposite of *honest*. Another derivation from *honest* is *honestly*. There is not really a change in meaning here, but there is a change in syntactic function: *honest* is an adjective and *honestly* is an adverb. Other examples of derivational morphology include the following: *act*, *actor, actress; kitchen, kitchenette; transport, transportation; sentiment, sentimental, unsentimental, sentimentally.* English offers countless examples.

Inflectional morphology refers to adding elements to a word that do not change the word's function or meaning, but might serve as a grammatical device to indicate things like person, number, tense, plurality, and so on. Thus, plural *-s* in English is an inflection added to count nouns to indicate more than one: *dog, dogs. -ed* is an inflection in English added to verbs that indicates pastness: *watch, watched.* English overall has weak inflectional morphology on verbs, whereas languages like Spanish, Italian, and Russian are morphologically rich when it comes to verbal inflections.

Acquisition of language involves acquisition of the morphological properties of the language, and, as such, morphology is an important area within L2 research. Acquisition of tense-aspect systems, for example, may include the acquisition of morphological features as well as the meanings/functions they express. Early L2 research (1970s) focused a good deal of attention on the acquisition of morphemes. This research is often referred to as the **morpheme studies** or the research on **acquisition orders**. What this research showed was that L2 learners, regardless of L1, acquired a particular set of morphemes in a particular order over time, thus challenging a major role for L1 at the time as well as challenging a significant role for instruction.

Motivation 动机

Motivation is one of a number of what researchers call **individual differences** (traits that vary across individuals). Motivation to learn another language is, simply conceived, the degree and type of "wanting to learn" and has been shown to correlate significantly with how far learners get (e.g., how much language they acquire, the skills they develop with the language). For a long period of time, L2 researchers discussed two distinct motivations in the SLA context: *integrative* and *instrumental*. Integrative motivation refers to the internal impetus that learners have to relate to, identify with, or integrate into another L2 culture. It involves the psychological and emotional dimensions of how people construct identity and how they interact with others. Instrumental motivation is related to purposeful use of language, such as wanting language for educational, economic, or other benefits. With this kind of motivation, language is seen as a tool to get goods, and to derive benefits from the environment that are not psychological in nature (even though we might feel good after we derive the benefit). Since the 1970s, the field of motivation research has become more complicated by including such things as the possible and ideal selves, motivation as process, demotivation, and the evolution of motivation over time, among other concepts. Early names associated with motivation are Wallace Lambert and Richard Gardner. More recently, Zoltán Dörnyei has emerged as a major scholar in the research on individual differences, including motivation.

Native language 本族语   native-like 类似本族语的

Everyone with normal language capacity acquires a native language. A native language is generally considered to be any language acquired since birth, be it one language in a monolingual household or environment or two languages in a bilingual home or environment. This situation contrasts with languages that are acquired later, especially after the native language(s) is/are "in place." This time frame is normally 4–5 years of age. Being a native speaker of a language, though, should not be confused with having the same ability or knowledge as every other native speaker of that language. For example, two people from New York—one with a high school education only and one with a Ph.D. in literary studies—most likely will have different abilities with **lexicon** (vocabulary), **discourse** and rhetoric, **pragmatics**, and other domains.

However, both people will have similar mental representations of **syntax** and **morphology**, for example, as these systems are finite in nature and governed by **Universal Grammar**.

We should also note that nativeness is contextually bound in that being a native speaker of English from New York may or may not be the same as being a native speaker of English from London, New Delhi, or Melbourne. Nativeness is somewhat tied into speech communities, especially in the domains of language that lay outside of syntax, morphology, and the other purely formal properties of language. For this reason, the concept of World Englishes emerged in linguistic circles. World Englishes refers to the fact that varieties of English are spoken around the world by both native and non-native speakers.

The term *native-like* refers to whether or not L2 learners either behave in a qualitatively similar manner to native speakers or possess qualitatively similar underlying mental representations of language. It is not clear to what extent L2 learners can become native-like. (See the Key Question **Can L2 learners become native-like?**)

Nativism/Nativist Theory 先天论

In linguistics, nativism is a term associated with Noam Chomsky, who developed the theory that all humans are born with an innate capacity and a knowledge system specifically designed for language and language acquisition. This contrasts with those who hold that language is purely a result of someone's interaction with the environment. Under linguistic nativism, a normally functioning human being is said to be born with **Universal Grammar** that constrains the shape of the language he or she will be exposed to as a child. Thus, even though the child does interact with the environment, Universal Grammar will restrain the hypotheses the child can make about language. For example, under nativism, the child is prohibited from making unconscious rules that are predicated on the serial ordering of words (A comes before B). Instead, the child must make unconscious rules that are predicated on syntactic structures that exist in certain relationships to each other (A can only replace A-like structures or occupy a place in a sentence designated for A-like structures).

Linguistic nativism contrasts with what might be called general nativism, in which children aren't born with something like Universal Grammar but are born with something like **processing** constraints that are tied to structural distance among elements. Syntactic structure emerges because of these processing constraints.

Opposite nativism are the positions that claim all language emerges from a person's interaction with the environment and is a result of more general cognitive capacities. An example of non-nativism would be **skill** theory or the now-defunct **behaviorism**. Under these positions, children acquire language not because they are born with any innate capacity or knowledge, but because they interact with the environment in particular ways and the general mechanisms of cognition and learning take care of language acquisition just as they would do to the learning of anything else.

One argument that seems to bolster linguistic nativism is the **poverty of the stimulus**. According to this argument, people (including children by the age of 5) come to know much more about language than what they could gather from the linguistic environment around them. Because people only hear possible sentences, how do they know what is impossible? For example, how do they know that *Should I've done it?* is not a possible contraction of *have* in English when all they've heard are the possible contractions with *have*? Nativists argue that people can do this because they are hardwired to rule out certain possibilities, that Universal Grammar provides them with what is impossible in language more generally. For linguistic nativism and Universal Grammar, see scholars such as Lydia White and many others. For general nativism, see William O'Grady.

Natural Order Hypothesis 自然顺序假说

The Natural Order Hypothesis is associated with Steven Krashen and forms part of his Monitor Theory. According to the Natural Order Hypothesis, learners proceed in a predictable order of acquisition of grammatical features of language, regardless of the L1 and regardless of the context in which they acquire languages (e.g., classroom vs. non-classroom, foreign language vs. second language). In English, for example, progressive -*ing* is acquired before regular past tense -*ed*, which is acquired before third-person -*s*. Although Monitor Theory itself has fallen out of favor, the idea that learners follow predictable paths and sequences is an accepted fact of SLA. (See **developmental sequences**, **morphemes/morpheme studies**, and the Key Question **What does development look like?**)

Naturalistic 自然的

Naturalistic is a term that one often sees or hears in relationship to learners who acquire language without any classroom instruction. Thus, immigrants to a country who do not enroll in language courses and basically learn the language "on the streets" or "on the job" are referred to as naturalistic learners. Naturalistic learners have been compared to classroom learners in order to address the issue of the effects of instruction (see the Key Question **Does instruction make a difference?**). For example, Schumann's research subject, Alberto, was a naturalistic learner (see **pidginization**). *Naturalistic* as a term now alternates with the term *non-classroom* (as in non-classroom vs. classroom), largely because some professionals objected to the idea that classrooms were being tagged as "unnatural" under the earlier distinction of naturalistic versus classroom.

Negative evidence 反面证据

Negative evidence is a term related to the type of feedback that language learners get, and specifically refers to information that a learner's utterance is ill-formed in some way. Negative evidence comes in two types: direct and indirect. Direct negative evidence refers to feedback in which the learner is explicitly told his or her utterance is incorrect in some way. Examples include "No. We don't say it that way. We say …" and "You mean *talked*. You forgot to put the past tense marker on." Direct negative evidence happens largely in classrooms but not exclusively.

Indirect negative evidence refers to conversational interactions in which the person speaking with the learner implicitly points out something is wrong (see **negotiation of meaning**). Here are some of the most commonly researched types of indirect negative evidence (appearing in italics). (NNS = non-native speaker and NS = native speaker.)

- Confirmation check: used to verify what one heard
  NNS: He grabbed by the craws.
  NS: *The claws? You mean with its hands?*
  NNS: Yes, yes.
- Clarification request: asking the person to clarify
  NNS: I can find no [ruddish].
  NS: *I'm sorry. You couldn't find what?*
- Recast: restating what the person says as part of the normal interactional flow
  NNS: And so he buy a car.
  NS: *He bought a car!*
  NNS: Yes, he bought a car.
  NS: Wow, how nice.

Unlike direct negative evidence, indirect negative evidence does not normally interrupt the flow of communication and is focused on meaning. In both L1 and SLA, researchers have questioned whether negative evidence—in particular indirect negative evidence—is either necessary or beneficial to language acquisition. In L1 research, negative evidence is widely viewed as being unhelpful and certainly not necessary for language growth in the child. In SLA circles, it is not clear what the role of negative evidence is. Although there is some consensus that direct negative evidence does not advance acquisition, researchers dispute the role of indirect negative evidence. The research suggests it may be useful for lexical growth as well as other aspects of meaning-making (e.g., pragmatics), but it is far from clear whether negative evidence of any kind is useful for the growth of the formal properties of language (e.g., syntax, morphology). The argument for indirect negative evidence is that it brings acquisitional problems into the learner's focal awareness during communication, thus increasing the salience of a grammatical or lexical form. There are several arguments against indirect negative evidence, the two most important being that (1) indirect negative evidence is haphazard and not frequent enough to be important (i.e., interlocutors just don't provide enough negative evidence, and it isn't consistently provided), and (2) learners don't always perceive indirect negative evidence as an indication that they did something wrong.

The names most associated with indirect negative evidence are Susan Gass, Michael Long, Roy Lyster, and Alison Mackey, although there are many people who have written about **negotiation of meaning** and have discussed indirect negative evidence.

Negotiation of meaning 意义协商

Negotiation of meaning is a term related to conversations and interactions. Specifically, it refers to when there is a communication breakdown that triggers some kind of clarification of a speaker's intended message. That is, negotiation of meaning is triggered when there is a mismatch between a speaker's intended message and what the listener interprets as the intended meaning. The purpose of negotiation is to resolve the perceived mismatch, and such negotiations can occur in just about any kind of interaction. Even natives speaking to other natives may say something like "What're you getting at?" because they're not quite sure what the other person's intention is. Such negotiations are usually the result of pragmatic problems or a lack of background knowledge. With second language learners, negotiation of meaning can be triggered by a variety of things, including pronunciation, vocabulary, morphosyntactic matters, pragmatics, and so on, and the quality and quantity of negotiation may change depending on the level of the learner. Following is a sample from Teresa Pica's research, published in 1994 (NS = native speaker; NNS = non-native speaker).

NNS: The windows are crosed.
NS: The windows have what?
NNS: Crosed.
NS: Crossed? I'm not sure what you're saying here.
NNS: Windows are closed.
NS: Oh, the windows are closed, oh, OK, sorry.

The mispronunciation of *closed* by the NNS the first time triggered the response by the NS, which was a type of clarification request. The rest of the interaction quoted above demonstrates the negotiation and how the miscommunication was resolved.

Negotiation of meaning is deemed important not just for communicative reasons but potentially for acquisitional reasons. Negotiation of meaning provides indirect **negative evidence**, clues to the learner that he or she did something wrong. Thus, interaction potentially provides useful feedback about vocabulary, syntax, and so on. However, researchers are not in agreement about the role that indirect negative evidence plays (see earlier discussion on this term). Nonetheless, negotiation of meaning is important for maximizing comprehension on the part of the learner. Not all miscommunications are a result of what learners do wrong; they can result when learners don't understand someone else. Thus, negotiation helps to ensure comprehension. With increased comprehension, there are increased chances for acquisition, because acquisition is a by-product of comprehension to a certain degree. The scholars most associated with interaction and negotiation of meaning are Susan Gass, Michael Long, Alison Mackey, and Teresa Pica, among others. (See also **Interaction Hypothesis** and **output** as well as the Key Question **What are the roles of input and output in SLA?**)

Neurolinguistics 神经语言学

Neurolinguistics is a field of study that involves the role of brain functioning in language comprehension, production, and storage. Neurolinguists have mapped out areas of the brain involved in language development and language processing, and have highlighted the role that Broca's area (a part of the brain) plays in language. One of the major tools of neurolinguistics is brain imaging, and to this end neurolinguists have borrowed from medical science by using techniques such as PET (positron emission tomography) and MRI (magnetic resonance imaging). These techniques provide "snapshots" of brain activity.

An area closely related to neurolinguistics is neurocognition, a field where researchers study the brain basis of human learning more generally. However, many neurocognitivists are interested in language and are specialized neurolinguists. Although some neurocognitivists use MRIs as research tools, ERPs (event-related potentials) tend to dominate the research in the neurocognition of language.

Neurolinguists have studied brain activity in L2 learners and bilinguals. Overall, this research shows that highly proficient L2 learners with extensive communicative exposure to the L2 demonstrate increasing overlap of the areas of the brain that also serve L1 processing. Similar findings have been obtained in the neurocognitive research on SLA. However, some research in neurolinguistics suggests that age may play a factor in terms of the extent to which both the L1 and L2 involve the same parts of the brain.

Some names associated with the neurolinguistics of SLA include David Green, Peter Indefrey, Michel Paradis, and Daniela Perani. Names associated with neurocognition include Lee Osterhout and Michael Ullman.

Noticing 注意　Noticing Hypothesis 注意假说

Noticing is a term attributed largely to Richard W. Schmidt. Specifically, he claims that the only linguistic elements in the input that learners can acquire are those elements that they notice. By *noticing*, Schmidt means that learners are paying attention, that there is some level of awareness in learning. He contrasts this to implicit learning, learning without awareness, subliminal learning, and other scenarios. In many respects, Schmidt's claim is a reaction to Krashen's idea that acquisition involves subconscious learning (see **acquisition**). Because Schmidt believes in some level of awareness on the part of the learner, he tends to reject a major role for any kind of implicit or unconscious learning. The concept of noticing and the role of noticing are not universally accepted within SLA and remain controversial. (See the Key Question **What are the roles of implicit and explicit learning in SLA?**)

On-line tasks 线上任务　off-line tasks 线下任务

Generally, off-line tasks are those used to measure learner knowledge and often involve paper-and-pencil-type tests. They are the most generally used tasks to get at what learners know and are ubiquitous in the L2 literature. Some classic off-line tasks include **grammaticality judgment** tests in which learners indicate whether they believe a sentence is possible or not in a given language, truth-value judgments in which learners determine which of two sentences logically follows or fits with something they just read, cloze tests in which learners fill in missing gaps in a text, and sentence combining tests, among others.

By contrast, on-line tasks tend to be moment-by-moment measures of what learners are doing with language. They tend to measure underlying processes (such as the interface between the learner's grammar and the **parsing** mechanisms). Classic examples of on-line tasks include (1) the moving-window technique, in which learners read bits and pieces of a sentence on a computer screen, advancing through the sentence as they push a button, and (2) eye-tracking, in which the movement of people's pupils is tracked while they read a sentence on a computer screen. In both moving-window and eye-tracking, the measurement that is recorded is the time it takes learners to read a particular part of a sentence that is of interest to the researcher. Longer reading times (measured in milliseconds) generally indicate longer processing time and a point at which people are resolving a linguistic dilemma while reading. Names often associated with on-line measures include Paola E. Dussias, Claudia Felser, Alan Juffs, Cheryl Frenck-Mestre, and Harald Clahsen.

Output 输出 　 Output Hypothesis 输出假说

Output, of course, refers to the language that learners produce during communicative interactions or for the purpose of expressing a message. The Output Hypothesis (also known as the Comprehensible Output Hypothesis) is associated with Merrill Swain. In the mid-1980s, she expressed concern that the field placed too much emphasis on the role of **input** in SLA, claiming that learners in Canadian immersion programs still demonstrated significant divergence from natives after years of study. She claimed that what was missing was output, and in direct contrast to Krashen's concept of comprehensible input, she argued that learners need to be pushed to make comprehensible output during acquisition. According to her, pushed output moves learners to greater reliance on syntax and less reliance on semantics; that is, they will pay more attention to how something is supposed to be said and not just to the message.

In the 1990s, Swain expanded the Output Hypothesis and suggested that there were three roles that learner output might play in acquisition. The first role causes more **noticing**. The second allows learners to test hypotheses they have about the language. If the hypothesis "works," then they will be inclined to continue using it. If it doesn't, then they will be more inclined to abandon it and search for a better hypothesis. Hypothesis testing happens during communicative interactions. Positive feedback about what learners are doing in terms of communicating well confirms hypotheses. **Negative evidence** might push learners away from their hypotheses. The third function of output, according to Swain, lies in the use of metatalk. Metatalk is the use of language about language, for example, when learners ask overt questions about language during interactions such as "I think that word needs a *se*, doesn't it?" Swain has argued that any one or all of these roles of output can aid acquisition in some way. (See the Key Question **What are the roles of input and output in SLA?**) Other names associated with output and the Output Hypothesis include Shinichi Izumi and Sharon Lapkin.

Overgeneralization 过度概括

Overgeneralization, a concept related to **regularization**, is the extension of a rule or linguistic form to domains where it is not appropriate. It is an attested phenomenon both in first and second language acquisition. The best and classic example of overgeneralization comes from work on the acquisition of the past tense in English. The first past tense forms to be acquired are a handful of the irregulars such as *came, went, left*, and *ate*. At this point, learners tend not to produce endings on regular verbs and may say *talk* for *talked*. As the regular forms creep in and the learner gains control over them, the correct irregular forms tend to drop out and are replaced with forms that look like regularized verbs or the overgeneralization of the rule for regular past tense verb endings. This is when we see verb forms such as *ated/eated* or *wented/goed*. These overgeneralized forms tend to drop out with additional exposure to language.

Overgeneralization is not restricted to verb inflections or **morphology** more generally. Overgeneralization can happen with **semantics** and **lexicon**, as in the case where child L1 learners might overgeneralize the word *doggie*, using it to refer to all four-legged creatures. Overgeneralization in **syntax** is less common and is often conflated with either a morphological feature or the interface between semantics and sentence structure. For example, learners in the early stages of acquiring the copular verbs *ser* and *estar* in Spanish often overgeneralize *ser* to the contexts in which *estar* is required as in *Juan es muy contento* rather than *Juan está muy contento* (for "John is very happy"). In French, learners may overgeneralize the verb *avoir* in the beginning stages of the acquisition of the *passé composé* (past tense), using it where the verb *être* should appear (e.g., *J'ai descendu* instead of *Je suis descendu* for "I descended").

Overgeneralization was widely studied in the early days of SLA research but currently does not receive the kind of attention it once did. It is taken as a fact of SLA.

Parameters 参数   parameter setting 参数定值

Parameters are mostly associated with syntactic theory, specifically Chomskyan theory and **Universal Grammar**. Parameters are particular variations on a type of syntactic feature, and these features are finite in number. One such parameter is the null subject parameter. A null subject refers to the fact that verbs can appear without an explicit or overt subject, and the sentence is grammatical. For example, in Spanish *Hablo* "I speak" and *Habla* "he speaks" are allowed. In addition, *Está lloviendo* "It's raining" is allowed; in fact, it is required that weather expressions in Spanish have no equivalent of it. These are all grammatical sentences. In English, however, such sentences are prohibited: "*Speaks," "*Is raining."

In short, languages vary as to whether they allow null subjects or not, and linguists talk about the parameter being set one way or another. Spanish and Italian, for example, are null subject languages and thus have the parameter set to +null subjects. English and French are not null subject languages and have the parameter set to −null subjects. Developments in syntactic theory have led to increasingly abstract notions of parameters, such as +/−strong agreement, which may affect word order.

In SLA, the question has been whether or not learners can "reset" parameters to the L2 value if their L1 value is different. In the case of going from Spanish to English, the learner would have to reset from + to −null subject, while the English speaker learning Spanish would have to reset from − to +null subject. Resetting of parameters occurs when appropriate input data from the environment interact with the information contained in Universal Grammar. Research to date suggests that parameter resetting can occur, but it is not a given. Some scholars have argued that only certain kinds of parameters can be reset. And, of course, there has been discussion of the degree to which L1 parameters are transferred into SLA from the beginning. (These topics are touched upon in the various sections of Key Questions, but see especially **Can L2 learners become native-like?**) One of the most widely read and cited scholars working within parametric matters in SLA (as well as Universal Grammar) is Lydia White, although there are many others who have examined SLA from a Universal Grammar framework.

Parsing 分解

Parsing is a psycholinguistic term that refers to the real-time computation of syntactic structure during comprehension. For example, the moment a listener hears "The man ...," that listener immediately projects a determiner phrase (DP) while simultaneously tagging it as "subject of sentence." If the listener hears "reduced" next, then that listener most likely tags the word as "verb," "past tense," thus projecting a verb phrase and confirms that "the man" is the subject of the verb. However, if the listener next encounters "to tears," then the listener's parsing mechanism stops and reanalyzes "The man reduced to tears ..." as a reduced relative clause that is the subject of a sentence. If a verb comes next, say, "told," then the listener's parser projects a new verb phrase with "The man reduced to tears" as the subject of "told." And so the analysis progresses as each word is encountered. Parsing, then, is this moment-by-moment (real-time) process of tagging words with syntactic roles, projecting syntactic structure, and making sense of the sentence.

Parsing research in SLA has been minimal to date but is taking on increasing importance, the question being whether L2 learners come to resolve ambiguity the same way native speakers do. For example, in Italian the sentence *Giovanni escriveva a Stefano cuando era negli Stati Uniti* "Giovanni wrote to Stefano while he was in the United States" is ambiguous as to who was in the United States: Giovanni or Stefano. Because Italian is a null subject language, the verb *era* can be either bare (have a null subject) or not (have an overt subject, in this case *lui*). Thus, the sentence can also be *Giovanni escriveva a Stefano cuando lui era negli Stati Uniti*. The question becomes how native speakers interpret null and overt subjects in the embedded clause. Research has shown that they overwhelmingly tend to link null subjects with the subject of the first clause (in this case, null subject = Giovanni) but tend to link overt subjects with non-subjects of the first clause (in this case, *lui* = Stefano). Research on this particular feature (interpretation of null and overt subjects) has shown that even very advanced speakers of Italian L2 do not resolve ambiguity like native speakers. A good deal of research has been conducted on ambiguous relative clauses and what they "attach to" during parsing. For example, in *Someone shot the maid of the actor who was on the balcony*, if asked "Who was on the balcony, the maid or the actor?," native speakers of English tend to say the actor (i.e., they "attach" the relative clause to "the actor"). But given the exact same sentence in Spanish, Spanish speakers tend to say the maid was on the balcony (i.e., they "attach" the relative clause to "the maid"). Research on L2 learners of Spanish and French have shown that in the case of relative clauses, L2 learners parse such sentences using L1 preferences but by very advanced stages can become indistinguishable from native speakers. The most associated names with parsing research in SLA include Paola E. Dussias, Eva Fernández, and Cheryl Frenck-Mestre.

Performance 语言运用

Performance is a term that stands in direct contrast to **competence** or underlying **mental representation of language**. Whereas these latter terms refer to implicit knowledge that speakers have about language, performance refers to what people do with language when communicating. A speaker "knows" what a language allows and disallows, even though through that person's speech, one might not be able to discern the full range of allowances and disallowances. Recursion is one example. Recursion refers to embedding as in *The horse fell*; *The horse that was raced past the barn fell*; *The horse that was raced past the barn that was built by Farmer McKenzie fell*; *The horse that was raced past the barn that was built by Farmer McKenzie who was killed in 2009 fell*; and so on. A speaker knows all these sentences are possible and that theoretically one could indefinitely embed. However, in terms of performance, no one embeds indefinitely. Performance is limited by such things as **working memory** (how much information can be stored on a millisecond by millisecond basis), fatigue (resulting in slips of the tongue, errors in usage), and style of language. In other words, there are performance factors that limit what people do with language even though they know more than what they can do.

In research, the distinction between competence and performance becomes important because if the researcher is interested in what an L2 learner implicitly knows about language, then speech may not be the best indicator of that underlying competence. Just because a learner doesn't produce something doesn't mean he or she doesn't know something. As for understanding what learners' competences disallow, collected speech samples would not reveal such information. A researcher can only find out what learners' competences disallow by creating tests that specifically tap that knowledge.

Phonology 音系学

Phonology is a branch of linguistics that studies sound systems. It is similar to other branches of linguistics that focus on "what's in the brain" and includes the study of what sounds exist in a language and what makes them different from other sounds (i.e., why is /p/ different from /b/ in English so that "pop" and "bop" are two different words), as well as how sounds combine to make syllables. Phonology also involves the study of when sound contrasts cease to be contrastive. For example, /z/ and /s/ are contrastive in that "zipper" and "sipper" are two different words. However, when pluralizing nouns, the sounds that correspond to -s vary depending on the sound that precedes the plural marker, and the /s/ versus /z/ distinction is no longer contrastive. In a sense, phonology is the study of how sounds work to help languages make meaning.

Phonetics is related to phonology and refers to how sounds are made by the vocal tract. For example, phonetics studies the placement of the tongue during the articulation of the sound or how open the mouth is.

Phonology is, of course, important to SLA in that L2 learners have to develop a phonology that allows them to speak in the L2. This may involve learning contrasts non-existent in their L1, such as the notorious /l/ and /r/ distinction in English that is often a problem for Japanese L1 speakers (/l/ and /r/ are not contrastive in Japanese). It may involve learning new sounds all together, such as the Spanish trill "r" (for English L1 speakers) or English "th" as in "booth" for French speakers. How learners deal with syllable construction is also an important area of L2 phonology research, as learners who come from languages with mostly open syllables (syllables that end in a vowel) must learn to deal with closed syllables (that end in consonants) in a language like English. Phonological issues may affect morphological issues, at least in terms of real-time speaking. Learners who come from languages with open syllables may have difficulty with words in English that require a consonantal inflection such as a plural marker as in "hat" and "hats." Learning to put two consonants at the end of a syllable may present quite a challenge for such learners, and even though intuitively (in their implicit systems) pluralization exists along with its markers, the phonological component of their grammars might not permit the actual realization of plurality on nouns or might cause them to insert "dummy" vowels to break up the consonant cluster. A number of scholars work in phonological acquisition, among them John Archibald, Fred Eckman, and James Flege. A good deal of research on phonological acquisition has looked at the issue of ultimate attainment (see the Key Question **Can L2 learners become native-like?**) and includes not only the scholars mentioned above but also Theo Bongaerts, Roy Major, Arlene Moyer, and Martha Young-Scholten, again, among others.

Pidginization 皮钦语化

Pidginization refers to a process by which non-native speakers develop a linguistic system in contact language situations to effect communication. The result is a pidgin, a linguistic system with reduced vocabulary and reduced grammar when compared to the two languages that come into contact to form it. Pidgins exist all around the world, with some of the most studied ones being in the Pacific and Caribbean Islands (e.g., Tok Pisin which is a pidgin in Papua New Guinea). Pidgins often exhibit commonalities as they develop, regardless of the languages that come into contact. Some of these commonalities include subject-verb-object word order, lack of relative clauses, reduction of closed syllables (see **phonology**), reduction of verbal inflections with words often taking the place of inflections, reduced inventory of phonemes (sounds), among others.

John Schumann applied the concept of pidginization to SLA in the mid-1970s when he asserted that some learners, who do not get beyond the very basic level of acquisition, may speak a kind of pidgin as a result of two languages coming into contact. His famous research subject, Alberto, was an immigrant from Costa Rica who lived in Massachusetts but had limited contact with English speakers. During the course of Schumann's research, Alberto had not advanced beyond the earliest stages of negation (e.g., *no like beer, I no like beer, He don't like beer*) and, for example, showed evidence of non-marking of past tense (e.g., *Yesterday my country change the president*). Schumann concluded that Alberto, compared to the other research subjects, showed little development over time and was speaking a pidgin-like version of English, largely because Alberto was engaged in the communication of purely denotative referential information and not integrative and expressive information. In other words, Alberto was not using language to become part of a society or culture, one of the aspects that Schumann claimed fostered pidginization.

Pidginization applied to SLA hit its apex in the late 1970s and early 1980s but has since fallen out of favor for various theoretical and practical reasons. In addition to John Schumann, other names associated with pidginization (and the related term *creolization*) in discussions of SLA are Roger Andersen and Albert Valdman. For pidginization more generally, some associated names are Derek Bickerton, Mark Sebba, and Loreto Todd.

Positive emission tomography/PET 正电子发射断层成像

Positive emission tomography—usually called by the acronym PET—is another technique used in **neurolinguistic** research. PETs are 3D images created by injecting someone with a short-lived radioactive isotope along with a glucose molecule. When the molecule is situated in the area of interest (in this case, somewhere in the brain), the isotope begins to decay and emits a positron (hence part of the name "positive emission"). The positron travels until it can combine with an electron and this activity (blood flow) is measured by the scanning device used by the researcher. The participant usually engages in some kind of comprehension test or **grammaticality judgment** and the researcher examines what part of the brain is active during the process.

Positive evidence 正面证据

Positive evidence is a term that stands in contrast to **negative evidence** and explicit information (e.g., telling a learner how something works in a language). Positive evidence is, essentially, the **input** that learners hear in communicative settings, in both L1 and L2 situations. It contains any and all utterances that learners might hear from more proficient or native speakers of the language. It can also be input that learners get from written texts (in the L2 context, of course, given that child L1 learners don't read). Some people refer to it as primary linguistic data. It is called positive because it does not contain direct negative feedback, such as error correction. According to theories of acquisition that work with **Universal Grammar**, only positive evidence can be used by the language-learning mechanism; that is, the language-learning mechanism cannot make use of negative evidence. The language-learning mechanism also cannot make use of explicit information such as rules provided to the learner. In short, what the language-learning mechanism needs is samples of language from the communicative environment. Positive evidence is also implicated in the **poverty of the stimulus** situation, meaning that learners come to know far more about language than what is evident in the language they are exposed to.

Poverty of the stimulus 刺激贫乏

Poverty of the stimulus (POS) is a situation in which people come to know more than what they could have gleaned from the data provided to them and is traceable back to Greek philosophers, most notably Plato. Plato was concerned with the issue of the relationship between knowledge and experience. He wanted to know how it is that a person could come to know something that was never learned explicitly. As part of his reasoning, he concluded that people must be born with innate ideas or at least some innate knowledge.

In language acquisition terms, the POS was outlined by Noam Chomsky and means that people come to have an underlying **competence** or **mental representation of language** greater than what the **input** data should have allowed them to have. The best example of this comes from knowledge about what is disallowed in a language. For example, speakers of English know that *I've done it* is a fine sentence but that the contraction of *I've* is disallowed in the question **Should I've done it?* One can only say *Should I have done it?*

How does a person come to know that *I've* (and contractions more generally) is allowed in some instances and disallowed in others? No one teaches a child this, and **negative evidence** on grammar and **syntax** is virtually absent or at best haphazard in interactions with child L1 learners. And yet every speaker of English comes to know what is disallowed with contractions. What makes the POS particularly interesting is that learners only get **positive evidence** in the input; that is, they only get examples of what languages allow. How then do they come to know what is disallowed? In short, the input underdetermines the grammatical and syntactic knowledge that a speaker comes to have about a language.

In addition, people do not always speak in complete sentences. They also create false starts, they make what looks like surface grammatical errors as they change the nature of a sentence in the middle of speaking it, they slur, they abbreviate, they chop words, and so on. Spoken language does not look like well-written prose, for example. Thus, when we say the input to children is impoverished, there is a poverty of the stimulus: The input doesn't always look good, and it only contains positive evidence.

Poverty of the stimulus is the bedrock of **Universal Grammar**, which says that people are born with an innate specification for language; that is, certain principles about language come hardwired at birth. These principles are what constrain language and serve as the internal and unseen "negative" information that guides speakers into what is allowed and disallowed in a language. In the case of contractions, we begin with the concept that Universal Grammar allows movement of constituents in a language. *I should have done it* and *Should I have done it* are related in that the *should* has moved from one position in the sentence to another in order to form the question version. What Universal Grammar contains, though, is also the concept that movement leaves traces. When the *should* moves, it leaves behind its trace where it originated from. Imagine a small *t* standing for trace so that in the speaker's mind the question has this structure: Should I *t* have done it? This trace blocks contraction; it literally occupies the space, and thus *I* and *have* can't merge to form a contraction. Therefore, Universal Grammar contains two things that are relevant in this instance: the possibility of movement and traces left behind by movement. Such an explanation means, then, that anyone born with normal capabilities for language has access to this information, and this is what helps the speaker come to know what is disallowed.

The POS has been applied to SLA as well, most notably by Bonne Schwartz, Lydia White, and others who work from a Universal Grammar perspective.

Pragmatics 语用学

Pragmatics is a branch of linguistics that studies **meaning**, specifically how people use sentences to intend something. Some sentences are straightforward, such as *Pass me that glass*. This is a clear directive, and there is sort of a one-to-one mapping of the speaker's intent (a command, a directive) and the shape of the sentence (the speaker actually used a command form of the verb). Other sentences are less straightforward in terms of their mapping. The same person who uttered *Pass me that glass* could also have said *The glass, please*. The listener, if the context is clear, would interpret this as a directive even though no verb was used and certainly no verb in a command form. As one more example, look at the following interchange:

Joe: I need ten bucks.

Harry: Forget it.

Joe: But it's really important. I'm in a jam.

Joe's declarative utterance is not just a description of his needs; it's actually a request. Overlaying the words is "Can I borrow ten dollars?" Harry's "command" does not literally mean that Joe should suddenly not remember something; his response is a refusal. He means he won't lend him the money and yet doesn't need to say "I won't lend you the money." That is understood by Joe, as indicated in his response.

Pragmatics is thus concerned with the role of context in language and how speakers and listeners rely on it for successful communication. People who say they can't "read between the lines" are suggesting that they may be pragmatically deficient compared to others, given that reading between the lines means understanding the true meaning of what someone said. As one more example, a boss could say *The company would be in grave danger if this were to leak out*. While this is syntactically nothing more than a declarative statement and could be taken literally, the context in which it is uttered could lead to the interpretation that it is a warning for the people in the room to keep their mouths shut and to ensure that others do as well.

Pragmatics has become an increasingly important part of SLA in terms of cross-cultural communication and how it is that L2 learners make and interpret meaning. In English, for example, speakers use *wh*-questions all the time to make suggestions, as in *Why don't you come by at 5:00?* Other languages might not make suggestions in the same way, and some L2 learners of English might interpret this as a literal *wh*-question requiring some kind of explanation. Thus, learners could have underlying competence that helps them compute sentences they hear but lack the pragmatic competence to interpret the sentence as it was meant by the speaker. They may misinterpret what they hear. The person most associated with pragmatics in SLA is Kathleen Bardovi-Harlig. (See also **speech acts**.)

Principles (of Universal Grammar) （普遍语法的）原则

Universal Grammar is a set of innate constraints on language that every unimpaired human brings to the task of language acquisition. Included within Universal Grammar are principles. Principles are constraints on language that are invariant and apply to all natural human languages. An example of a principle is that all languages have a basic structural feature called a phrase that consists of a head and its complement. A head can be a lexical item, such as noun, verb, or preposition, resulting in noun phrases, verb phrases, or prepositional phrases. Thus, *a man of few words* is a noun phrase with *man* = head and *of few words* = complement. Such a principle is important because syntactic operations must obey structural relationships (another principle). So when *a man of few words* appears in a sentence, we cannot just move *man* but must move the entire noun phrase in order to maintain grammaticality. Thus, *I saw a man of few words* is questioned as *Was a man of few words what you saw?* and not **Was a man what you saw of few words?*

Some principles of Universal Grammar involve abstract notions that are too complicated to get into here. It is enough to say that principles apply to all languages. However, if all languages obey all the principles, why don't all languages look alike? One reason is that languages may vary in how the principles are instantiated. For example, the fact that all languages contain the basic structural feature called the phrase and that syntactic operations must observe the integrity of phrases does not mean that all languages have phrases that are the same. A simple example will illustrate. Phrases can come in two basic orders: head first (head + complement) or head final (complement + head). English is a head first language, whereas Japanese is a head final language. Thus, for verb phrases, English follows verb (head) + complement (*John hit the ball*), while Japanese follows complement + verb (*John the ball hit*). This gives English its characteristic subject-verb-object word order, while giving Japanese its characteristic subject-object-verb word order. However, operations in both English and Japanese must observe the integrity of their phrases. Such variations are called **parameters**. Thus, languages are shaped by both invariant principles and parameters. When one considers all the possible combinations of parameters along with principles, we can see why the world's languages differ, albeit within restricted ways.

In SLA, principles of Universal Grammar are believed by many scholars to constrain and govern the development of underlying competence just as they do in first language acquisition. Thus, no mental representation of the L2 should violate a principle of Universal Grammar, even if the mental representation is not native-like. So far, this seems to be the case. However, where scholars disagree is on whether or not learners can get the right parameter for the L2 where this varies from the L1. (See **parameters/parameter setting** as well as the Key Question **Can L2 learners become native-like?**)

Procedural knowledge 程序性知识

See **declarative/procedural knowledge**.

Processability 可加工性

See **Processability Theory** in the section Key Theories and Frameworks.

Processing 加工

Processing is a cover term used for how syntactic and grammatical computations are made during language performance. Processing happens both during comprehension (see, for example, **parsing** and **input processing**) and during output (see, for example, **processability**). As one example, when someone hears *John told me that she was coming*, even though *she* is third-person singular, the listener rules out that John is talking about himself because *John* contains the feature [+masculine, –feminine] while *she* contains the feature [–masculine, +feminine]. (Note: [–masculine, –feminine] would be neuter.) The listener searches for possible antecedents for *she* and eliminates *John*. This searching and ruling out during comprehension is part of processing. Sometimes there is ambiguity, as in *John told me he wasn't coming*. Theoretically, *he* can be John or someone else. The listener may use context, such as something previously said, real word knowledge, or something else to determine the antecedent for *he*.

Something similar happens during speaking. When people put together a sentence, they first conceptualize what they want to say. Then, they must (1) access the **lexicon** to pull down the words they want, and (2) compute the syntactic relationships among all the words to get the sentence in the form they intend it to have (i.e., to indicate what they mean to say). Accessing words and computing syntactic relationships is part of processing, but we might call this "output processing" or "sentence production."

Processing contrasts with **competence** and **mental representation**

of language. The latter two refer to unconscious and abstract knowledge in the speaker's mind, while processing refers to what speakers and listeners do in real-time **performance.**

Processing instruction 输入加工教学法

Processing instruction, usually abbreviated as PI, was launched by a seminal publication by Bill VanPatten and Teresa Cadierno in 1993. It is a unique instructional intervention based on VanPatten's model of **input processing** (see the section **Key Theories and Frameworks in Second Language Acquisition**). The idea behind PI is that because acquisition is input-dependent, it is important to understand learners' basic strategies governing and constraining how learners make **form-meaning connections.** These strategies result in less-than-optimal **intake** for acquisition. Therefore, PI involves the manipulation of input in particular ways to push learners away from these less-than-optimal strategies. In this way, PI is clearly distinct from other pedagogical interventions that are predicated on **noticing** (see also **input enhancement**), which does not account for actual learner strategies for processing input. PI is perhaps the most researched pedagogical intervention in instructed second language acquisition. The scholar most associated with PI is Bill VanPatten, although Alessandro Benati, James F. Lee, Wynne Wong, and others have made significant contributions to the research on PI.

Projection 投射　　Projection Hypothesis 投射假说

Projection is a concept related to linguistic approaches to understanding acquisition and was formalized in the Projection Hypothesis by Helmut Zobl. What the hypothesis predicts is that because some structures are related by **markedness**, the learner may not need **positive evidence** (input) from the environment to know (implicitly, of course) that something exists. The learner's internal mechanisms can "project" it based on the data at hand. Normally, this means that the learner's mechanisms project from marked to unmarked or lesser marked features. So, if Z is more marked than T and the two are related, once the learner acquires Z, the learner can infer that T exists even if T hasn't appeared in the input. We can take a concrete example from relative clauses. Relative clauses exist in a markedness relationship, and there is a well-known hierarchy that lists them from unmarked to most marked (see **markedness** for a definition):

- subject relative clause: Tom is the man *who studied SLA*;
- object relative clause: SLA is the subject *that Tom studied*;
- indirect object relative clause: Tom is the guy *who I gave the SLA book to*;
- object of preposition clause: Tom is the guy *who I studied SLA with*;
- genitive clause: Tom is the guy *whose SLA book I borrowed*;
- object of comparison clause: Tom is the guy *who I am taller than*.

Under the Projection Hypothesis, when learners encounter and acquire genitive relative clauses, their grammars can project the existence of everything from subject relative clauses to object relative clauses if any of these have not been acquired. Note that projection is unidirectional: a grammar can only project from more marked to lesser marked. Thus, learners cannot project the existence of genitive clauses if they have acquired object clauses.

Zobl applied this concept to features related to **Universal Grammar**; however, since his initial hypothesis the concept of markedness within Universal Grammar has received little attention, largely because the theory of Universal Grammar has evolved. But within non-Universal Grammar–related structures, such as relative clauses and certain phonological contrasts, projection remains a valid construct. It has even been exploited in some experiments on instructed SLA. Susan Gass conducted an experiment in the early 1980s in which she taught learners more marked relative clauses. When she tested the learners afterwards, she found that they had projected lesser marked relative clauses that were absent in their pretest performance. Thus, learners' grammars could be affected by teaching more marked elements of language and letting the lesser marked ones get projected by the learners' own internal capacities.

Psycholinguistics 心理语言学

Psycholinguistics is a branch of psychology that investigates how people comprehend language as well as how people formulate messages in real time. Unlike formal linguistics, which is concerned with **competence** and **mental representation of language**, psycholinguistics is concerned with the performance side of things. However, it differs from **sociolinguistics** in that it does not concern itself with social factors that influence language use or language change. Child L1 acquisition research is often referred to as developmental psycholinguistics.

Although psycholinguistics has focused on things such as slips of the tongue, malapropisms, access of the mental **lexicon**, and speech formulation, one important area in psycholinguistic research is ambiguity resolution during real-time comprehension; that is, how listeners/readers make sense of something that could be interpreted in more than one way. This issue is an area within **parsing** research. As an example, the sentence *John saw Robert after he returned from Patagonia* is ambiguous in terms of who returned from Patagonia: Either John or Robert could have been in Patagonia. What do listeners/readers prefer as an interpretation in this instance? Did John return or was it Robert? In languages like Spanish and Italian, such ambiguity is more complicated because of the dual pronoun system. That is, Spanish and Italian have null and overt subject pronouns, whereas English only has overt pronouns. Thus, the same sentence could be in Spanish *Juan vio a Roberto después que regresó de Patagonia* or *despues que él regresó de*

Patagonia, with *él* being the overt subject pronoun. Do listeners/readers have a preference for how they interpret these pronouns in terms of who they refer to? Note that this is not the stuff of formal linguistics: From a syntactic perspective, these sentences are all legitimate, and there is nothing about **syntax** (e.g., **Universal Grammar**) that would dictate one interpretation over another. So, the resolution of ambiguity as a psycholinguistic phenomenon is due to something other than the formal properties of the subject pronouns of these statements.

In addition, psycholinguistics is concerned with the relative contribution of syntax, lexicon, and **semantics** in how sentences are interpreted. For example, does the listener rely exclusively on syntax until a problem is encountered and he or she has to "backtrack" to resolve an interpretation problem, or does the listener rely on syntax, semantics, and lexicon in parallel fashion while parsing sentences?

The psycholinguistics of SLA has gained importance over the years. Scholars have been studying ambiguity resolution among L2 learners to see if they coincide with how L1 speakers resolve ambiguity. Work in **input processing** and **processability** are additional examples of areas within SLA that take a psycholinguistic approach. It is becoming increasingly clear in the field that both formal linguistics and psycholinguistics are needed to fully understand how learners come to have linguistic systems in another language. Some names associated with the psycholinguistics of SLA are Harald Clahsen, Paola E. Dussias, Cheryl Frenck-Mestre, and Bill VanPatten. Recent theories that incorporate psycholinguistics into discussions of L2 development include John Truscott and Michael Sharwood Smith's Acquisition by Processing, Harald Clahsen and Claudia Felser's Shallow Structures Hypothesis, and Susanne Carroll's Autonomous Induction Theory.

Recasts 重铸反馈

Recasts are restatements of learners' utterances that occur naturally in **interactions**. They usually occur when the learner has produced some kind of non-native-like utterance, and the other interlocutor is confirming what the learner intended to say, as a kind of confirmation check. For example, in the following interchange, the recast appears in italics. The two speakers are talking after an intramural tennis match for men's doubles, and one is inquiring about the other's partner (NS = native speaker; NNS = non-native speaker).

> NS: So where's Dave?
> NNS: He vacation.
> NS: *He's on vacation.*
> NNS: Yeah, on vacation.
> NS: Lucky guy.

The native speaker's recast in this example is a natural reaction that shows he understood what the learner meant. It was even said with a bit of rising intonation to indicate "Is this what you said?" Thus, it was a communicative event within the interaction. Unlike what teachers may do in classrooms, it was not intended as a correction.

However, recasts are classified in research under **negative evidence** as indirect negative evidence. This means that they are considered subtle indicators to learners that they have produced something less than target-like. The claim by proponents of recasts is that these communicative events can help focus learners' attention at a given time on something that is non-native-like and may aid in pushing acquisition along. But there is debate as to whether or not this is the case. Those who argue against any important role for recasts (and negative evidence more generally) have argued that recasts are infrequent and inconsistent, just as they are in child L1 acquisition situations. Thus, they cannot form an important part of acquisition for L2 learners. Scholars whose names are associated with recasts are Michael H. Long and Roy Lyster, among others. (See also **negotiation of meaning** and the Key Question **What** are the roles of input and output in SLA?)

Redundancy 羡余

Although redundancy is an everyday term, within linguistics and SLA, it takes on a particular use. Here we mean it to be the redundancy of grammatical features, that is, features that repeat themselves in an utterance or are copies of something else. We'll illustrate with several examples.

Our first example concerns grammatical features that are copies (redundant) of information provided lexically. In English, third-person -*s* is a redundant feature as far as person-number is concerned. Because English almost invariably includes either a subject or a subject pronoun, third-person -*s* on the verb is redundant: It marks the same information. Thus, *John* includes information that we are talking about a third-person singular and so does *talks* in the following sentence: *John talks too much.* As an additional example, past tense markers such as -*ed* in English can be redundant, as when they co-occur with an adverbial that expresses a past time reference: *Yesterday John talked a lot.* In this sentence, *yesterday* encodes pastness and thus -*ed* is redundant. This situation contrasts with -*ing* as a signal of progressive aspect (i.e., an action in progress). Note that in the following sentence, there is nothing else in the utterance that signals that the action is in progress: *Quiet! John is talking.* -*ing* carries the sole burden of providing this information.

Redundancy need not occur solely with lexical items. A grammatical feature can be redundant, say, due to word order. For example, let's say that a language has a normal or expected word order of subject-verb-object. At the same time, that language marks nouns or their articles for case (e.g., nominative case = subject, accusative case = object). Because subject-verb-object is the expected and normal order, marking nouns for case becomes redundant; the word order tells us who did what to whom. This does not mean case markings are always redundant. In many languages with case marking, word order can be inverted to object-verb-subject or some other permutation, depending on context and discourse. In such cases, then, case marking ceases to be redundant as word order is not the reliable indicator of who did what to whom.

So far, our examples have been of grammatical features that are redundant markers of meaning or semantic information (e.g., "in progress" contrasts meaningfully with "is completed" or "happens every day"; "pastness" contrasts meaningfully with "present" or "future"; case indicates who did what to whom). Some grammatical markers are redundant and do not carry meaning. An example comes from Spanish. Spanish, like all Romance languages, has grammatical gender. Thus, *el auto* is masculine but *la casa* is feminine. There is nothing semantic or meaningful about gender; it is a purely grammatical concept. Redundancy comes in because adjectives and determiners must agree with the noun, as in *Esa casa blanca es vieja* "That white house is old." Here, the feature of gender (feminine) is copied onto the determiner (the demonstrative *esa*) and two adjectives (*blanca* and *vieja*).

Interestingly, redundancy is the norm for grammatical markings; that is, the majority of them tend to be redundant and few aren't. Redundancy has been shown to be an issue in SLA because redundant features experience delayed acquisition compared to non-redundant features. And redundant features that don't carry meaning are the most delayed. Redundancy is an important aspect of **input processing** as well as some other models of acquisition.

Regularization 规则化

Regularization, a term related to **overgeneralization**, is concerned with how learners in both first and second language acquisition treat irregular forms or exceptional rules. It is common in both L1 and L2 contexts for learners to regularize the irregular past tense forms, and both children and adults produce such things as *wented* and *goed* instead of *went* at a particular stage of acquisition. Although many teachers may view such things as errors, in terms of SLA they are viewed as progress. Such forms show that the regular past tense endings, which were most likely missing in an earlier stage (e.g., the learner said "talk" instead of "talked"), are now firmly entrenched in the learner's grammar.

Outside of SLA, regularization is an attested phenomenon of language change and historical linguistics. Much of language change over time is a result of regularization, as speakers (particularly undereducated or illiterate speakers, but not always) begin to weed out irregularities. In contemporary English, there is vacillation between such forms as *dived/ dove* and *strived/strove*, for example, and it is not atypical for a native speaker to sometimes stop and check himself or herself when trying to use the past tense or even past participle of these and other verbs. This is because languages are living things whose evolution continues with each generation of speakers. In some dialects of English, *was* has replaced *were* ("So we was walkin' down the street mindin' our own business ...") as these speakers regularize the past tense of *be*. Although regularization is most easily exemplified in what happens to verbal inflections, regularization can and does happen in all parts of language, including syntax. Regularization is thus not surprising or unexpected in an L2 context. (See also the Key Question **What does development look like?**)

Reinforcement 强化

Reinforcement is most associated with **behaviorism** and involves the kind of feedback learners get from their environment. In the days when language was seen as stimulus-response, the response was the reinforcement. Both L1 and L2 learners were believed to get either positive reinforcement or negative reinforcement. Positive reinforcement was continued conversation, looks of approval, and verbal reactions such as "very good" and others. Negative reinforcement was interrupted conversation or problematic comprehension on the part of the person listening to the learner, looks of disapproval, and verbal reactions such as "No, say it this way," among others.

Under current psychological accounts of language acquisition (which differ from linguistic accounts), strengthening has replaced reinforcement. Learners build up linguistic information that consists of connections between things. Each time the learner hears the same thing in the input, a connection is strengthened. Each time the learner uses a connection successfully, it is strengthened. Strengthening is thus tied to frequency; more frequent linguistic items get stronger connections in the mind/brain. Less frequent items get weaker connections. This is one way in which psychologists explain **regularization,** the elimination of irregular forms and rules. In the examples from past tense, forms such as *went* and *had* are highly frequent and tend to stay in the language over generations. They have strong connections in speakers' minds/brains. Such is not the case for less frequent or highly infrequent words such as the past tense of *dive*. Is it *dove* or *dived*? Native speakers of English will vacillate because the connections in the mind/brain for these forms are much weaker compared to *went* and *had*, for example.

In the L2 context, reinforcement has fallen to the wayside as a construct, but strengthening has not. Those who take psychological approaches will often talk of strong and weak connections in SLA as well as the nature of strengthening as a process. Scholars associated with these concepts include Nick Ellis and Judith Kroll.

Repetition 重复

Repetition in SLA refers to either a learning strategy or a teaching strategy. As a learning strategy, it refers to learner self-generated repetition—for example, when studying grammar or vocabulary. As a teaching strategy, repetition was a widely popular technique used under audio-lingual methodology, and teachers still use it today to varying degrees as part of their eclectic approaches. Some self-study programs (e.g., using CDs or computer software) may build in repetition as a feature of student practice.

Repetition as a means for developing a mental representation of language is suspect, given that such a representation is built on how learners engage input and not on any kind of output practice they engage in, especially repetition. Research on the contribution of repetition to more general proficiency and skill development also leads us to think that this technique is suspect, if not useless overall. In some cases, the research shows only the slightest contribution. In other cases, repetition negatively correlates with proficiency. The reason for the lack of effects of repetition on acquisition of both competence and skill may lie in the process of repetition itself. Because repetition is a meaningless activity (i.e., there is no communication of information), it lacks a basic requirement for the kind of activity that contributes to acquisition. Acquisition occurs because of learner engagement with processing meaningful language in some kind of communicative context, in or out of classrooms. Also, repetition may aid the development of **explicit knowledge** in the short run, and explicit knowledge exists as a separate system from the implicit knowledge that forms competence.

Restructuring 重构

Under cognitive approaches to language acquisition, as learners' internal grammars (mental representations, competences) evolve, they may undergo restructuring. What this means is that as a piece of new data is processed and accommodated by the developing grammatical system, that piece of data may have repercussions for the grammar. In most cases, this means that learners move from exemplar-based knowledge (knowledge in which only examples exist in the system and not rules) to rule-based system. U-shaped learning curves (see **U-shaped acquisitions**) are a classic example of restructuring. When U-shaped learning happens, learners seem to unlearn something as they incorporate new data. For example, when regular past tense endings are processed and make their way into the system, we begin to see a decline in learners' accuracy with previously acquired irregular forms. Thus, *went* may become *wented* or even *goed*. In order to accommodate the newly acquired feature of *-ed*, the system restructures itself. In this particular case, the restructuring is reflected in **regularization** or **overgeneralization**. At the same time, we see the shift from an exemplar-based system to a rule-based system. Irregular past tense verbs exist as lexical items and aren't formed by any rules. When the regular past tense ending enters the system, it spreads as a rule throughout the concept of "pastness," and thus even irregulars become subject to a rule. This is what cognitivists mean by moving from exemplar- to rule- based systems. The name most associated with the concept of restructuring is Barry McLaughlin.

Salience 突出性

Salience is one of those concepts that escapes easy description or definition. In general, salience refers to the degree to which something stands out in the crowd or catches a person's attention. In linguistics and language acquisition, salience is used to talk about grammatical features and to what extent they catch a person's eye or ear. The problem in its definition is that we are not completely sure what contributes to salience. Some of the features purported to underlie salience follow.

Salience could be a result of phonological properties. In general, features that carry stress are said to be more salient than those that do not. Thus, salience is partly tied to syllabicity as only syllables (units with a vowel) can carry stress. So, we would say that verb inflections that are syllabic are more salient than those that are not and those inflections that carry stress are more salient than those that do not carry stress. Other phonological properties that could be associated with salience are pitch and rhythm.

Somewhat related to phonological properties is the issue of location in words and sentences. Things that occur at the beginning of words and sentences are said to be more salient than things that occur in other positions. Following this, things that occur at the end of words and sentences are more salient than things that occur in the middle. More generally, some researchers have posited that it is pausing that makes something salient. That is, a word or feature that is bounded on one or more sides by a pause is more salient than one that is not. Because the beginnings and ends of sentences are bounded on at least one side by a pause, these positions are said to be more salient. But here's where salience as an operative construct becomes problematic. How do we compare an unstressed item at the beginning of a sentence to a stressed item in the middle? Is location more important than stress, or is it the other way around?

Some scholars have advocated that salience may relate to novel properties or features. That is, something that is new might receive attention or catch the eye/ear simply because it's new. At the same time, some scholars have suggested that similarity to L1 (making the feature closer to "old stuff") may contribute to salience; for example, words that sound like L1 words may be more salient for learners. Again, we are confronted with how salience might be operationalized for research or even exploited for teaching. What is the relative contribution of "novelty" compared with stress, location, rhythm, and so on, as discussed earlier?

Finally, researchers have asked the question to what degree learners control salience. Is salience, perhaps, a property that evolves because of the state of the learner's linguistic system and/or processing mechanisms? Could it be that something that otherwise might be salient is ignored in the input until the learner has reached a stage where it can be processed and incorporated into the linguistic system? If so, then what makes something salient?

The construct of salience has been applied in instructed SLA to written input via text enhancement. Text enhancement is a technique by which grammatical features are consistently highlighted in a text in some way by bolding, italicizing, capitalization, underlining, and other means. The idea is to make the feature more salient, thus drawing learner attention to it and increasing the likelihood that learners will notice and process it. For example, to make third-person -s more salient to learners, an instructor might give them reading passages that look like this:

> John like**s** SLA. He think**s** it is very interesting. He read**s** books on it, and he attend**s** lectures on SLA at the university. His roommate, Bob, disagree**s**. He think**s** SLA is boring. Bob studie**s** English literature.

Thus, by consistently bolding the third-person ending in these passages, the instructor presumably is making the inflection more salient.

Scaffolding 支架

Scaffolding is a term used to describe what happens in some interactions with both first and second language learners. Because such learners may not have the linguistic tools necessary to express their ideas, their interlocutors may sometimes help to build the conversation or topic by providing crucial bits of language. In this way, the more proficient speaker is providing assistance. An example follows (NNS = non-native speaker; NS = native speaker):

NNS: Look.

NS: Look? At what?

NNS (pointing): That.

NS: It's a bug.

NNS: Bug.

NS: Yeah, a bug. And it's crawling very slowly.

NNS: Crawling.

NS: Yeah, crawling slowly. Maybe it's looking for food.

In this interchange, what is worth noting is how much the NS talks to fill in what the NNS can't do. While the NNS is basically speaking in one-word utterances, the NS is speaking in full sentences, fleshing out the conversational topic and providing key linguistic information, such as vocabulary, at particular points. This is what is referred to as scaffolding.

Scaffolding has been claimed to assist learners' development. By providing needed language, scaffolding may increase the **salience** of some aspects of language, for example. Learners may be getting critical data at the right time, and because they are actively engaged in the conversation, they are paying attention to both what is said and how it is said. Some might claim, however, that scaffolding could delay acquisition. Learners could use scaffolding to compensate for weaknesses in their own productive abilities and thus rely on others to "do the work." Either way, scaffolding appears to be a normal part of interactions.

Second language 二语   foreign language 外语

Some people make the distinction between second and foreign language based on the context in which languages are learned. A second language is one that is learned where the language is spoken, such as English in the United States or Japanese in Japan. A foreign language is one that is learned (primarily in classrooms) where the language is not normally spoken, such as English in Japan and Japanese in Des Moines, Iowa. Although it is clear that the social contexts are different whether the language is spoken or not, and that the quantity and quality of input and interaction for the learner may be different in different contexts, it is also clear that the linguistic, psycholinguistic, and cognitive dimensions of language acquisition do not change depending on context. Thus, all learning contexts are grouped under one umbrella term, *second language acquisition*, for the purpose of theory and research.

Selective attention 选择性注意

Selective attention refers to how people attend to the stimuli around them. We are constantly bombarded by stimuli, both visual and auditory, and yet we keep from going crazy. This is because we have built-in filters so that when we focus on a task, we do not attend to unnecessary stimuli such as the buzzing of fluorescent lights overhead or traffic noise on the streets. However, even when focused on a task, we do not attend to and pick up all the information we have focused on. We select certain bits of information depending on a variety of factors, while other bits of information fall to the wayside. When approaching a traffic light, for example, we focus on the color of the light as well as the flow of traffic and may ignore the fact that a building on the right has a broken window even though the building is clearly within our peripheral vision. In short, in our daily lives selective attention is the norm. We filter out what we don't need at a given moment.

Some scholars working with cognition applied to SLA have used the construct of selective attention to discuss what learners do when processing language. Clearly, learners do not process all of the linguistic data that confront them at a given time. If so, acquisition would be much quicker than it is—in fact, almost instantaneous. As they do with everything else, learners focus on particular things depending on tasks, demands, prior knowledge, and a variety of other factors. They selectively attend to linguistic data. At this point, those working within a cognitive framework cannot predict what elements of language learners select and which ones go unattended, so the potential for spotting problems in language acquisition is limited. Under several accounts, early-stage learners selectively attend to vocabulary and chunks of the language that help them grasp meaning as quickly as possible, while ignoring grammatical devices that do not immediately aid them in getting meaning. How selective attention can be applied to later stages of acquisition is unclear. Selective attention is also used as a rationale for focus on form and grammatical intervention in classrooms. If learners are selectively attending to stimuli and filtering out linguistic data, then perhaps instruction can bring those data into the attentional realm. Researchers often associated with selective attention include Susan Gass, Peter Robinson, Richard Schmidt, and Bill VanPatten. (See also **attention** and **noticing**.)

Semantics 语义学

Semantics is a branch of linguistics related to **meaning**. In general, there are two kinds of semantics: lexical semantics and compositional semantics. Lexical semantics refers to the meanings of words, and compositional semantics refers to how more complex meanings are built up from simpler ones.

Lexical semantics involves the stuff of words. For example, we may all know what the verb *eat* means: someone or something consumes something. But note that animals can both feed and eat, but plants can only feed. Thus, there is something different about *eat* compared to *feed*. People working in lexical semantics would break down the meanings of these words and show that *eat* might require not only the feature [+animate] but also the feature [+animal] ("animal" entailing both +/– human). *Eat* is thus more restrictive in meaning than *feed*. Although lexical semantics is important for all words, its importance becomes especially clear with verbs. Compare *eat* with *seem*, for example. *Eat* requires some kind of agency or purposeful action: An "eater" must be involved. However, *seem* excludes any kind of agency: There is no "seemer." Instead, *seem* requires something else. This could be an experiencer, someone or something experiencing a condition, such as *John seems tired*. What lexical semantics tells us about verbs is that they are not all actions, they are not all states, they are not all processes, and thus they require different things. This may have an impact on how they are used grammatically and why there is an *eater* but no *seemer*. This, in turn, impacts **syntax**, making *The apple was eaten by John* possible but not **Tired was seemed by John.*

Compositional semantics tends to focus on sentences and is concerned with how the individual semantic components of a unit (e.g., words in a sentence) add up to make a meaning larger than any individual unit. For example, in *Mary hit the ball*, we have three divisible units of meaning: *Mary, hit, ball.* Each of these units "means something" but combined, they mean something in particular. For example, *hit* has a general meaning but can be used with a variety of nouns: *hit the button, hit the child, hit on my boyfriend,* and so on. However, it takes on a particular meaning in a particular context, as in *hit the ball.* This phrase, in turn, means something even more particular when combined with *Mary.* In addition, the composite of these sentences makes the most sense if the listener (reader) knows who Mary is and knows which ball is being talked about. (We are being necessarily simplistic in order to illustrate the basics of compositional semantics; the field is rather more complicated than what we can present here.)

The acquisition of semantics has received relatively scant attention in SLA research compared to things such as **syntax**, **phonology**, **morphology**, and even **pragmatics**. One area that has received some (but not a great deal) of attention is lexical semantics and its interface with syntax. Researchers are concerned with the L1 transfer of both semantic and syntactic properties of verbs and how this transfer impacts SLA. Two names associated with such issues are Alan Juffs and Eric Kellerman.

Sensitive period 敏感期

The concept of a sensitive period is related to—and, in part a reaction against—the notion of a critical period. Under the **Critical Period Hypothesis**, language acquisition is impossible after a biologically predetermined time frame, often said to be around puberty. Strictly speaking, prior to the "cutoff" point, successful language acquisition is possible; afterwards, it is not. Here we should be clear that successful language acquisition means access to and use of the specialized language mechanisms that each non-impaired child is born with. People who seek to acquire a second language after puberty, according to the CPH, do not have access to the same language acquisition mechanisms that children have. Thus, they must rely on other cognitive capabilities that are nonlinguistic in nature.

Those who advocate a sensitive period differ from those who advocate a strict critical period in that under a sensitive period, the cutoff point is not clear and loss of language-learning abilities is gradual. There is no "onset" or cutoff point. The sensitive period allows for more variation in **ultimate attainment** as well as variation in when we see age effects in learners. In a certain sense, then, the concept of a sensitive period is a weaker and less restrictive version of the critical period. Scholars who have worked extensively with the idea of both the critical and sensitive periods (for and against) are David Birdsong, Theo Bongaerts, Robert DeKeyser, and Julia Herschensohn, among others.

Silent Period 沉默期

The Silent Period is a term made popular by Steven Krashen in the early 1980s. It refers to the early stages of SLA during which learners may not produce any language at all or produce the most minimal language. The Silent Period is readily observable in child L2 learners and less so in older learners, largely because the communicative demands made on older learners from the beginning is greater (e.g., they may have to use the L2 on the job, they are in classrooms that demand production, people may simply expect adults to talk). According to Krashen, the language learner is building up competence during the Silent Period by actively listening and processing the input data around him or her. The learner needs not be speaking to be acquiring language. Transferred into language pedagogy under the Natural Approach, the recommendation was to allow learners to have a silent period in the early stages of classroom learning. Thus, students should not be forced to speak until they are ready to do so. Presumably, early forced speaking would raise the learner's levels of anxiety and other negative emotions, perhaps inhibiting acquisition more generally. In addition, the idea was that by forcing learners to speak before they are ready, they would learn to rely on L1 rules to produce utterances as a communicative strategy. This strategy, too, might impede language acquisition more generally.

The Silent Period is not a concept that one hears much these days outside of discussion of Krashen's **Monitor Theory** or outside of the Natural Approach. This does not mean that it is not a relevant concept or that the recommendations made under the Natural Approach are necessarily wrong. It may be more reflective of how the field of SLA has moved on to other issues since the early 1980s and how theory development has progressed since Krashen's proposals.

Skill/skills 技能

Skill refers to the ability to perform, and in SLA, skill is generally conceptualized as speaking, listening, reading, and writing. Skill entails the interaction of two concepts or features: accuracy and fluency. Accuracy refers to the ability to do something correctly, while fluency refers to the speed with which a person can do something. Theoretically, the features of accuracy and fluency can develop independently of each other so that someone could be highly accurate but exceedingly slow at doing something, or exceedingly fast but highly inaccurate. In reality, research on skill development has shown that the two tend to develop in tandem. As accuracy increases, so does speed. In classic skill learning research in educational psychology, there is a rapid increase in accuracy and speed at the outset. This increase tapers off relatively soon such that there is a much slower progression after the outset with a possible plateauing of performance after time (i.e., there is relatively no change in skill). Research in various domains of language use and language **processing** (e.g., real-time syntactic computation during comprehension of sentences), however, suggests that even very advanced L2 learners are often not as fast as native speakers at doing something, even if they are indistinguishable from native speakers in terms of accuracy.

Skill is said to develop with appropriate "practice." In terms of language learning, appropriate practice means doing the kinds of things from the outset that resemble what a person is supposed to do in the end. For speaking, to take one example, this means engaging in tasks from the outset that require a learner to make meaning while producing language, because speaking is generally about making meaning. Thus, mechanical drills in which the learner can function "in rote" do not move the learner toward the skill of speaking. Instead, tasks in which the learner must put together language to communicate an idea (language appropriate for the learner's level, to be sure) would constitute appropriate practice. The same would be true of reading. Reading aloud for the sake of pronunciation does not help reading skill. Reading skill develops by reading for meaning—engaging the text in some way for what it has to say.

Skill can be juxtaposed to underlying competence or **mental representation of language**. The latter refers to the "stuff" that learners have in their heads about language: the unconscious, implicit, and generally abstract knowledge of language. Skill in speaking (or writing) does not always demonstrate what is in this mental representation. A learner may know, for example, that *You should've come* and *You've come* are fine sentences in English, but **Should you've come?* as a question is not possible, and yet that learner might not produce contractions regularly like a native speaker. It is generally understood that learners always know (unconsciously) much more about language than what they produce, at least in terms of syntax. The name most associated with skill and skill development in SLA is Robert DeKeyser. (See also **Skill**

Acquisition Theory in the section **Key Theories and Frameworks in Second Language Acquisition**.)

Social factors 社会因素

Social factors are exactly what the term implies: factors related to social circumstances that may affect language acquisition. There are many these factors, and we provide just a few here. One such factor is the context of acquisition itself and the nature of the language being learned. Is the language spoken outside the home (i.e., in the community/ society)? And if so, is it a prestige language? Learners are more likely to gain greater proficiency with prestige languages than non-prestige languages. (Note that prestige language is tightly bound to context, and a prestige language in one domain may not be prestige in another.)

Another factor is social distance. How does the language learner perceive himself or herself vis-à-vis the speakers of the second language? Social proximity would mean that the learner perceives a certain "kinship" measured by such variables as level of education, socioeconomic class, or perhaps skin color. Social distance would mean that the learner perceives a lack of kinship. The prediction is that there would be an inverse relationship between social distance and proficiency: the greater the social distance, the lesser the proficiency. A related concept is perceived power relationships. A person perceived to be inferior in terms of social status and power may be in a more difficult position to attain higher levels of L2 ability.

One theme underlying all social factors is access to **input** and **interaction**. Because such great importance is put on both input and interaction in the acquisition of a second language, social factors can positively or negatively affect access to these key ingredients. Returning to social distance, for example, if a learner is socially distant from the L2 community, that learner will have fewer opportunities to get input and interaction. What is clear from the research on social factors, however, is that the predictive ability of the factors is not always supported. For example, it is possible that for a particular individual social distance is not a significant factor in the development of proficiency. Those who work in and study social context in language acquisition often claim that social factors interact, may cancel each other out, or one may prove to be more important in context A than in context B. In short, social factors have to be studied on the micro as well as macro level. One name associated with research on social factors in SLA is Jeff Siegal. (See also **sociolinguistics**.)

Sociolinguistics 社会语言学

Sociolinguistics is a branch of linguistics concerned with **social factors** that affect language use and to a certain extent, language change. Sociolinguists study, for example, how context affects the choices people make with language. People may speak differently in a formal context compared with how they speak in an informal context. They may speak differently to a superior than to a colleague. These adjustments affect **lexicon**, pronunciation, and sometimes even **syntax**. As an example, a person might say "You got any cash on you?" in one context but "Do have any change I can borrow?" in another. The person might use more *gonna*s in some contexts and more *going to*s in others.

Sociolinguists also study how group identity affects the choices that people make with language. When people strongly identify with a particular group, they may resist adopting the way another group speaks. Or, if they perceive that the way another group speaks is more prestigious, they may adopt aspects of that speech or try to emulate it. Factors that affect group identity include ethnicity, socioeconomic class, region, and age, among others. Groups may also be responsible for novel developments with language, especially lexicon. In short, sociolinguists are interested in how people adjust their language depending on who they speak with and are also interested in dialects and how they are used. Because people can and do adjust their language, sociolinguists often talk of **variability** or **variation** in language use.

Sociolinguists also study language in contact situations, such as bilingualism. They are interested in issues such as which language a person prefers to speak with which people, how code-switching (the use of two languages in the same conversation between two bilinguals) occurs, and how the contact between two languages influences the development of the languages themselves. Because bilinguals are not two monolinguals in one, they present interesting cases about "leakage" between languages in a person's mind, and bilingualism is an important ingredient in language change over time. For example, although Latin was bound to evolve like all languages do, successive generations of bilingualism with Latin and local languages throughout the Roman Empire accelerated the changes and pushed them in some directions as opposed to others. Thus, Spanish, French, Italian, Portuguese, and other Latin-originated languages are the products of internal and external (social) factors, including language contact due to bilingualism.

Sociolinguistics is relevant to SLA because of the importance attributed to social factors within SLA. However, strictly speaking, few scholars apply sociolinguistic methods of research to the L2 context these days. (For more discussion, see **variability**.)

Speech acts 言语行为

A speech act is related to what is called "speaker intent" and thus is part of **pragmatics** and **meaning**. When someone says something, that person is performing a kind of action. For example, person A says to person B "There's a bear sneaking up behind you." In terms of grammar, this is a declarative sentence. But person A intends to warn person B. Thus, the speech act is a warning. If person C says to person D "I'll kill you if you leave me," again in terms of grammar, we have a declarative sentence that is called an *if–then* sentence. As a speech act, it is a threat.

Traditionally, linguists talk of three kinds of speech acts: locutionary, illocutionary, and perlocutionary. Locutionary acts refer to grammar and pronunciation (e.g., a declarative sentence is a locutionary act). Illocutionary acts are those that attempt to communicate something like a promise, a warning, a compliment, a request, and so on. The examples given above are illocutionary acts. Perlocutionary acts are those that go beyond communication such as the use of language to frighten someone or the use of language to cajole someone into doing something. Thus, saying something like "He shouldn't get away with it," as part of goading someone to take revenge on someone else is a perlocutionary act.

Although pragmatics has occupied some interest in L2 research, it has not occupied the interest of scholars as much as the formal properties of language have. Thus, research on speech acts and how L2 learners realize them is not as common as research on, say, the role of **Universal Grammar** in SLA. However, pragmatics and speech acts would be indispensable tools for studying how learners communicate and the devices they use to do so.

Stabilization 稳定化

Stabilization is a concept related to development in SLA and refers to learners reaching a certain stage and apparently not progressing. Originally posited by Larry Selinker in his groundbreaking essay on **interlanguage**, stabilization is a precursor to **fossilization**. As such, stabilization means that a learner's linguistic system has begun to reach stasis and that fluctuation and **variation** are no longer the norm. If stabilization persists (becomes permanent), then the linguistic system is said to have fossilized. Development has ceased.

Over the years, researchers have concluded that it is inappropriate to talk of entire linguistic systems stabilizing (and fossilizing). Rather, subsystems may stabilize while others continue to develop and/or show variation in learner performance. Thus, a learner may evidence stabilization with morphological properties of language and yet show native-like development with syntax. In addition, some researchers have argued that fossilization is a difficult construct to support empirically (e.g., how long does a linguistic system or subsystem have to be stabilized before we say it is fossilized?). On the other hand, evidence for stabilization is abundant. These researchers claim, then, that stabilization avoids a number of methodological problems for research and is a more valid construct. Because stabilization is not seen as something permanent, researchers do not need to worry about length of time as a defining feature of the construct. Stabilization can last a short time or a long time. The idea is, however, that stabilized systems can change; there is no permanence with stabilization.

Stages of development 发展阶段
staged development 阶段性发展

See **developmental sequences**.

Subjacency 邻接

Subjacency is a syntactic term related to what is called movement. In syntactic theory, phrases are said to move from particular locations in a sentence to a position "higher up" in the sentence. For example, the verb *kicked* normally requires two arguments: an agent (the kicker) and a theme (the kickee). In English, these are usually realized as subjects and objects, respectively. In addition, subjects normally precede verbs in English while objects normally follow: *John kicked the ball.* When asking a *wh*-question about this particular event, we might say *What did John kick?* Intuitively, we know that *what* is an object in this sentence, and we can state the question another way: *John kicked what?* Clearly, these two forms of questions are related, and *what* is the object of the verb in each one. What syntacticians say is that in the *What did John kick?* version, the *what* has moved out of its normal position to occupy a position higher up in the sentence. This is called *wh*-movement.

However, there are restrictions on movement that keep phrases from traveling too far from their origin ("too far" meaning how many syntactic boundaries they cross). For example, *Who did Mary say that the man saw?* is fine but **Who did Mary meet the man who saw* is not fine. Hidden within the structure of these two sentences are syntactic boundaries, and in the bad sentence, there are too many for the *wh*-phrase to travel from its position behind the verb. It must remain "subjacent" to the verb, hence the term *subjacency*. Such movements are called subjacency violations. (The concept of subjacency has evolved over the years within **syntax**, but the general point about crossing syntactic boundaries has not.)

Subjacency has been an important focus of research within SLA. A number of studies have examined to what extent L2 learners can come to know about subjacency violations. Although from a theoretical perspective all languages are capable of allowing phrases to move, not all languages actually do move phrases around. In Chinese, for example, *Who did Mary see?* is not a possible sentence. It can only be said as *Mary saw who?* with the *wh*-phrase remaining in its position by the verb. The question of interest to SLA scholars is what happens with speakers of Chinese when they learn English. Clearly, they must learn that *wh*-phrases can move in order to form questions, but do they acquire the abstract knowledge related to subjacency? Do they come to learn that *Who did Mary meet the man who saw?* is not permissible in English? This is an important test case for the question of **parameters** and parameter resetting in SLA as L1 **transfer** can be ruled out as an intervening variable in the case of Chinese learners of English L2. A general review of the literature would yield a number of studies and analyses on this matter, and it would appear that learners can indeed acquire the subtle aspects of syntax related to subjacency, although not all do.

Syntax 句法

The study of syntax deals with sentence structure. Whether or not a sentence is well formed and why it is or isn't is the concern. For example, syntacticians are interested in why *Who do you wanna invite to the party?* is fine but **Who do you wanna fire John?* is not. Why is *wanna* fine in one instance but not in another? As another example, syntacticians want to know what brings about the differences in the placement of negation in French and English. French has post-verbal negation as in *Jean ne boit* **pas** *de bière*, whereas English has preverbal negation with main verbs *John does* not *drink beer* and post-verbal negation with copular verbs and auxiliaries: *John has* **not** *drunk any beer* and *John is* **not** *a drunk*. Neither language can do what the other does: **Je ne* **pas** *boit de bière* and **John drinks* **not** *beer*. Why is this?

For the layperson, syntax deals with transparent and ordinary matters dealing with "good use of language" such as *who* versus *whom* and the avoidance of *ain't*. But syntacticians are not concerned with "good use" of language; they are concerned with what a language actually allows and disallows. So, while people may say *ain't* is not good language use, the syntactician notes that people can and do use *ain't* but that there are restrictions on well formedness with *ain't*. For example, *He ain't got no sense* is fine but *He ain't have no sense* sounds weird at best. So, even "bad language" has properties that must obey syntactic rules.

The dominant approach to syntax today is generative syntax, founded by Noam Chomsky. In the Chomskyan approach, scholars believe that there are universal properties of language that all human languages must obey. These are called **principles**. Scholars also believe that there are dimensions on which languages vary, these dimensions being sanctioned by principles of language. These variations are called **parameters**. The goal of syntactic research is to uncover these principles and parameters to account for language behavior. Many of these principles involve abstract constructs that a person does not readily see in everyday examples of language. They're there, but we have to look for them. The study of syntax, then, involves peeling back the layers of language to find the "hidden stuff" that regulates sentence structure. (See also **Universal Grammar**, **mental representation of language**, and **competence**.)

To be sure, there are non-Chomskyan approaches to syntax. Three of these are Lexical Functional Grammar, Cognitive Grammar, and Construction Grammar. These latter approaches are more popular among linguists who are interested in how people speak or how they come to make meaning with grammar. Chomskyan approaches are more concerned with the abstract implicit knowledge system that speakers have in their head and much less with how people use language to communicate information.

Systematicity 系统性

Systematicity refers to behavior in which learners perform consistently with a particular form or structure. For systematic behavior to occur, the learner does not have to be accurate; the learner just has to be consistent. So, for example, if a learner is in the early stages of the acquisition of negation and consistently produces structures of the type no + X (e.g., *no drink beer, no want go, no like soup*), we would say that behavior is systematic. Systematicity stands in contrast to **variability/variation**, in which learner behavior with a particular form or structure is not consistent.

Target-like use 类似目的语的用法

Target-like use is concerned with how learners perform with particular features of language and is mostly associated with **morpheme studies** and **acquisition orders**. When learners use language, they create what are called obligatory occasions for use. For example, the moment a learner begins a sentence with a third-person subject, that learner is creating an obligatory occasion for third-person -s. The minute the learner creates an utterance with -ing, that learner is creating an obligatory occasion for auxiliary be.

In the early days of research on acquisition orders and morphemes, researchers tended to count obligatory occasions and then note the percentage of suppliance of the obligatory item. Thus, a score of 70 percent for past tense -ed meant that the learner supplied past tense -ed in 70 percent of the occasions in which it was required. A major criticism of this scoring technique was that it ignored the use of morphemes in incorrect environments (e.g., **overgeneralizations**). What if a learner scores 95 percent with past tense -ed, and yet if we look at the data more closely, we see such things as *He didn't liked it too much*, in which the past tense marker is added to the main verb *like* when it shouldn't be? Or what if the learner has overgeneralized to the irregulars and is producing items such as *wented* and *eated*? The 95 percent score sounds like the learner has the past tense marker under control, and yet we see evidence that this particular learner doesn't have it under control.

This challenge to accuracy scores was met by Teresa Pica in her target-like use analysis in the early 1980s. She piloted a scoring method in which the occasions in which learners used a morpheme incorrectly were added to those in which learners used them correctly. She then used the result of this addition as the denominator in her calculation of the percentage of correct use. This method of scoring learner performance was viewed as a major improvement over the simple accuracy score.

Task 任务

A task in second language acquisition can be defined as an activity with the following prerequisites: the meaning is the main focus; there is some communication problem that learners needs to solve; and the task must relate to a real-world situation. Usually learners are asked to perform tasks using a number of language skills: listening, speaking, reading or writing, or any combination of them. It is crucial to distinguish between a "language task" and a language practical "exercise" which mainly requires a primary focus on form rather than meaning. These practical exercises usually ask L2 learners to manipulate language given to them rather than to attempt to communicate using their own linguistic and nonlinguistic resources. Three very common types of tasks found in second language research are: information-gap tasks; opinion-gap tasks; and collaborative output tasks. Researchers have used tasks to measure whether particular tasks can facilitate second language acquisition processes considering factors such as type of tasks, real-time processing, and complexity. In instructed SLA research, names associated with this research are Martin Bygate, Michael Long, Peter Skehan, Virginia Samuda, David Nunan, and Pauline Foster.

Teachability 可教性

Teachability is a concept related to Manfred Pienemann's work on **processability** and the development of output processing procedures. According to the theory, learners develop the ability to produce certain kinds of grammatical structures over time in a hierarchical order. What this means is that learners progress from stage 1 to stage 2 to stage 3, and so on, with each stage implying the learner has traversed the stages below it—but not necessarily the stages above it. Thus, if we collect data and find evidence of stage 3 behavior in a learner, we can infer he or she has passed through stages 1 and 2 but we cannot infer that he or she is at stage 4.

Each stage is marked by particular processing procedures (described under **processability**), and a learner must have acquired the processing procedure for each stage before going on to the next stage. The theory holds that learners cannot skip stages and thus cannot acquire processing procedures for which they are not ready. Thus, a learner cannot skip stage

4 and go from stage 3 to stage 5. That learner cannot skip the processing procedures of stage 4 to acquire those at stage 5.

This restriction on staged development and that the processing procedures for each stage are hierarchically ordered have implications for language teaching. Because learners cannot skip stages, they cannot learn and spontaneously produce grammatical structures for which they are not ready in terms of processing procedures. Teachability, then, refers to the idea that the effects of instruction are also constrained. Instruction in grammar can only make a difference if the learner is at the point at which he or she would naturally acquire the processing procedure needed to produce the grammatical structure in question. In his research, Manfred Pienemann offers evidence that this is so. Learners taught structures that were too far beyond their current level of processing ability did not acquire the structures in question. In some cases, learners backslid (i.e., regressed to a previous stage), suggesting they were cognitively overloaded by the processing demands of the new structure. (See the Key Question **Does instruction make a difference?**)

Tense 时

As a linguistic term, tense refers to the relative temporal reference of an event. Simply put, tense refers to whether an event occurs in the present, the past, or the future. Within each of these time frames there can be indications of other things. For example, in the past we can indicate anteriority with *had* + participle in English, as in *John had eaten by the time I arrived*. But both *had eaten* and *arrived* occurred in the past. In the future, we can do the same, as in *By the time I arrive, John will have eaten*. Both *arrive* and *will have eaten* fall within the scope of future events. In pedagogical grammars, tense is sometimes used loosely to refer to verbal features, which is a bit misleading. In the Romance languages, for example, one often hears of the preterit and imperfect tenses used to narrate past events.

However, strictly speaking, preterit (e.g., something equivalent to *ate*) and imperfect (e.g., something equivalent to *was eating*) are not distinct tenses but ways of reporting events with the same tense, in this case, the past (see **aspect**). The same would be true of the present, as in the difference between *I generally eat at 5:00* and *I am eating right now*. In both cases, *eat* and *am eating* fall within the present tense, but they are two ways of reporting different kinds of present tense events.

The Shallow Structure Hypothesis 浅结构假说

The Shallow Structure Hypothesis (SSH) is concerned with the ability of second language learners to create full syntactic representations during **parsing**. The SSH acknowledges that native speakers may either parse sentences with full syntactic representation ("deep" or "detailed" processing) or parse them without full syntactic representation ("shallow" or "less detailed" processing). A classic example involves parsing complex sentences in which question words as *who, which*, and so on, have moved out of one spot of the sentence into a high spot leaving "gaps" along the way. An example is the following in which the *who* has moved out of the lowest spot, landed somewhere else, and then moved up to the highest spot possible in the sentence. Its origin and landing spots are represented by the blank line ___: *The captain who the officer decided ___ that the young adult soldier had displeased ___ will write a formal report next week*. Native speakers make use of the hidden information contained in these gaps to process and comprehend the sentence. However, the SSH claims that non-natives are prone to shallow processing and may even rely exclusively on it. This does not mean that non-native speakers cannot successfully comprehend the sentence, but they may do so relying on non-syntactic information. The scholars most associated with the SSH are Harald Clahsen and Claudia Felser.

Transfer 迁移

In SLA, transfer refers to a psychological process by which learners rely on the L1 system to construct the L2 system. Generally speaking, this reliance means that the learner unconsciously assumes that the L2 is like the L1, and thus the mechanisms responsible for language acquisition use the L1 as the starting point. In its original conceptualization, transfer was seen as a process that acted on both productive and receptive processes, that is, in speaking/writing and reading/listening as these relate to acquisition. However, transfer as a concept has changed as has the role of L1 in SLA. Sketched here are the major phases:

- *Pre-SLA research*: under **behaviorism**, transfer was seen as rampant; it underlay every aspect of acquisition, and the L1 was seen as the major problem to overcome;
- *Early SLA research*: with the appearance of the **morpheme studies** and **acquisition order** in the 1970s, transfer came into question; it was seen as much less important;
- *1980s*: transfer as a concept was revived and gained ground in importance, but at the same time, scholars suggested that it was constrained by universal aspects of language (e.g., **markedness**);
- *Post-1980s*: although SLA specialists generally rejected behaviorism, the field saw a resurgence of transfer as a major component of SLA, especially from those who took a linguistic perspective on acquisition as well as those who took a processing perspective. However, under Processability Theory (see **processability**), transfer remains constrained.

Truth-value tasks 真值判断任务

A truth-value task is often used to test people's underlying **mental representation** of syntax and morphology. In this kind of task, the participant hears or reads a short narrative and then decides if the sentence that follows is logical or not. An example is the following in

Spanish (translation provided), in which participants are asked whether the comment made by the character is logical: *Mencha cumple años el viernes. Desea recibir muchos regalos. Mencha dice: "Quiero que reciba muchos regalos."* (Mencha is having a birthday on Friday. She hopes to get lots of gifts. Mencha says: "I want (someone) to receive lots of gifts.") In this example, Mencha's comment is not logical because in Spanish an embedded clause with a tensed verb in the subjunctive only makes sense if Mencha is talking about someone else. To make sense, the comment should be *Quiero recibir muchos regalos.* The crucial point here is that both comments are grammatical sentences, but only one makes sense in this context. Here the researchers were testing learners' underlying knowledge about the subjunctive and constraints on interpretation of null subjects. (This example comes from research conducted by Joyce Bruhn de Garavito.)

Typological universals 类型共性

Within the framework of **Universal Grammar**, universals are abstract **principles** that apply to all languages. These are generally derived by deduction as scholars examine how a language behaves and then posit generalizations that can later be checked against other languages. In the framework of linguistic typology, however, universals are less abstract and are based on readily observable data. Such universals are determined by surveying world's languages and then arriving at a conclusion about what might constitute a universal. An example of a typological universal is something like the following: *in languages with prepositions, the genitive almost always follows the governing noun, while in languages with postpositions, it almost always precedes the noun.*

Other typological universals are implicational in nature. That is, what the universal states is that if X is present, Y is also present—but not necessarily the other way around. Thus, X implies Y, but Y does not necessarily imply X. An example would be voiced consonants. If a language has voiced consonants, it must have voiceless consonants. However, the presence of voiceless consonants does not necessarily imply the existence of voiced consonants. An example from sentence structure would be relative clauses. The existence of object relative clauses (*the man who I followed*) implies the existence of subject relative clauses (*the man who followed me*). But subject relative clauses do not imply object relative clauses. Linguists most associated with typological universals are Joseph Greenberg and Bernard Comrie, among others.

Typological universals are important in SLA research because research has demonstrated that L2 learners' linguistic systems seem to obey typological universals during development, and such universals may even constrain their development, especially constraining the influence of the L1. For example, learners may acquire subject relative clauses before object relative clauses but never object relative clauses before subject relative clauses. Or, they may produce more errors with object relative clauses than with subject relative clauses. Learners might have more difficulty with the production of voiced consonants at the ends of words than voiceless consonants, and we would expect words ending in voiceless consonants to be "easier" to acquire and produce than words ending in voiced consonants. In SLA research, the names most associated with the application of typological universals to research are Fred Eckman and Susan Gass. (See also **markedness**.)

Ultimate attainment 最终习得状态

Ultimate attainment refers to the point at which learners seem to stop progressing. We say that their grammar (linguistic system) has reached stasis. Ultimate attainment for all unimpaired L1 learners is a native system. The great question in SLA is whether L2 learners' ultimate attainment can be native-like or whether it will always be different in some way from what native speakers possess as a linguistic system. Concepts integral to the notion of ultimate attainment include **fossilization** and **stabilization** (see also **Can L2 learners become native-like?**).

Universal Grammar 普遍语法

Within the linguistic tradition—at least since Noam Chomsky's arrival on the scene in the 1950s—has been the idea that children do not come to the task of language acquisition as *tabulae rasae*. That is, children are not blank slates upon which linguistic data imprint themselves. They are not little mimics who merely repeat what they hear around them. Instead, children are seen to be active creators of a linguistic system and are guided by innate knowledge called **Universal Grammar**. The role of Universal Grammar is to constrain and guide acquisition, to limit the "hypotheses" that children can make about how language behaves. Universal Grammar is innate, meaning that children are born with Universal Grammar as part of their biological makeup. The human species is thus DNA-coded for language.

Universal Grammar consists of abstract **principles** as well as variations on principles called **parameters**. An example of a principle might be "All sentences must have subjects that have a particular structural relationship to verbs." (The structural relationship is an abstract notion defined by Universal Grammar.) A parameter related to this principle might be "Languages may allow null subjects. If they do, then X, Y, and Z must happen. If they do not allow null subjects, then X, Y, and Z don't happen." Null subjects refers to the absence of overt subject pronouns, such as in Spanish, Italian, and Arabic, where a simple verb *habla* means "he speaks" and no overt "he" is needed. (We will ignore X, Y, and Z in order to not get swamped by technical details about the null subject parameter.) Thus, both principles and parameters account for the variation we see in the world's languages. For example, let's imagine there are ten principles (there are more in actuality). Let's further imagine that these ten principles all have some kind of parametric variation such that there are *a* and *b* versions of each. This would mean that just with these ten principles with their two variations each, we can account for $2 \times 2 \times 2 \times 2 \times 2 \times 2 \times 2 \times 2 \times 2 \times 2 = 1{,}024$ possible languages.

If we take the case of sentential subjects, children are born "knowing" that languages require subjects. They are not born knowing, however, that the language they are learning is a null subject language or not a null subject language. Linguistic data they hear provide the evidence for the possibility of null subjects. Once the child's grammar determines the language is null subject, X, Y, and Z are automatically "triggered" as additional properties of the grammar. This kind of process greatly reduces the time it would take to learn languages and constrains the development of the child's grammar. This is why children make only certain possible errors while not making other equally possible errors if they were, say, merely calculating frequencies or making hypotheses based on linear word order. (See also **innatist position**, as well as **Universal Grammar and Linguistic Theory** in the section **Key Theories and Frameworks in Second Language Acquisition**.)

Although Universal Grammar is pretty much accepted as part of the child's L1 language making capacity, its status in SLA has been hotly debated. Some have taken the side that it is completely available to L2 learners, others that it is not available at all, and still others take various middle positions. Many scholars are associated with the application of Universal Grammar to SLA research including Lydia White, Julia Herschensohn, Bonnie Schwartz, and Rex Sprouse. An excellent overview is Lydia White's 2003 book *Second Language Acquisition and Universal Grammar*. (See also the Key Questions **Is there a critical period?** and **What constraints are there on acquisition?**)

Uptake 领会

Uptake is a term used in research on interaction, recasts, and other related phenomena to describe a particular learner behavior. During interaction, learners sometimes receive some kind of indication that their conversational partners may not have understood something correctly (see **negative evidence**). Uptake refers to learners' immediate reactions to such indications. For example, in the following interchange, the NS (native speaker) signals something to the NNS (non-native speaker) by recasting what the learner said and putting it in native-like form.

> NNS: And so he buy a car.
> NS: *He bought a car!*
> NNS: Yes, he bought a car.
> NS: Wow, how nice.

In this interchange, the uptake is the learner's response in which he says "Yes, he bought a car." His response signals that he noticed the correct past tense form of *buy*.

Uptake is generally differentiated from **intake**. Uptake is always visibly manifested in learner behavior during interaction. However, intake is something that occurs in the learner's mind and is normally not readily observable.

U-shaped acquisition U 型发展

U-shaped acquisition, also known as U-shaped behavior, is a particular kind of developmental pattern. During U-shaped acquisition, learners' performance suggests they are doing something rather well. Then, there is a drop-off during which their performance indicates a loss of ability or knowledge. Subsequently, they regain the ability or knowledge. When plotted over time, the graph of accuracy looks like that in the figure below, with a U-shape to it.

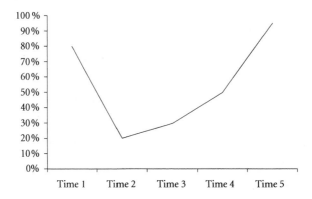

A classic example of U-shaped acquisition is the acquisition of irregular past tense forms in English. Both children and adults (in L1 and L2 situations) begin by producing highly frequent irregular forms correctly: for example, *went, ate*. As they begin to acquire regular past tense forms, learners go through a process of **regularization** and begin to produce incorrect irregular past tense forms such as *wented/goed, eated/ated*. With time, they reacquire the correct irregular forms.

Variability/variation 变异

As learners produce language, they may not be consistent in what they do. Although sometimes they might produce a form or structure accurately in a consistent manner or they might produce it inaccurately in a consistent manner, very often learners vacillate. That is, during a given time frame, they may produce something both accurately and inaccurately, and even their inaccurate productions might vary in terms of what they produce. This behavior is known as variability or variation in the **interlanguage**. For example, a learner might produce the following two utterances during the same game of bingo: *No look my card* and *Don't look my card* (from a study by Rod Ellis). Variability and variation stand in contrast to systematicity, that is, when learners are consistent in what they do. At the same time, there can be what is called systematic variation. This occurs when the learner uses two versions of the same form or structure but under two different conditions or meanings. Thus, one variation does not occur where the other does.

The source of variability has been hotly debated, as has its status as a theoretical construct. For various reasons, it has fallen from the focus of SLA inquiry, having reached its peak as an object of study in the 1980s. This does not mean, however, that variability does not exist in learner production. Clearly, it does. The name most associated with variation is Elaine Tarone.

Working memory 工作记忆

Working memory is a psychological construct that refers to the "processing space" in the mind/brain when a person computes information. The term has replaced the older and now outdated concept of short-term memory. Working memory is, for example, where listeners fleetingly store and process linguistic data to analyze it for comprehension. There are multiple theories and models of working memory, but what they all have in common is the idea that working memory has a limited capacity. That is, a person can only process and store in working memory a limited amount of information before it must be dumped so that the person can continue processing new incoming information. Working memory has been explored most in the context of comprehension.

Working memory has become a semi-important construct within SLA since the 1990s. One idea is that because working memory capacity varies from individual to individual, this might account for differential outcomes in terms of rate of acquisition. If person X has greater working memory capacity compared to person Y, then X should acquire language faster. This follows from the fact that acquisition is input-dependent and also comprehension-dependent; people have to comprehend input in order to acquire language. Those who can comprehend more at a given time ought to be able to acquire language more quickly than others. Whether this is true or not is a matter of research. Working memory, then, has become one of a number of factors related to **individual differences**.

Key Readings

Andersen, R. W. (1991). Developmental sequences: The emergence of aspect marking in second language acquisition. In T. Huebner & C. Ferguson (Eds.), *Crosscurrents in second language acquisition and linguistic theories* (pp. 305–324). Amsterdam: John Benjamins.

Andersen, R. W., & Shirai, Y. (1996). The primacy of aspect in first and second language acquisition: The pidgin-creole connection. In W. C. Ritchie & T. K. Bhatia (Eds.), *Handbook of Second Language Acquisition* (pp. 527–570). San Diego, CA: Academic Press.

Anderson, J. (1982). Acquisition of cognitive skill. *Psychological Review, 89,* 369–406.

Anderson, J. (2000). *Learning and Memory: An Integrated Approach.* 2nd edition. New York: John Wiley & Sons.

Archibald, J. (1998). Second language phonology, phonetics, and typology. *Studies in Second Language Acquisition, 20,* 189–211.

Bachman, L. F., & Palmer, A. S. (1996). *Language Testing in Practice.* Oxford: Oxford University Press.

Bailey, N., Madden, C., & Krashen, S. (1974). Is there a natural sequence in adult second language acquisition? *Language Learning, 24,* 235–243.

Bardovi-Harlig, K. (1999). The interlanguage of interlanguage pragmatics: A research agenda for acquisitional pragmatics. *Language Learning, 49,* 677–713.

Bardovi-Harlig, K. (2000). *Tense and Aspect in Second Language Acquisition: Form, Meaning and Use.* Oxford: Blackwell.

Bardovi-Harlig, K., Félix-Brasdefer, C., & Omar, A. S. (Eds.) (2006). *Pragmatics and Language Learning L1.* Honolulu: University of Hawai'i, National Foreign Language Resource Center.

Benati, A., & Lee, J. F. (2008). *Grammar Acquisition and Processing Instruction: Secondary and Cumulative Effects.* Clevedon: Multilingual Matters.

Benati, A., & Lee, J. F. (2015). Processing instruction: New insights after twenty years of theory, research and application. Special Issue in the *International Review of Applied Linguistics in Language Teaching, 53.*

Bialystok, E. (1990). *Communication Strategies.* Oxford: Blackwell.

Bialystok, E., & Hakuta, K. (1994). *In Other Words: The Science and Psychology of Second Language Acquisition.* New York: Basic Books.

Bickerton, D. (1988). Creole languages and the bioprogram. In F. Newmeyer (Ed.), *Linguistics: The Cambridge Survey* (pp. 267–284). Cambridge: Cambridge University Press.

Bickerton, D. (1990). *Language and Species.* Chicago: University of Chicago Press.

Bickerton, D. (2008). *Bastard Tongues.* New York: Hill and Wang.

Birdsong, D. (1992). Ultimate attainment in second language acquisition. *Language, 68,* 706–755.

Birdsong, D. (Ed.) (1999). *Second Language Acquisition and the Critical Period Hypothesis.* Mahwah, NJ: Lawrence Erlbaum.

Birdsong, D. (2005). Interpreting age effects in second language acquisition. In J. Kroll., & A. M. B. de Groot (Eds.), *Handbook of*

Bilingualism: Psycho-linguistic Approaches (pp. 109–127). Oxford: Oxford University Press.

Bley-Vroman, R. (1989). What is the logical problem of foreign language learning? In S. M. Gass & J. Schachter (Eds.), *Linguistic Perspectives on Second Language Acquisition* (pp. 41–68). New York: Cambridge University Press.

Bongaerts, T. (1999). Ultimate attainment in L2 pronunciation: The case of very advanced late L2 learners. In D. Birdsong (Ed.), *Second Language Acquisition and the Critical Period Hypothesis* (pp. 133–159). Mahwah, NJ: Lawrence Erlbaum.

Bongaerts, T. (2005). Introduction: Ultimate attainment and the critical period hypothesis for second language acquisition. *International Review of Applied Linguistics, 43*, 259–267.

Canale, M., & Swain, M. (1980). Theoretical bases of communicative approaches to second language teaching and testing. *Applied Linguistics, 1*, 1–47.

Cancino, H., Rosansky, E. J., & Schumann, J. H. (1978). The acquisition of English negatives and interrogatives by native Spanish speakers. In E. Hatch (Ed.), *Second Language Acquisition: A Book of Readings* (pp. 207–230). Rowley, MA: Newbury House.

Carroll, J. B. (1981). Twenty-five years of research on foreign language aptitude. In K. C. Diller (Ed.), *Individual Differences and Universals in Language Learning Aptitude* (pp. 83–117). Rowley, MA: Newbury House.

Carroll, J. B., & Sapon, S. (1959). *Modern Language Aptitude Test-form A.* New York: Psychological Corporation.

Carroll, S. (2001). *Input and Evidence: The Raw Material of Second Language Acquisition.* Amsterdam: John Benjamins.

Cazden, C., Cancino, H., Rosansky, E., & Schumann, J. (1975). *Second Language Acquisition Sequences in Children, Adolescents, and*

Adults. Washington, DC: Final report submitted to the National Institute of Education.

Chamot, A. U., Barnhardt, S., El-Dinary, P. B., & Robbins, J. (1999). *The Learning Strategies Handbook*. New York: Longman.

Chomsky, N. (1959). A review of B. F. Skinner's *Verbal Behavior*. *Language, 35*, 26–58.

Chomsky, N. (1965). *Aspects of the Theory of Syntax*. Cambridge, MA: MIT Press.

Chomsky, N. (1995). *The Minimalist Program*. Cambridge, MA: MIT Press.

Clahsen, H. (1984). The acquisition of German word order: A test case for cognitive approaches to L2 development. In R. Andersen (Ed.), *Second Languages: A Cross-linguistic Perspective* (pp. 219–242). Rowley, MA: Newbury House.

Clahsen, H., & Felser, C. (2006). Grammatical processing in language learners. *Applied Psycholinguistics, 27*, 3–42.

Coady, J., & Huckin, T. (Eds.) (1997). *Second Language Vocabulary Acquisition*. Cambridge: Cambridge University Press.

Cohen, A. D. (1998). *Strategies in Learning and Using a Second Language*. Harlow: Longman.

Comrie, B. (1981). *Language Universals and Linguistic Typology: Syntax and Morphology*. Chicago: University of Chicago Press.

Cook, V. (1991). *Second Language Learning and Language Teaching*. London: Edward Arnold.

Coppieters, R. (1987). Competence differences between native and near-native speakers. *Language, 63*, 544–573.

Corder, S. Pit. (1967). The significance of learners' errors. *International Review of Applied Linguistics, 5*, 161–170.

Corder, S. Pit. (1981). *Error Analysis and Interlanguage*. Oxford: Oxford

University Press.

DeKeyser, R. M. (1997). Beyond explicit rule learning: Automatizing second language morphosyntax. *Studies in Second Language Acquisition, 19,* 195–221.

DeKeyser, R. M. (2000). The robustness of critical period effects in second language learners. *Studies in Second Language Acquisition, 22,* 499–533.

DeKeyser, R. M. (2007). Introduction: Situating the concept of practice. In R. M. DeKeyser (Ed.), *Practice in a Second Language: Perspectives From Applied Linguistics and Cognitive Psychology* (pp. 1–18). Cambridge: Cambridge University Press.

DeKeyser, R. M. (2015). Skill acquisition theory. In B. VanPatten & J. Williams (Eds.), *Theories in Second Language Acquisition: An Introduction* (pp. 94–112). 2nd edition. Mahwah, NJ: Lawrence Erlbaum.

DeKeyser, R. M., & Larson-Hall, J. (2005). What does the critical period really mean? In J. Kroll & A. M. B. de Groot (Eds.), *Handbook of Bilingualism: Psycholinguistic Approaches* (pp. 88–108). Oxford: Oxford University Press.

Donato, R. (2000). Sociocultural contributions to understanding the foreign and second language classroom. In J. P. Lantolf (Ed.), *Sociocultural Theory and Second Language Learning* (pp. 27–50). Oxford: Oxford University Press.

Dörnyei, Z. (2005). *The Psychology of the Language Learner: Individual Differences in Second Language Acquisition.* Mahwah, NJ: Lawrence Erlbaum.

Dörnyei, Z., & Skehan, P. (2003). Individual differences in second language learning. In C. J. Doughty & M. H. Long (Eds.), *The Handbook of Second Language Acquisition* (pp. 589–630). Oxford: Blackwell.

Doughty, C., & Williams, J. (Eds.) (1998). *Focus on Form in Classroom Second Language Acquisition*. Cambridge: Cambridge University Press.

Doughty, C. J., & Long, M. H. (Eds.) (2003). *The Handbook of Second Language Acquisition*. Oxford: Blackwell.

Dulay, H., & Burt, M. (1974). Natural sequences in child second language acquisition. *Language Learning, 24*, 37–53.

Dulay, H., & Burt, M. (1975). Creative construction in second language learning and teaching. In M. Burt & H. Dulay (Eds.), *On TESOL '75: New Directions in Second Language Learning, Teaching and Bilingual Education* (pp. 21–32). Washington, DC: TESOL.

Dulay, H., Burt, M., & Krashen, S. (1982). *Language Two*. New York: Oxford University Press.

Dussias, P. E. (2003). Syntactic ambiguity resolution in L2 learners (some effects of bilinguality on L1 and L2 processing strategies). *Studies in Second Language Acquisition, 25*, 529–557.

Dussias, P. E., & Sagarra, N. (2007). The effect of exposure on syntactic parsing in Spanish-English bilinguals. *Bilingualism: Language and Cognition, 10*, 101–116.

Eckman, F. (1977). Markedness and the contrastive analysis hypothesis. *Language Learning, 27*, 315–330.

Eckman, F. (1981). On predicting phonological difficulty in second language acquisition. *Studies in Second Language Acquisition, 4*, 18–30.

Eckman, F., Bell, L., & Nelson, D. (1988). On the generalization of relative clause instruction in the acquisition of English as second language. *Applied Linguistics, 9*, 1–20.

Eckman, F., Moravcsik, E., & Wirth, J. (1989). Implicational universals and interrogative structures in the interlanguage of ESL learners.

Language Learning, 39, 173–209.

Ehrman, M., & Leaver, B. L. (2003). Cognitive styles in the service of language learning. *System, 31,* 391–415.

Ehrman, M., & Oxford, R. L. (1990). Adult language learning styles and strategies in an intensive training setting. *Modern Language Journal, 54,* 311–327.

Ellis, N. (2002a). Frequency effects in language processing: A review with implications for theories of implicit and explicit language acquisition. *Studies in Second Language Acquisition, 24,* 143–188.

Ellis, N. (2002b). Reflections on frequency effects in language processing. *Studies in Second Language Acquisition, 24,* 297–339.

Ellis, N. (2003). Constructions, chunking, and connectionism: The emergence of second language structure. In C. Doughty & M. H. Long (Eds.), *The Handbook of Second Language Acquisition* (pp. 63–103). Oxford: Blackwell.

Ellis, N. (2005). At the interface: Dynamic interactions of explicit and implicit language knowledge. *Studies in Second Language Acquisition, 27,* 305–352.

Ellis, N. (2007). The associative-cognitive CREED. In B. VanPatten & J. Williams (Eds.), *Theories in Second Language Acquisition* (pp. 77–95). Mahwah, NJ: Lawrence Erlbaum.

Ellis, R. (1994). *The Study of Second Language Acquisition.* Oxford: Oxford University Press.

Eubank, L., & Gregg, K. (1999). Critical periods and (second) language acquisition: Divide et impera. In D. Birdsong (Ed.), *Second Language Acquisition and the Critical Period Hypothesis* (pp. 65–99). Mahwah, NJ: Lawrence Erlbaum.

Faerch, C., & Kasper, G. (Eds.) (1983). *Strategies in Interlanguage Communication.* London: Longman.

Felser, C., Roberts, L., Marinis, R., & Gross, R. (2003). The processing of ambiguous sentences by first and second language learners of English. *Applied Psycholinguistics, 24*, 453–489.

Ferguson, C. (1971). Absence of copula and the notion of simplicity: A study of normal speech, baby talk, foreigner talk, and pidgins. In D. Hymes (Ed.), *Pidginization and Creolization of Languages* (pp. 141–150). Cambridge: Cambridge University Press.

Fernández, E. M. (2003). *Bilingual Sentence Processing: Relative Clause Attachment in English and Spanish*. Amsterdam: John Benjamins.

Flege, J. E. (1987). A critical period for learning to pronounce foreign languages? *Applied Linguistics, 8*, 162–177.

Flege, J. E. (1999). Age of learning and second language speech. In D. Birdsong (Ed.), *Second Language Acquisition and the Critical Period Hypothesis* (pp. 101–131). Mahwah, NJ: Lawrence Erlbaum.

Flege, J. E. (2009). Give input a chance! In T. Piske & M. Young-Scholten (Eds.), *Input Matters* (pp. 175–190). Bristol: Multilingual Matters.

Flege, J. E., Yeni-Komshian, G., & Liu, S. (1999). Age constraints on second-language acquisition. *Journal of Memory and Language, 41*, 78–104.

Freeman-Larson, D. (2002). Making sense of frequency. *Studies in Second Language Acquisition, 24*, 275–285.

Frenck-Mestre, C. (2002). An on-line look at sentence processing in a second language. In R. Heredia & J. Altarriba (Eds.), *Bilingual Sentence Processing* (pp. 217–236). Amsterdam: North-Holland.

Frenck-Mestre, C. (2005). Eye-movement recording as a tool for studying syntactic processing in a second language: A review of methodologies and experimental findings. *Second Language Research, 21*, 175–198.

Fries, C. (1945). *Teaching and Learning English as a Foreign Language*. Ann Arbor: University of Michigan Press.

García, Mayo., Gutierrez, M., & Martínez, A. (Eds.) (2014). *Contemporary Approaches to Second Language Acquisition.* Amsterdam: John Benjamins.

Gardner, R. (1985). *Social Psychology and Second Language Learning: The Role of Attitudes and Motivation.* London: Edward Arnold.

Gardner, R., & Lambert, W. E. (1972). *Attitudes and Motivation in Second Language Learning.* Rowley, MA: Newbury House.

Gass, S. (1979). Language transfer and universal grammatical relations. *Language Learning, 29,* 327–344.

Gass, S. (1984). A review of interlanguage syntax: Language transfer and language universals. *Language Learning, 34,* 115–132.

Gass, S. (1997). *Input, Interaction, and the Second Language Learner.* Mahwah, NJ: Lawrence Erlbaum.

Gass, S. (2003). Input and interaction. In C. J. Doughty & M. H. Long (Eds.), *The Handbook of Second Language Acquisition* (pp. 224–255). Oxford: Blackwell.

Gass, S., & Mackey, A. (2006). Input, interaction and output: An overview. In K. Bardovi-Harlig & Z. Dörnyei (Eds.), *Themes in SLA Research* (pp. 3–17). Amsterdam: John Benjamins.

Gass, S., & Mackey, A. (2012). *The Routledge Handbook of Second Language Acquisition.* New York: Routledge.

Gass, S., Behney, J., & Plonsky, L. (2013). *Second Language Acquisition: An Introductory Course.* 4th edition. New York: Routledge.

Goldschneider, J., & DeKeyser, R. (2001). Explaining the natural order of L2 morpheme acquisition in English: A meta-analysis of multiple determinants. *Language Learning, 51,* 1–50.

Green, D. W. (1998). Mental control of the bilingual lexico-semantic system. *Bilingualism: Language & Cognition, 1,* 67–81.

Green, D. W. (2003). The neural basis of the lexicon and the grammar in L2 acquisition: The convergence hypothesis. In R. van Hout, A. Hulk, F. Kuiken, & R. Towell (Eds.), *The Interface Between Syntax and the Lexicon in Second Language Acquisition* (pp. 197–218). Amsterdam: John Benjamins.

Greenberg, J. H. (Ed.) (1963). *Universals of Language*. Cambridge, MA: MIT Press.

Gregg, K. (1984). Krashen's monitor and Occam's razor. *Applied Linguistics, 5*, 79–100.

Han, Z.-H. (2004). *Fossilization in Adult Second Language Acquisition*. Clevedon: Multilingual Matters.

Han, Z.-H., & Odlin, T. (Eds.) (2006). *Studies of Fossilization in Second Language Acquisition*. Clevedon: Multilingual Matters.

Hatch, E. M. (1983). Simplified input and second language acquisition. In R. W. Andersen (Ed.), *Pidginization and Creolization as Language Acquisition* (pp. 64–86). Cambridge, MA: Newbury House.

Hawkins, R. (2001). *Second Language Syntax*. Oxford: Blackwell.

Herschensohn, J. (2008). *Language Development and Age*. Cambridge: Cambridge University Press.

Higgs, T. V., & Clifford, R. (1982). The push toward communication. In T. V. Higgs (Ed.), *Curriculum, Competence, and the Foreign Language Teacher* (pp. 7–79). Lincolnwood, IL: National Textbook.

Huckin, T., & Coady, J. (1999). Incidental vocabulary acquisition in a second language: A review. *Studies in Second Language Acquisition, 21*, 181–193.

Hulstijn, J. (2001). Intentional and incidental second language vocabulary learning: A reappraisal of elaboration, rehearsal and automaticity. In P. Robinson (Ed.), *Cognition and Second Language Instruction* (pp. 258–287). Cambridge: Cambridge University Press.

Hulstijn, J. (2005). Theoretical and empirical issues in the study of implicit and explicit second language learning: Introduction. *Studies in Second Language Acquisition, 27*, 129–140.

Hymes, D. (1972). On communicative competence. In J. B. Pride & J. Holmes (Eds.), *Sociolinguistics* (pp. 269–293). Harmondsworth: Penguin.

Indefrey, P. (2006). A meta-analysis of hemodynamic studies on first and second language processing: Which suggested differences can we trust and what do they mean? In M. Gullberg & P. Indefrey (Eds.), *The Cognitive Neuroscience of Second Language Acquisition* (pp. 279–304). Oxford: Blackwell.

Ioup, G., Boustagui, E., El Tigi, M., & Moselle, M. (1994). Reexamining the critical period hypothesis. *Studies in Second Language Learning, 16*, 73–98.

Izumi, S. (2002). Output, input enhancement, and the noticing hypothesis. *Studies in Second Language Acquisition, 24*, 541–577.

Johnson, J., & Newport, E. (1989). Critical period effects in second language learning: The influence of maturational state on the acquisition of ESL. *Cognitive Psychology, 21*, 60–99.

Johnson, J., & Newport, E. (1991). Critical period effects on universal properties of language: The status of subjacency in the acquisition of a second language. *Cognition, 39*, 215–258.

Juffs, A. (1996). *Learnability and the Lexicon: Theories and Second Language Acquisition Research*. Amsterdam: John Benjamins.

Juffs, A. (1998). Main verb versus reduced relative clause ambiguity resolution in L2 sentence processing. *Language Learning, 48*, 107–147.

Keenan, E., & Comrie, B. (1977). Noun phrase accessibility and universal grammar. *Linguistic Inquiry, 8*, 63–99.

Kellerman, E. (1979). Transfer and non-transfer: Where we are now.

Studies in Second Language Acquisition, 2, 37–57.

Kellerman, E. (1983). Now you see it, now you don't. In S. Gass & L. Selinker (Eds.), *Language Transfer in Language Learning* (pp. 112–134). Rowley, MA: Newbury House.

Klein, W. (1986). *Second Language Acquisition.* Cambridge: Cambridge University Press.

Kolb, D. A. (1984). *Experiential Learning: Experience as the Source of Learning and Development.* Englewood Cliffs, NJ: Prentice-Hall.

Krashen, S. (1982). *Principles and Practice in Second Language Acquisition.* Oxford: Pergamon.

Krashen, S. (1985). *The Input Hypothesis: Issues and Implications.* New York: Longman.

Krashen, S. (2009). The comprehension hypothesis extended. In T. Piske & M. Young-Scholten (Eds.), *Input Matters* (pp. 81–94). Bristol: Multilingual Matters.

Kroll, J. F., & de Groot, A. M. B. (Eds.) (2005). *Handbook of Bilingualism: Psycho-linguistic Approaches.* New York: Oxford University Press.

Kroll, J. F., & Stewart, E. (1994). Category interference in translation and picture naming: Evidence for asymmetric connections between bilingual memory representations. *Journal of Memory and Language, 33,* 149–174.

Lado, R. (1957). *Linguistics Across Cultures: Applied Linguistics for Language Teachers.* Ann Arbor: University of Michigan.

Lantolf, J. P. (Ed.) (2001). *Sociocultural Theory and Second Language Learning.* Oxford: Oxford University Press.

Lantolf, J. P., & Thorne S. L. (2006). *Sociocultural Theory and the Genesis of Second Language Development.* Oxford: Oxford University Press.

Lardiere, D. (2007). *Ultimate Attainment in Second Language Acquisition.* Mahwah, NJ: Lawrence Erlbaum.

Larsen-Freeman, D. (1976). An explanation for the morpheme acquisition order of second language learners. *Language Learning, 26*, 125–134.

Larsen-Freeman, D., & Cameron, L. (2008). *Complex Systems and Applied Linguistics.* Oxford: Oxford University Press.

Laufer, B., & Hulstijn, J. (2001). Incidental vocabulary acquisition in a second language: The construct of task-induced involvement. *Applied Linguistics, 22*, 1–26.

Leow, R. P. (1997). Attention, awareness, and foreign language behavior. *Language Learning, 47*, 467–506.

Lightbown, P. (1985). Great expectations: Second language acquisition research and classroom teaching. *Applied Linguistics, 6*, 173–189.

Lightbown, P., & Spada, N. (2006). *How Languages are Learned.* 3rd edition. Oxford: Oxford University Press.

Long, M. H. (1981). Input, interaction, and second language acquisition. In H. Winitz (Ed.). *Native Language and Foreign Language Acquisition: Annals of the New York Academic of Sciences, 379*, 259–278.

Long, M. H. (1983a). Does second language instruction make a difference? *TESOL Quarterly, 17*, 359–382.

Long, M. H. (1983b). Linguistics and conversational adjustments to non-native speakers. *Studies in Second Language Acquisition, 5*, 177–193.

Long, M. H. (1991). Focus on form: A design feature in language teaching methodology. In K. de Bot, R. B. Ginsberg, & C. Kramsch, (Eds.), *Foreign Language Research in Cross-cultural Perspective* (pp. 39–52). Amsterdam: John Benjamins.

Long, M. H. (1996). The role of the linguistic environment in second language acquisition. In W. C. Ritchie & T. K. Bhatia (Eds.),

Handbook of Second Language Acquisition (pp. 413–468). San Diego, CA: Academic Press.

Long, M. H. (2003). Stabilization and fossilization in interlanguage. In C. J. Doughty & M. H. Long (Eds.), *The Handbook of Second Language Acquisition* (pp. 487–535). Oxford: Blackwell.

Long, M. H. (2007). *Problems in SLA*. Mahwah, NJ: Lawrence Erlbaum.

Lyster, R. (1998). Recasts, repetition, and ambiguity in L2 classroom discourse. *Studies in Second Language Acquisition, 20,* 51–81.

Lyster, R. (2004). Differential effects of prompts and recasts in form-focused instruction. *Studies in Second Language Acquisition, 26,* 399–432.

Lyster, R., & Ranta, L. (1997). Corrective feedback and learner uptake: Negotiation of form in communicative classrooms. *Studies in Second Language Acquisition, 19,* 37–66.

Mackey, A. (1999). Input, interaction, and second language development: An empirical study of question formation in ESL. *Studies in Second Language Acquisition, 21,* 557–587.

Mackey, A. (2006). Feedback, noticing and instructed second language learning. *Applied Linguistics, 27,* 405–430.

Mackey, A., Gass, S., & McDonough, K. (2000). How do learners perceive interactional feedback? *Studies in Second Language Acquisition, 22,* 471–497.

Mackey, A., & Philp, J. (1998). Conversational interaction on second language development: Recasts, responses, and red herrings? *Modern Language Journal, 82,* 338–356.

MacWhinney, B., Bates, B., & Kliegl, R. (1984). Cue validity and sentence interpretation in English, German and Italian. *Journal of Verbal Learning and Behavior, 23,* 127–150.

MacWhinney, B., & Bates, E. (Eds.) (1989). *The Cross-linguistic Study of*

Sentence Processing. Cambridge: Cambridge University Press.

McLaughlin, B. (1978). The monitor model: Some methodological considerations. *Language Learning, 28*, 309–332.

Meisel, J., Clahsen, H., & Pienemann, M. (1983). On determining developmental stages in natural second language acquisition. *Studies in Second Language Acquisition, 3*, 109–135.

Mitchell, R., Myles, F., & Marsden, E. (2012). *Second Language Learning Theories.* 3rd edition. New York: Routledge.

Moyer, A. (2004). *Age, Accent, and Experience in Second Language Acquisition.* Clevedon: Multilingual Matters.

Norris, J. M., & Ortega, L. (2000). Effectiveness of L2 instruction: A research synthesis and quantitative meta-analysis. *Language Learning, 50*, 417–528.

Ochs, E. (1982). Talking to children in Western Samoa. *Language in Society, 11*, 77–104.

O'Grady, W. (2003). The radical middle: Nativism without universal grammar. In C. J. Doughty & M. H. Long (Eds.), *The Handbook of Second Language Acquisition* (pp. 43–62). Oxford: Blackwell.

Ohta, A. S. (2000). Rethinking interaction in SLA: Developmentally appropriate assistance in the zone of proximal development and the acquisition of L2 grammar. In J. P. Lantolf (Ed.), *Sociocultural Theory and Second Language Learning* (pp. 51–78). Oxford: Oxford University Press.

Ohta, A. S. (2001). *Second Language Acquisition Processes in the Classroom: Learning Japanese.* Mahwah, NJ: Lawrence Erlbaum.

O'Malley, J. M., & Chamot, A. U. (1990). *Learning Strategies in Second Language Acquisition.* Cambridge: Cambridge University Press.

Ortega, L. (2015). *Second Language Acquisition.* London: Routledge.

Osterhout, L., McLaughlin, J., Pitkanen, I., Frenck-Mestre, C., &

Molinaro, N. (2006). Novice learners, longitudinal designs, and event-related potentials: A means for exploring the neurocognition of second language processing. In M. Gullberg & P. Indefrey (Eds.), *The Cognitive Neuroscience of Second Language Acquisition* (pp. 199–230). Oxford: Blackwell.

Oxford, R. L. (1990). *Language Learning Strategies: What Every Teacher Should Know.* New York: Newbury House.

Oxford, R. L. (1993). *Style Analysis Survey (SAS).* Tuscaloosa: University of Alabama.

Oxford, R. L. (1999). "Style Wars" as a source of anxiety in language classrooms. In D. J. Young (Ed.), *Affect in Foreign Language and Second Language Learning* (pp. 216–237). New York: McGraw-Hill.

Paradis, M. (2004). *A Neurolinguistic Theory of Bilingualism.* Amsterdam: John Benjamins.

Perani, D., & Abutalebi, J. (2005). The neural basis of first and second language processing. *Current Opinion in Neurobiology, 15,* 202–206.

Peters, A. M. (1985). Language segmentation: Operating principles for the analysis and perception of language. In D. Slobin (Ed.), *The Crosslinguistic Study of Language Acquisition, vol. 2.* (pp. 1029–1067). Hillsdale, NJ: Lawrence Erlbaum.

Pfaff, C. (1987). Functional approaches to interlanguage. In C. Pfaff (Ed.), *First and Second Language Acquisition Processes* (pp. 81–102). Rowley, MA: Newbury House.

Pica, T. (1983). Adult acquisition of English as a second language under different conditions of exposure. *Language Learning, 33,* 465–497.

Pica, T. (1988). Interlanguage adjustments as an outcome of NS-NNS negotiated interaction. *Language Learning, 38,* 45–73.

Pica, T. (1994). Research on negotiation: What does it reveal about second language learning conditions, processes, and outcomes?

Language Learning, 44, 493–527.

Pienemann, M. (1987). Psychological constraints on the teachability of languages. In C. Pfaff (Ed.), *First and Second Language Acquisition Processes* (pp. 143–168). Rowley, MA: Newbury House.

Pienemann, M. (1998). *Language Processing and L2 Development.* Amsterdam: John Benjamins.

Pienemann, M., Di Biase, B., Kawaguchi, S., & Hakansson, G. (2005) Processability, typological distance, and L1 transfer. In M. Pienemann (Ed.), *Cross-linguistic Aspects of Processability Theory* (pp. 85–116). Amsterdam: John Benjamins.

Pimsleur, P. (1966). *The Pimsleur Language Aptitude Battery.* New York: Harcourt Brace Jovanovich.

Pinker, S. (1994). *The Language Instinct: How the Mind Creates Language.* New York: Harper Collins.

Platzack, C. (1996). The initial hypothesis of syntax: A minimalist perspective on language acquisition and attrition. In H. Clahsen (Ed.), *Generative Perspectives on Language Acquisition* (pp. 369–414). Amsterdam: John Benjamins.

Richards, J. (Ed.) (1974). *Error Analysis.* London: Longman.

Riding, R. (1991). *Cognitive Styles Analysis User Manual.* Birmingham: Learning and Training Technology.

Robinson, P. (2001a). Individual differences, cognitive abilities, aptitude complexes and learning conditions in second language acquisition. *Second Language Research, 17,* 368–392.

Robinson, P. (Ed.) (2001b). *Cognition and Second Language Instruction.* Cambridge: Cambridge University Press.

Robinson, P. (2003). Attention and memory during SLA. In C. Doughty & M. H. Long (Eds.). *The Handbook of Second Language Acquisition* (pp. 631–679). Oxford: Blackwell.

Robinson, P. (Ed.) (2012). *Routledge Encyclopedia of Second Language Acquisition*. New York: Routledge.

Salaberry, M. R., & Shirai, Y. (Eds.) (2002). *Tense-aspect Morphology in L2 Acquisition*. Amsterdam: John Benjamins.

Sanz, C., & Leow, R. (2011). *Implicit and Explicit Bilingualism & SLA: Conditions, Processes, and Knowledge*. Washington, DC: Georgetown University Press.

Savignon, S. (1998). *Communicative Competence: Theory and Classroom Practice*. 2nd edition. New York: McGraw-Hill.

Schachter, J. (1974). An error in error analysis. *Language Learning, 24*, 205–214.

Schachter, J. (1986). In search of systematicity in interlanguage production. *Studies in Second Language Acquisition, 8*, 119–134.

Schmidt, R. (1990). The role of consciousness in second language learning. *Applied Linguistics, 11*, 129–158.

Schmidt, R. (Ed.) (1995). *Attention and Awareness in Foreign Language Learning*. Honolulu: University of Hawai'i, National Foreign Language Center.

Schmidt, R. (2001). Attention. In P. Robinson (Ed.), *Cognition and Second Language Instruction* (pp. 3–32). Cambridge: Cambridge University Press.

Schumann, J. (1978). *The Pidginization Process: A model for Second Language Acquisition*. Rowley, MA: Newbury House.

Schumann, J. (1979). The acquisition of English negation by speakers of Spanish: A review of the literature. In R. Andersen (Ed.), *The Acquisition and Use of Spanish and English as First and Second Languages* (pp. 3–32). Washington, DC: TESOL.

Schumann, J. (1986). Research on the acculturation model for second language acquisition. *Journal of Multilingual and Multicultural*

Development, 7, 379–392.

Schwartz, B. (1993). On explicit and negative data effecting and affecting competence and linguistic behaviour. *Studies in Second Language Acquisition, 15,* 147–163.

Schwartz, B. (1998). The second language instinct. *Lingua, 106,* 133–160.

Schwartz, B., & Sprouse, R. (1996). L2 cognitive states and the full transfer/full access model. *Second Language Research, 12,* 40–72.

Sebba, M. (1997). *Contact Languages: Pidgins and Creoles.* London: Macmillan.

Selinker, L. (1972). Interlanguage. *International Review of Applied Linguistics, 10,* 209–231.

Selinker, L. (1992). *Rediscovering Interlanguage.* London: Longman.

Sharwood Smith, M. (1986). Comprehension versus acquisition: Two ways of processing input. *Applied Linguistics, 7,* 239–274.

Sharwood Smith, M. (1993). Input enhancement in instructed SLA: Theoretical bases. *Studies in Second Language Acquisition, 15,* 165–179.

Shirai, Y., & Andersen, R. W. (1995). The acquisition of tense/aspect morphology: A prototype account. *Language, 71,* 743–762.

Siegal, J. (2003). Social context. In C. J. Doughty & M. H. Long (Eds.), *The Handbook of Second Language Acquisition* (pp. 178–223). Oxford: Blackwell.

Skehan, P. (1989). *Individual Differences in Second Language Learning.* London: Edward Arnold.

Skehan, P. (1998). *A Cognitive Approach to Learning Language.* Oxford: Oxford University Press.

Skinner, B. (1957). *Verbal Behaviour.* New York: Appleton-Century Crofts.

Snow, C. (1977). The development of conversations between mothers and babies. *Journal of Child Language, 4,* 1–22.

Snow, C., & Ferguson, C. (Eds.) (1977). *Talking to Children: Language Input and Acquisition.* Cambridge: Cambridge University Press.

Sorace, A. (2003). Near-nativeness. In C. J. Doughty & M. H. Long (Eds.), *The Handbook of Second Language Acquisition* (pp. 130–151). Oxford: Blackwell.

Spada, N. (1997). Form-focused instruction and second language acquisition: A review of classroom and laboratory research. *Language Teaching, 30,* 73–87.

Sparks, R., & Ganschow, L. (1991). Foreign language learning differences: Affective or native language aptitude differences? *Modern Language Journal, 75,* 3–16.

Sparks, R., & Ganschow, L. (2001). Aptitude for learning a foreign language. *Annual Review of Applied Linguistics, 21,* 90–111.

Stockwell, R., & Bowen, J. (1965). *The Sounds of English and Spanish.* Chicago, IL: University of Chicago Press.

Stockwell, R., & Bowen, J. (1983). Sound systems in conflict: A hierarchy of difficulty. In B. J. Robinett & J. Schachter (Eds.), *Second Language Learning: Contrastive Analysis, Error Analysis, and Related Aspects* (pp. 20–31). Ann Arbor: University of Michigan Press.

Stockwell, R., Bowen, J., & Martin, J. (1965). *The Grammatical Structures of English and Spanish.* Chicago, IL: University of Chicago Press.

Swain, M. (1985). Communicative competence: Some roles of comprehensible input and comprehensible output in its development. In S. Gass & C. Madden (Eds.), *Input in Second Language Acquisition* (pp. 235–253). Rowley, MA: Newbury House.

Swain, M. (1995). Three functions of output in second language learning. In G. Cook & B. Seidlhofer (Eds.), *Principles and Practice in Applied Linguistics* (pp. 125–144). Oxford: Oxford University Press.

Swain, M. (1998). Focus on form through conscious reflection. In C. J. Doughty & J. Williams (Eds.), *Focus on Form in Classroom Second Language Acquisition* (pp. 64–81). Cambridge: Cambridge University Press.

Swain, M., & Lapkin, S. (1995). Problems in output and the cognitive processes they generate: A step towards second language learning. *Applied Linguistics, 16*, 371–391.

Tarone, E. (1977). Conscious communication strategies in interlanguage. In H. D. Brown, C. A. Yorio, & R. C. Crymes (Eds.), *On TESOL '77: Teaching and Learning English as a Second Language* (pp. 194, 203). Washington, DC: Teachers of English to Speakers of Other Languages.

Tarone, E. (1979). Interlanguage as chameleon. *Language Learning, 29*, 181–191.

Tarone, E. (1988). *Variation in Interlanguage*. London: Edward Arnold.

Todd, L. (1991). *Pidgins and Creoles*. London: Routledge and Kegan Paul.

Tomlin, R., & Villa, V. (1994). Attention in cognitive science and second language acquisition. *Studies in Second Language Acquisition, 16*, 183–203.

Truscott, J. (1998). Noticing in second language acquisition: A critical review. *Second Language Research, 14*, 103–135.

Truscott, J. (2004). The effectiveness of grammar instruction: Analysis of a meta-analysis. *English Teaching and Learning, 28*, 17–29.

Truscott, J., & Sharwood Smith, M. (2004). Acquisition by processing: A modular perspective on language development. *Bilingualism: Language and Cognition, 7*, 1–20.

Ullman, M. T. (2001a). The neural basis of lexicon and grammar in first and second language: The declarative/procedural model. *Bilingualism: Language and Cognition, 4*, 105–122.

Ullman, M. T. (2001b). A neurocognitive perspective on language: The declarative/procedural model. *Nature Reviews Neuroscience, 2*, 717–726.

Vainikka, A., & Young-Scholten, M. (1996). The gradual development of L2 phrase structure. *Second Language Research, 12*, 7–39.

Valdman, A. (1977). *Pidgin and Creole Linguistics*. Bloomington: Indiana University Press.

VanPatten, B. (1996). *Input Processing and Grammar Instruction: Theory and Research*. Norwood, NJ: Ablex.

VanPatten, B. (2000). Thirty years of input (or intake, the neglected sibling). In F. Morris Swierzbin, M. E. Anderson, C. A. Klee, & E. Tarone (Eds.), *Social and Cognitive Factors in Second Language Acquisition* (pp. 287–311). Somerville, MA: Cascadilla Press.

VanPatten, B. (2003). *From Input to Output: A Teacher's Guide to Second Language Acquisition*. New York: McGraw-Hill.

VanPatten, B., & Fernández, C. (2004). The long-term effects of processing instruction. In B. VanPatten (Ed.), *Processing Instruction: Theory, Research, and Commentary* (pp. 273–289). Mahwah, NJ: Lawrence Erlbaum.

VanPatten, B., & Williams, J. (Eds.) (2015). *Theories in Second Language Acquisition*. 2nd edition. Mahwah, NJ: Lawrence Erlbaum.

Varonis, E., & Gass, S. (1985). Non-native/non-native conversations: A model for negotiation of meaning. *Applied Linguistics, 6*, 71–90.

Wagner-Gough, J., & Hatch, G. (1975). The importance of input data in second language acquisition studies. *Language Learning, 25*, 297–307.

White, L. (1989). *Universal Grammar and Second Language Acquisition*. Philadelphia, PA: Benjamins.

White, L. (2003). *Second Language Acquisition and Universal Grammar*. Cambridge: Cambridge University Press.

White, L. (2007). Linguistic theory, universal grammar, and second language acquisition. In B. VanPatten & J. Williams (Eds.), *Theories in Second Language Acquisition* (pp. 37–55). Mahwah, NJ: Lawrence Erlbaum.

White, L., & Genesee, F. (1996). How native is near-native? The issue of ultimate attainment in adult second language acquisition. *Second Language Research, 11*, 233–265.

Wode, H. (1976). Developmental sequences in naturalistic L2 acquisition. Working papers in bilingualism. Reprinted in E. Hatch (Ed.), *Second Language Acquisition: A Book of Readings* (pp. 102–117). Rowley, MA: Newbury House.

Wong, W. (2005) *Input Enhancement: From Theory and Research to the Classroom*. New York: McGraw-Hill.

Young-Scholten, M. (1994). Positive evidence and ultimate attainment in L2 phonology. *Second Language Research, 10*, 193–214.

Young-Scholten, M., & Archibald, J. (2000). Second language syllable structure. In J. Archibald (Ed.), *Second Language Acquisition and Linguistic Theory* (pp. 64–101). Oxford: Blackwell.

Zobl, H. (1981). Markedness and the projection problem. *Language Learning, 33*, 293–313.

Zobl, H. (1982). A direction for contrastive analysis: The comparative study of developmental sequences. *TESOL Quarterly, 16*, 169–183.

Zobl, H. (1985). Grammars in search of input and intake. In S. M. Gass & G. Madden (Eds.), *Input in Second Language Acquisition* (pp. 329–344). Rowley, MA: Newbury House.

Index

*For terms with multiple page references, **bold font** indicates the page where the main definition or discussion can be found.*